USING THE INTERNET

in easy steps
.compact

BRIAN AUSTIN

in easy steps and **in easy steps.compact** are imprints of Computer Step
Southfield Road . Southam . Warwickshire CV47 OFB . England
Web site: http://www.ineasysteps.com
Email: books@ineasysteps.com

Notice of Liability

Every effort has been made to ensure that this book contains accurate and current
information. However, Computer Step and the author shall not be liable for any loss or
damage suffered by readers as a result of any information contained herein.

Trademarks

All trademarks are acknowledged as belonging to their respective companies.

Printed and bound in the United Kingdom

ISBN 1-84078-110-6

Contents

Modems 55

Getting online 69

Exploring the Web *107*

A closer look at Web browsers *123*

Maintaining your security online *147*

Finding what you want on the Net *157*

Shopping online *171*

Children and the Internet *177*

On the road and using the Net *187*

Speeding up your Internet connection *193*

Part II: Using Email

Getting started with email *203*

Sending and receiving email messages *233*

Managing your email messages *267*

Mailing lists 277

Part III: Interactive Internet

Playing online games 287

Internet newsgroups 291

Talking and viewing on the Internet 313

Downloading and uploading information 321 and software

Part IV: Creating Web Pages

Software for creating Web pages *341*

Creating simple Web pages *347*

Creating fancy Web pages 359

Part V: Doing Business on the Internet

Web business basics 369

Creating a profitable e-commerce Web site 381

Making money on the Internet 393

Internet marketing secrets revealed 401

Internet Service Providers, domain name *411* registers and Web hosts

The Newsgroups Directory *415*

The Web Directory *421*

The Internet: yesterday and tomorrow *483*

Jargon buster *489*

Index *501*

ReadMe.first

Perhaps one hundred years from now, historians will look back at the start of the 21st Century as an incredibly significant period! We're seeing the last days of the industrial revolution as we move into the dawn of a new digital age, one that is having a momentous effect on the entire world in all sorts of ways. The Internet is a key component of this emerging digital era and is affecting millions of people worldwide including you and me.

In this book, we seek to help as many people as possible make use of the Internet to enhance the quality of their lives. First, we're seeking to provide an incredible, value-packed resource affordable to as many people as possible. Secondly, Computer Step editors invest a lot of time and effort to create easy-to-understand products with clear and concise plain-English explanations. We've also included lots of examples to help you learn more easily and discover what the Internet really means to you and how you can benefit from it.

Researching and writing this book has been a huge task and like any large complex project has its own special challenges! Although my name is on the cover, like all Computer Step books, "Using the Internet in easy steps dot compact" is the end result of a carefully planned team effort, from researching, writing, editing and finalising to printing and distribution to you our valued reader. I want to thank my long-suffering publisher Harshad Kotecha, the ever-helpful staff at Computer Step, international distributors Penguin Books, my wonderful wife Ann for her support and for maintaining a creative environment, and my children for understanding. Enjoy and prosper through awareness!

Dealing with dead links

We carefully research Web site addresses and related information. However, the chaotic nature and fast pace of change on the Internet have a way of confounding even the most determined efforts. If you find that some of the links mentioned no longer work, I promise they were working correctly at the time of our research. Often, you can still find the page you want easily by using the following method. (If you're new to the Internet, don't worry if our explanation below doesn't make much sense to you: all that you need is in the book.) So let's imagine you want to find the following page:

- http://www.ineasysteps.com/updates/latest.html
  (a fictional Web address created for illustration purposes only).

Now if your Web browser were to return a "Page not found" error message, you could try modifying your entry to:

- http://www.ineasysteps.com/updates/

or simply

- http://www.ineasysteps.com/

Get the picture? By navigating "backwards" in this way, you may find that the Web site providers have created a new link that leads to the page you want. Alternatively, just email the Web site and ask your question.

With that said, let's get started. Sit back and enjoy your journey into a new land of amazing colour, vibrancy and opportunity: it's YOUR Internet!

Part I
Getting Started on the Internet

Introducing
the Internet

What is the Internet?

Imagine: millions of computers and other electronic devices around the world that can connect with each other using ordinary telephone lines! On a basic level, that's the Internet, a complex network of different types of electronic devices connected together and essentially "talking" the same language. However, on a deeper level, the Internet is much more than that: it's really millions of people connected together, each having the power to decide with a couple of mouse clicks.

Originally a communications system designed to survive a global nuclear war, the Internet is the first human system that puts power back into the hands of individuals and limits the power of governments – so far. (Debatable, I know). A few individuals have coined other more colourful words and phrases to describe the Internet: "Cyberspace", "The Information Superhighway" or simply the "Net" if you feel like cutting out the excess! The Internet today is really a shorthand way of describing several key technologies, the four most important currently being:

- The World Wide Web – or just The Web: this is the most popular "click-and-go" face of the Internet today (page 107).
- Email – or more formally electronic mail (page 203).
- Newsgroups – also known as Usenet – providing popular places to discuss topics that interest you (page 291).
- Chat – often known as Internet Relay Chat (IRC) – unlike email or newsgroups is "live": you can immediately talk to other Internet

users – a little like the futuristic video phones we see in science fiction movies (page 317).

Don't worry if these phrases don't make much sense to you now. These and other essential components that make the Internet function are covered in more depth throughout this book.

So why has the Internet changed our world? In a word: information! Individuals, companies and other organisations, governments, universities and colleges help provide at low cost (or make freely available) a huge range of information. Contributors to the Internet are responsible for ensuring their own connection, yet it's this freedom that is at the heart of why the Internet even works at all: we can only benefit when we connect!

Currently, computers are the most important electronic devices that make up the Internet and cover a wide range of different varieties, ranging from large "old" mainframe computers, to the more familiar desktop and notebook PCs many of us use today. Through the incredible progress of technology and the pace of electronic miniaturisation, many of today's desktop and notebook PCs are many times more powerful than the older, much larger mainframe computers built two decades ago!

However, many people don't have access to a computer or may not want to learn how to use one. As computing and mass communications power continues to increase while unit and running costs fall, other popular electronic devices like televisions, mobile phones, even washing machines and microwave ovens are also beginning to get hooked up to the Net!

So why is all this so exciting? Well, if you're fortunate enough to be reading books like this, you are living in what is possibly the most exciting time in the entire history of our world! The framework of the Internet breaks down barriers between countries and empowers ordinary people everywhere to do what they want, to discover what they want and, more often than not, to save money! To get on the Net, essentially, you just need three things:

- An Internet access device. Examples include: computers, special mobile phone or WebTV.
- A connection to the Internet: for most of us, this means an Internet Service Provider and a phone line.
- Software that lets you explore and use the Net.

More on these topics later. First, let's explore a few of the basic words and phrases you'll come across when getting involved in and travelling around this exciting new global landscape.

Essential topics and what they mean

Development of the Internet has brought with it many new and strange words and phrases. But never fear: we've also included a full *Jargon buster* on page 489. Don't feel intimidated: you can learn a few new terms at a time while having fun on the Internet. Before you realise it, you'll know more than you might have thought possible. In the following paragraphs, let's examine a few of the most important Internet-related words and phrases.

Computer network: a group of computers and other electronic devices connected together in some way for the purpose of sharing information. That's it: just plug the critters together, add some software to ensure they all talk the same language and there you have a computer network.

A computer network in the same building is often referred to as a Local Area Network or LAN. A network made up of devices in separate buildings or locations is referred to as a Wide Area Network or a WAN. The Internet is actually the largest computer network ever created; the mother of all networks. You'll never see a bigger network until we start colonising outer space!

Computer virus: a program designed to affect the normal working of a computer, PC or associated software applications. Some viruses are just plain annoying but nevertheless harmless, while others are highly devastating and can result in all information stored on a computer being lost.

Without doubt, viruses are spread more easily using the Internet. However, there are lots of steps you can take to protect your computer, and applying just a little key knowledge from this book can prevent a lot of heartache for yourself and others. See also page 147.

Downloading and Uploading: when we receive information from another computer on the Internet, we call this downloading. If we send information to another computer on the Net, we're uploading. When using the Internet, downloading and uploading often occur "in the background" automatically especially when using the Web.

Online/Offline: online – or on-line – is a shorthand way of saying: "I'm now electronically connected to the Internet." Offline is the opposite: when you're disconnected from the phone line or the Internet. The plugs and connectors between your various electronic devices can remain in place, and you simply use the commands in your software to actually connect and disconnect from the Net.

The Web: more formally called the World Wide Web (WWW), this is the largest and most popular "branch" of the Internet. The Web is made up of millions of "Web pages" or electronic documents stored on tens of thousands of Web computers (servers) around the world. You can click on special links in Web pages to go to other Web pages around the Internet, jumping or "surfing" from page to page within seconds usually.

Although much of the information provided on the Internet is free for anyone to use, you should always check copyright statements associated with the information you want – especially for Web-based material: the providers may limit what you can do with their information.

What's the Internet good for?

Wow, what a question! I know I'm probably biased but the Internet is just amazing. You can find out something about almost everything – in fact, practically any piece of information you might ever want to know is probably available somewhere on the Internet! Also, you won't need to know any complicated computer programming languages to use the Internet. If you're happy to cope with any basic computer word processing software, you should have no trouble getting online and having a lot of fun exploring Cyberspace.

If the ultimate guidebook to everything in existence were to exist, it would probably be the Net or stored somewhere on it! From the vast source of information – much of which is often freely available – you can probably solve any problem you're ever likely to come across using the Internet. To perhaps get a clearer picture, let's explore the Net a little more and consider some of the main components that make up the Net and the kinds of things you can do.

Email: you can send and receive email – more formally known as electronic mail – to anyone anywhere who has access to the Internet, using computers, mobile phone, WebTVs and other Internet-ready devices. See also page 203.

Shop till you drop: no longer necessary. There are clear benefits to shopping on the Net: no traffic, no queues and if you're careful, little hassle. More and more companies are making their goods and services available for sale online and passing on savings they make to canny Net customers. But you need to know how to get informed and learn a few ground rules. For more about Internet shopping, see page 171.

Go to the movies: before you go and see the latest films, why not go online and view extracts from current popular movies and read the reviews –

sometimes even before the films are on show at your local cinema! Find out what's going on behind the scenes and maybe even talk to some popular celebrities.

Computer software: you can obtain most computer software programs and regular updates on the Internet, for the IBM-compatible PC, Apple Mac, Atari Amiga and possibly others too. Therefore, if you're short on time, instead of visiting your local computer store, often you can choose to visit them on the Internet. This approach can mean less wear and tear on you, your bank balance, your car, the roads and has got to be good for the environment.

However, buying a full software product online may not always offer the best solution. For example, much of today's software is large in file size. If, like most people, you're using a standard computer-type modem to access the Net, you may decide that spending four hours or more downloading a large file is simply not worth the hassle! Nevertheless, technology has a habit of speeding things up while reducing prices, so perhaps when 4 hours become 1 hour...

Learn something new: discover key information on a huge range of topics! A variety of easy methods is available to help you find the kind of information you want – once you know how – and this book can help you. For example, you can:

- Find your favourite food recipe.
- Read about current events in online newspapers or magazines.
- Visit your government representatives and find out what they're up to.
- Give your brain a workout with a complex academic journal.
- Get help with school homework.
- Enrol on a college course or take a University degree – the Open University in Britain provides a wide range of courses and the Internet is an ideal way to deliver information.

- Get answers from an online encyclopaedia – a huge up-to-date information resource. You can use search tools to gain access to all relevant information or you can get quick "snapshot" answers instead of pages and pages of text to wade through.

Chill out, relax and play a game. Many generous sources on the Internet provide free games like chess, poker and football. Plus you can play many other more animated and interactive games live with opponents living locally or who may live thousands of miles away on another continent! See also page 287.

Newsgroups: known also as discussion groups, newsgroups enable you to discuss topics with other people from around the world. You can solve a problem, get advice, offer a solution, and so on, to freely help others and receive help when you need it. Newsgroups can also be useful for businesses to make a contribution and in return subtly advertise their products and services. See also page 291.

Business: starting any business is a hugely brave step and needs a lot of research and careful consideration. You can learn about what it takes to set up and run a business or start an Internet business! Free and low-cost resources on the Internet can help you get started, avoid expensive mistakes and promote your business to millions around the world for a low cost. You can also learn about Internet marketing, Web sites and e-commerce and how to provide and carry out safe and secure transactions on the Internet. See also page 371.

New communities: the current growing trend of providing free and low-cost access to the Internet is enabling many individuals from around the globe to communicate using a variety of different and interesting ways. This has led to the formation of new small communities in which people who share the same interests and beliefs can meet and discuss issues even though they may be based thousands of miles apart.

101 fun things to do on the Net!

Why not jump in? Here's a tiny sample of the wide range of fun topics covered in this book including some example Web links:

1. Ask the Butler! Ask Jeeves a question and get some answers – really!
    http://www.askjeeves.com/
2. Shop till you drop – without the traffic jams or queues!
    http://www.123.com/
3. Get low-priced or FREE software for your computer – PC, Apple Mac and others.
    http://www.freewareweb.com/newsindex.html
4. You're counting the days! Reserve your ticket on that exotic holiday once and for all – and get a great deal!
    http://www.pocruises.com/
5. Escape! Buy that new book you're curious about.
    http://www.amazon.co.uk/
6. Express gratitude and make a difference: feed a hungry person with a single mouse click. http://www.thehungersite.com/
7. Discover what the papers say. Want to stay informed? Read local or national newspapers from around the world.
    http://www.lineone.net/

8. In business? Check out those company accounts.
   http://www.companieshouse.com/
9. Phone anywhere for the cost of a local call – or less.
   http://www.mediaring.com/
10. Let the train take the strain? Reserve your ticket online.
    http://www.thetrainline.com
11. Find all sorts of key travel information.
    http://www.atuk.co.uk/index.html
12. Get savvy! Find cheaper life, home and car insurance.
    http://www.screentrade.co.uk/ and http://www.easycover.com/
13. Sell your car and buy a Porsche – or failing that, maybe just get a great
    replacement car.
    http://www.carbusters.com/

14. Beat the blues: discover the true secret of happiness.
    http://www.georgeparry.com.au/ & http://www.philiphumbert.com/
15. Perform some financial magic: visit your bank without queuing or leaving the house.
    Example: http://www.natwest.co.uk/
16. Discover once and for all if those aliens really are out there!
    http://www.ufomind.com/area51/
17. Strike gold: form a new dotcom company.
    http://www.GreatDomains.com/
18. Find your ideal partner and fall in love – then invite me to the wedding.
    http://www.match.com/
19. Watch your favourite sport online. http://www.sports.com/
20. Complain to your government. Let 'em know it's just not on! For example:
    (UK) http://www.pm.gov.uk/
    (USA) http://www.whitehouse.gov/
21. Sell that dusty Picasso lying in the attic – and retire to Hawaii!
    http://www.ebay.co.uk/
22. Discuss what really matters to you with others around the globe. Learn how to use Internet Relay Chat.
    http://www.irchelp.org/
23. Almost everyone has a book inside them. Discover how to write and sell a profitable eBook on the Web.
    http://www.InternetTIPS.com/
24. Don't get nervous Carrie: chill out with Stephen King.
    http://www.stephenking.com/
25. Discover the top 100 most popular Web sites. Find the Internet gems.
    http://www.web100.com/

26. Feeling literary and would like some bawdy culture (or not)? Read Shakespeare for free on http://the-tech.mit.edu/Shakespeare/

27. Play computer games with other users around the world. http://www.mpog.com/

28. Try some retail therapy while you sip a Tia Maria. http://www.shopsonthenet.com/shops/

29. Get key impartial financial advice. http://www.which.net/

30. Enough is enough! Find that dream job – then fire your overbearing boss! http://www.monsterboard.co.uk/ and http://www.gisajob.com/

31. Listen to the radio on the Net. http://windowsmedia.com/iradio/en_gb/radio.asp

32. Get a great domain name for your Web site. http://www.register.com/ http://www.nominet.org.uk/

33. Discover once and for all how to create a great Web site. Web page design in easy steps at http://www.ineasysteps.com/

34. Learn 50 ways to get rid of blind dates? http://www.cog.brown.edu/brochure/people/duchon/humor/blind.dates.html

35. Find God at http://www.jesussaves.cc/site_map.html

36. Invest in the stock market (but get professional advice first). http://www.esi.co.uk/

37. Read The Daily Telegraph newspaper online. http://www.dailytelegraph.co.uk/

38. Keep your finger on the pulse. Manage your financial investments. http://www.moneyworld.co.uk/ and http://news.ft.com/

39. You've seen it; you've saved for it, now buy your dream home. http://www.homehunter.co.uk/

40. Zoom down to your home from outer space (not all locations are yet covered). http://www.terraserver.com/

41. Check out what Manchester United Football Club are up to online. http://www.manutd.com/

42. Learn self-control with martial arts at http://www.bushido.ch/

43. Get help from the Samaritans at http://www.samaritans.org.uk/

44. Feel like you know something "they" don't? Learn how to become a White Witch at http://www.maxpages.com/witchesbook2

45. Carpe Diem. Seize the day! Have a daily motivational message sent to you. http://www.infoadvn.com/inspire/

46. Expecting a baby? find out more about motherhood – dad's too! http://www.ukmums.co.uk/

47. Keen to cut your gas, electricity, water and mobile phone bills? http://www.buy.co.uk/

48. Build on the University of life. Get a degree. http://www.open.ac.uk/

49. Wise up. Finish that homework sooner then relax: scan the superb Encyclopedia Britannica online for free at http://www.britannica.co.uk/

50. In business? get lots of free marketing help. http://www.marketinguk.co.uk/

51. Find your true life purpose: discover your destiny. http://www.lifeonpurpose.com/

52. Like trivia? Then get trivial at http://www.funtrivia.com/

53. Help your plants grow: play Mozart and other relaxing classical tunes. http://www.classicfm.co.uk/

54. Buy a computer online and save money at http://www.dell.co.uk/

55. Curious about anything and everything? Discover things about nothing in particular at http://www.letsfindout.com/

56. Chill out and find the best pubs with The Good Pub Guide.
http://www.goodguides.com/pubs/search.asp

57. Learn how to make money on the Internet from a respected expert with a proven record.
http://www.marketingtips.com/t.cgi/12939/

58. Help Amnesty International help someone who can't ask for help.
http://www.amnesty.org.uk/

59. Support your favourite charity:
http://www.childreninneed.com/

60. England, 1644. Smell the gunpowder as Oliver Cromwell's Roundheads meet Prince Rupert's Cavaliers at the Battle of Marston Moor.
http://www.sealedknot.org/history-1.htm

61. Want to kick the habit? Get practical advice and help to quit smoking.
http://www.quitsmoking.com/

62. Listen in while Police Special Forces catch the guys on the run!
http://www.policescanner.com/

63. Let the Internet update and upgrade your Windows software applications for you at http://www.manageable.com/

64. Escape to: "The most beautiful place on Earth."
http://www.yosemitepark.com/

65. Enter the time capsule. Key in a favourite date between 1900 to 1997 in the Time Capsule and discover the popular songs of the time, the big news around that date, birthdays of the famous, and so on.
http://www.dmarie.com/timecap/

66. Ask George and get some great gardening tips before you weed the borders at http://www.greenfingers.com/

67. Discover how to pay no tax – legally – at http://www.offshoreprofit.com/

68. Learn the most important useless knowledge (for example, how fish avoid drowning) at http://www.uselessknowledge.com

69. Is there more to coincidence? Learn about The Celestine Prophesy with James Redfield at http://www.celestineprophesy.com/

70. Feeling clever? Take an IQ test with MENSA.
http://www.mensa.com/

71. Listen to what's happening around the world with the BBC World Service at http://www.bbc.co.uk/worldservice/

72. If you're into aviation, check out the Boeing experience.
http://www.boeing.com/

73. Visit Number 10 Downing Street and join me in the Cabinet room.
http://www.number-10.gov.uk/

74. Pop in and say Hello to the First Lady at The White House.
http://www.whitehouse.gov/

75. Get spaced out: visit NASA and check out the Hubble telescope.
http://spacescience.nasa.gov/

76. Worship God in the Buff with the Christian Naturists.
http://home.vistapnt.com/markm/

77. Get into DIY and finally fix the house.
http://www.todayshomeowner.com/ and http://www.diy.co.uk/

78. Discover how to cook like my Grandmother.
    http://www.geocities.com/NapaValley/1111/
79. Fed up with traffic jams? Go vertical: get a Moller skycar.
    http://www.moller.com/skycar/
80. Confess your sins online at http://www.ulc.net/confession.html
81. Show that special person how much you love them, with flowers.
    http://www.interflora.co.uk/
82. Become fit and relaxed at the same time: learn yoga.
    http://www.sivananda.org/
83. Sell your house for nothing (no commission, no estate agents, no hassle)
    at http://www.easier.co.uk/
84. Cultivate green fingers. Brush up on your gardening skills.
    http://www.sierra.com/sierrahome/gardening/

85. Have a warped sense of humour? Then read what other warpies have to say in this comedy zine at http://www.fadetoblack.com

86. It's a new age in which more doesn't necessarily mean better. Learn the secrets of how to live simply at http://members.aol.com/DSimple/

87. Receive a free tips newsletter on your favourite topics. http://www.topica.com/tipworld

88. Ask an expert or become a guru yourself at http://www.guru.com/

89. Get cultural! Visit the Louvre in Paris at http://www.culture.fr/louvre

90. Experience London's Millennium Dome! http://www.dome2000.co.uk/static/flash/index.htm

91. Calm your mind and visit Tyburn Convent, London. Hear the bells toll and take a virtual tour at http://www.tyburnconvent.org.uk/

92. In a hurry? Need a gift fast? Looking for a great last minute holiday deal? http://www.lastminute.com/

93. Play safe: choose your condoms at Condomania. http://www.condoms4u.com/

94. Create your own digital films online. Sit in the Director's chair. http://www.dfilm.com/

95. This one's a surprise. Has serious multimedia eye-candy appeal including some amazing special video and sound effects. http://www.eye4u.com/

96. Get delicious Yorkshire cakes (from Elizabeth Botham at Whitby, North Yorkshire, England) at http://www.botham.co.uk/

97. Find out how things work at http://www.howstuffworks.com/

98. Visit Shakespeare at the Globe. http://www.reading.ac.uk/globe/ and http://shakespeare.eb.com/

99. Let your modem take the strain. Shop at Tesco's online (while relaxing in the garden with a fine wine) at http://www.tesco.co.uk/

100. Too much free time? Learn all about the bizarre art of "phone-bashing".
http://www.phonebashing.com/

101. OK, ready for a break now? Go Bed &Breakfast? Check out what's available around the world.
http://www.bedandbreakfast.com/

Who owns the Net?

A striking and sometimes confusing fact is that nobody and yet everybody "owns" the Internet! No single government or power has total control of the Internet – an unsettling reality for some authorities – and anyone with a PC/modem or other Internet device, and a phone connection, can gain access to it.

However, a number of large companies and organisations do have the power and influence to "steer" development of the Internet, including Microsoft, CompuServe/America Online (AOL)/Time-Warner and Netscape, plus several others. Other smaller organizations however, play a key role in the nuts and bolts development of the Internet, including: the World Wide Web Consortium (W3C) and domain naming bodies like InterNIC.

Some governments have tried and are still trying to control or censor the kind of information people can gain access to on the Internet – but usually with little success. Perhaps not a surprising outcome when we consider that the original purpose of the Internet was to create a communications system that could continue functioning even after a devastating global thermonuclear war.

The Internet at present is young and still forming, and in some ways it's much like a new "Wild West" or the Klondike of the 19th century. Like the gold fields of that era, the Internet and its "digital gold" are helping to create many multimillionaires. Internet success starts with having the right knowledge and know-how and if you have your eye on mining some Internet gold, books like this one can help you get started quickly. But like those early pioneers, you'll need to tread carefully to avoid unknown dangers!

The drive to bring the Net to everyone

Yesterday, most people had to have a "true" computer to access the Internet. Today, a computer can contain a plug-in TV card and televisions are being redesigned to include computer components that provide access to the Internet – WebTV for example. The differences between televisions and computers are slowly becoming hazy – and this trend is only just starting. Also, big changes are on the way with Internet access costs set to fall across the globe. This trend was made more evident to me even during the few months it took to write this book. More and more cable television operators and manufacturers around the world are forming alliances to further integrate the Internet into the most popular 21st Century communications medium: television.

Most new computers now come with built-in Internet access – which can now also be found in the latest mobile phones, personal organisers (Psion) and a whole host of other emerging Internet access devices.

Introducing Telnet

The various methods previously introduced are about connecting with potentially many different computers on the Internet and around the world.

Telnet, however, enables you to connect your computer with another single computer somewhere else around the world so that what you see on your screen is exactly the same as what appears on the monitor of the other computer to which you're Telnet-linked. Telnet is much like having two computers physically connected in the same room. The only difference is, you're using the Internet and where the other computer is physically situated is also not really relevant.

Imagine you're doing research in some obscure topic and you learn that a specific University computer somewhere on the other side of the world contains thousands of documents that might provide the key information you're looking for. If access through the more popular Internet channels like the Web is not available, ask about Telnet. However, not all Telnet computers give free public access; some are subscription-based but following up this method may still be worthwhile.

Once you're connected, you can search through folders, copy information and run programs. Many Telnet computers use the UNIX operating system, so if you're unfamiliar with UNIX, you'll need to spend some time learning the basics before starting to use Telnet.

As Telnet is largely text-based, it's not as "sexy" as the Web – which for most people has replaced any need to use Telnet. However, for some organisations that don't provide POP3 email or dial-up accounts to the Internet – like some educational establishments for example – Telnet may provide a solution.

Although you can Telnet using DOS or UNIX connections, software like Microsoft Windows or Apple Mac that have the necessary Telnet components built in are much easier to use as the software can remember host names automatically. (Here's an imaginary hostname: first.titan.net.)

Using Telnet in Microsoft Windows

In Microsoft Windows v9x, here's an easy way to use Telnet if you have already set up a working dial-up connection to the Internet. To open the Telnet window simply click the Start button, followed by the Run command and in the Run dialog box, type: telnet and click OK. Next in the Telnet window, choose the menu command Connect, followed by the Remote System command.

In the Connect dialog box, enter your desired host name – that is the address of the computer to which you want to connect – and click the Connect button to start your dialler. If you have multiple host names stored, you can use the drop-down arrow button next to the host name box to display a list of host names you previously entered.

Introducing Netiquette

When different people with varying outlooks are suddenly brought together, problems and misunderstandings can result. Throughout history, people across the world have developed acceptable methods with which to interact in a polite and positive way, in a spirit of tolerance, understanding and appreciation and acceptance of other views, habits and customs.

This general approach has also been transferred to the Internet to become known a little tongue-in-cheek as "Netiquette" or Net-etiquette – which is simply a way of acting with consideration for others. See page 291 (and elsewhere) for key information.

Copyright: how to become seriously rich or poor

Here's what to some is an obvious statement: every component on the Internet (text, graphics, programs, sound clips and video files) is owned by somebody. Compare this with the popular but dangerously false view among many

Internet users that everything on the Internet is free! Although much on the Internet is free of charge to use privately by individuals usually for non-commercial purposes, check the small print or risk being sued. As the Internet is becoming accepted into mainstream business life, sharp copyright and trademark lawyers are quickly learning the rules and can make their clients much richer at the expense of people who decide to "borrow" components from the Internet!

Often, an option is provided to download one copy, make a backup copy and print a single copy all for personal, non-commercial use. However, photocopying, re-selling or repeated printing is usually illegal. Arguably, copyright automatically applies to everything that is written, although including a copyright symbol does make ownership more clear. However, usually, even if Internet content is available free of charge, the ownership of that content stays with the copyright or trademark owner.

If in doubt, simple: just ask copyright or trademark owners before using their material and keep copies of all written communications to cover yourself if necessary during any possible future disputes – people may sometimes genuinely forget that they have given permission previously so you need to keep documentary evidence to avoid possible problems and misunderstandings.

As a result of copyright and trademark infringements, some organisations have found a highly lucrative addition to their income by setting up systems that regularly scan the Internet (sometimes automatically, 24 hours a day) and suing those parties who violate international copyright laws.

Nethead heaven:
how the Internet works

When you send or receive information on the Internet, an incredible chain of events occurs. To use the Net, you don't need to know how it works. However, sometimes a little key background knowledge can help clarify explanations provided later in the book. Here's a brief outline of what happens to information as it moves across the Internet.

What is TCP/IP and all that jazz?

Transmission Control Protocol/Internet Protocol –more sensibly referred to as TCP/IP – is part of a complex set of rules that computers on the Internet use to communicate. The TCP part first ensures information to be sent is chopped up into smaller chunks known as packets.

TCP/IP is responsible for creating the information packets, transmitting the information and then recombining the

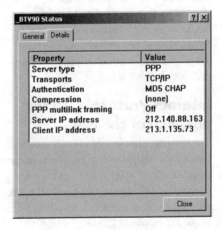

packets properly to recreate the original information at the receiving end. Your computer first sends the packets to your Internet Service Provider, or equivalent Internet connection service. From your Internet Service Provider, the packets travel across the computer networks and communications links that make up the Internet.

Each packet may travel a different route to the other packets that make up the same piece of information. At the receiving end the packets are recombined and the information re-formed to its original state. If one "connection" to the Internet is broken, information can use "connections" on other routes to ensure that all the information arrives at its destination.

Internet Protocol (IP): the postman of the Net

The Internet Protocol makes sure each packet is sent to the right destination. Each computer connected to the Internet is given a unique number or IP address. A typical IP address uses four sets of numbers separated by full stops, for example: 123.456.789.6.

When a computer connects to the Internet, it is assigned an IP address – if using an Internet Service Provider, the numbers that make up the address may change each time you connect. However, thankfully we users don't usually need to be concerned with these numbers, since an automatic system is in place on the Internet that translates a set of IP numbers to a Web address. The Domain Naming

System (DNS) allows you to enter a more user-friendly name for a Web site (like www.gardening.com) instead of something like 123.137.456.7 (imaginary DNS numbers simply picked at random to illustrate the DNS numbering pattern).

Routers – amazing Internet guides

A router is one of many special computers on the Internet that are responsible for controlling the continuous flow of information – often referred to as "traffic" – across the Internet.

When a router receives an information packet as discussed in previous paragraphs, it decides the most efficient route for that packet to take and sends the packet on its way to the next router if necessary. And so on. As a result, a single packet may go through a single router, several routers or many routers to ensure that the packet successfully reaches its final destination. Now isn't that amazing?

How Internet Backbones speed up the Net

Just like some roads are busier than others in our towns and cities, specific parts of the Internet now sometimes have a similar problem too. At "peak" times, say between 3pm - 7pm in the UK (when the USA "wakes up"), parts of the Internet have to move a lot more information in comparison to other parts of the Net, sometimes causing delays and jams. To help combat Internet traffic jams, high-speed "busy" communication lines – or "Backbones" as they are popularly known – have been developed and directly interconnect the most important computer networks around the world.

Preparing your computer for the Internet

Many different types of computer can be used to access the Internet. Whether you're using an IBM-compatible Personal Computer (PC), Apple Macintosh (iMac), company network terminal, Amiga, or whatever, providing the computer you want to use meets the minimum standards – and most do – then you can get connected. However, as many Web sites nowadays do contain a lot of animation and more demanding self-running programs, the most recent, faster computers generally give better results.

Buying a computer

Most computers today are either an IBM-compatible Personal Computer (PC) or an Apple Mac. Apple were the first computer maker to start using a Graphical User Interface (GUI) – a visual design made up of different types of boxes or "windows", icons (visual symbols), and so on, which when combined with a mouse, provide a point-and-click navigation approach. With the GUI, What-You-See-Is-What-You-Get (WYSIWYG, pronounced "Wiziwig") was born.

This same idea was later introduced to the PC with Microsoft Windows to provide the familiar look and feel that we see today in Windows 9x/2000/NT and later versions. When compared, both the PC and the Mac now offer a similar range of options, yet true Mac enthusiasts constantly argue with PC devotees over performance and look and feel issues. So which is best? The answer really depends on what you want. Apple Macs have an obvious designer look and feel, are usually more expensive than equivalent PCs, and are often especially popular with artists and designers. In terms of performance, arguably the PC is currently winning the race.

Today, the PC installed with the Microsoft Windows operating system is by far the most popular platform. However, Apple's fortunes may change again – as the rising level of recent sales figures shows. Many more varieties of PCs are made than Apple Macs. Therefore, a wider range of software is available and prices are often cheaper all round.

If you really want to examine the computer buying business in detail, shop around. Ask friends who already use a computer – just appreciate that your friends are almost certainly going to be biased either for or against a specific type; this is natural, but read the reviews and see demonstrations before making your final decision. My own choice is the PC simply because it offers the range of software I want, to perform the tasks I need to complete.

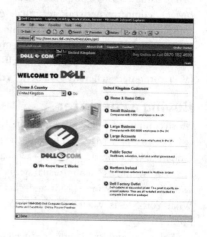

The most essential component in a computer needed to use the Internet is a modem or equivalent device. Most new computers now come with a modem or Internet access device; however, you may want to add a new modem or install a faster model. Modems and other fast Internet access devices are covered in "Modems" on page 55 and "Speeding up your Internet connection" page 193.

Although, you can probably browse the Internet with an older PC – for example, an IBM-compatible PC based on the Intel 486 chip – you may become frustrated with poor performance while viewing Web sites containing animations and self-running programs, and so on. Also if, like most people in the UK, you have to pay dearly for your Internet connection, a slower PC will almost certainly take longer to complete tasks and so probably increase your phone or Internet access costs generally. When buying a new or used computer, the two most important considerations that affect the speed at which you can use the Internet are:

• The speed of the computer (also known as the CPU speed).
• The amount and type of memory (RAM) installed.

These same performance considerations also apply to other devices that are used to access the Internet if these devices use a microprocessor and memory chips and other similar electronic components. The most important type of memory to affect the speed of your computer is the speed and capacity of the plug-in RAM chips your computer uses.

Get the fastest computer with the most amount of Random Access Memory (RAM) you can afford, to reduce the amount of time you need to spend finding, receiving and saving information. 32Mb as an absolute minimum, 64Mb is fine, 128Mb is better. And only buy a computer that allows you to upgrade/add more "standard" RAM modules easily. Get assurances that you can add more RAM in say 12-18 months, should you choose.

RAM chips hold information temporarily and lose their information when the PC is switched off. RAM is measured in megabytes (Mb) or millions of bytes. Remember, in computer terms, a byte is simply eight bits of information. A fast PC with lots of RAM can help make your journeys around the Internet more enjoyable, more stable and interesting. Coupled with a reliable fast link to the Internet, you can then concentrate on the Internet content without getting sidetracked into looking for ways to speed up your viewing experience.

The speed of a computer is only one component that helps determine how fast you can surf the Internet. If you have a slow connection to the Net, using a faster computer usually won't solve the problem – it will only allow interactive or multimedia components to play faster and run better. For faster Internet surfing, get the fastest connection you can afford: for example, leased lines, cable and ISDN provide faster Internet connections than a modem. For more information, see page 193.

If you decide to opt for a second-hand PC, the best advice I can offer is to choose a well known brand name if possible, like Dell, IBM, Dan, etc., that is less than 2 years old. Why? Older PCs may not be able to properly cope with the current demands of the Internet.

Getting up to speed

The most important electronic chip in a computer is the main microprocessor – often referred to as the Central Processing Unit (CPU). The CPU performs the most important number-crunching operations in a computer and therefore makes an enormous impact on its overall speed. The rate at which a CPU completes a series of tasks is measured in millions of cycles each second –

computer makers now use the term Hertz (Hz) meaning one cycle each second. So a powerful computer today might work at 700 million Hertz – often shown in advertisements as 700 MHz – or I GHz (1000 million Hertz), or even more.

Although you can "upgrade" some older computers by changing the main microprocessor (CPU) and perhaps adding more powerful RAM (memory) chips, check into the full costs of this option very carefully. After you consider the costs, benefits and drawbacks, as the price of PCs continues to fall, you may be better off simply selling your old PC and buying a new one.

How's your memory?

If you're upgrading, remember the absolute minimum amount of RAM you should aim for is 32Mb. Although 64Mb is better, ideally aim for 128Mb or more. Anything under 16 Mb will probably cause problems for today's Web browsers. As the Web and television merge, sound, video and computer or Internet games and entertainment usually work much better with more RAM memory.

Hard drive café

To keep information intact even when you switch your computer off, on most computers you "save" your data to the computer's hard disk drive. A hard drive typically has several disks or platters that spin very fast. The larger your hard drive, the more information can be stored and processed. Current versions of Web browser suites like Microsoft Internet Explorer need a considerable amount of hard disk space – typically 80 Mb or more. Netscape Web browser suites may need less while Apple Mac PCs generally need even less disk space. Check your Web browser documentation for the computer you're using.

Web pages are becoming ever more animated and interactive and generally these types of Web pages take up more storage space than that of a "simple" Web page. It's amazing how soon you can fill a hard disk while regularly saving information from the Internet. Therefore again, aim to get the largest capacity hard drive you can afford: ensuring plenty of empty hard drive space also ensures that you computer runs better. Try to aim for a minimum of 4Gb (Gigabytes) – ideally double that figure if possible.

If you are running out of hard drive space, you may be able to fit a second hard drive or install a larger capacity drive. If unsure of how to go about it, get advice from your computer dealer and if you want to know more about this topic, the plain English "Upgrading Your PC in easy steps" from Computer Step has been designed to help anyone who can use a screwdriver.

Choosing a display monitor

Your computer's monitor is your window onto the Internet. The screen size of your monitor affects how you see some Web pages – for example: if the screen is too small, you may be forced to use the horizontal scrollbars or keyboard more and this can become quite frustrating over time. Ideally, aim for at least a 17 inch screen minimum – as measured diagonally from corner to corner. But remember, Web page scrollbars and boxes also take up space. Computer operating systems like Microsoft Windows and the Macintosh MacOS can use lots of boxes on the screen at once and Web pages can contain lots of different components. Therefore, the "effective" screen size is only 15"!

Screen sizes smaller than about 15" can mean that you have to use your mouse or keyboard more often to complete your tasks. Ideally, a 17" or 19" screen is ideal for Internet use as these can easily display most Web pages properly and without the need for horizontal scrolling (if designed correctly). For more information on Web design, see "Web Page Design in easy steps" from Computer Step). Your computer monitor also uses a special type of video memory so again, more video memory generally means items display faster. Try to get the fastest and largest amount of video memory you can afford.

Finally make sure your display monitor can display as many different colours as possible so that you can see images that use many colours and shades, like photographs, clearly as they should appear. In practice this means up to 17 million colours, however, you computer's operating system usually allows you to set the exact level. If this level is set too low at, say, 16 colours, photographs on Web pages especially will probably look patchy and flat.

Change your settings to display at least "256 colours" or "thousands" of colours and the quality of the display should improve considerably. Although often you can set your display to "millions" of colours, this option may cause some Web pages to display more slowly as the monitor has to perform more work to meet the demands asked of it. Check your computer documentation on how to do this or speak to your computer dealer if unsure.

An ideal Internet-ready PC

Here's an ideal specification for a PC on the Internet today:

- Computer Speed: 450 MHz or faster microprocessor (CPU).
- RAM: 128 Mb of RAM upgradeable to 4 or 5 times that level.
- Hard drive: at least 4Gbyte capacity; 10 - 15Gbyte preferred.
- Video card/video chips: creates the electronic signals to drive your display monitor. To view video clips and possibly 3D Internet displays clearly, try to get a video card with at least 8Mb of fast video memory, to help minimise the amount of time your computer needs to spend processing these large routines.

- Display monitor: 17" or larger; 19" is a good option; 21" is a joy.
- Modem: a 56Kbps modem either built-in on-board, as a plug-in card or an external box. Most important: if you're buying a modem, make sure you choose one that is compatible with your computer and the phone system for your country.
- DVD drive: a Digital Video Disk (DVD) drive can also play Compact Discs for computers (CD-ROMs) as well as audio Compact Discs (CDs). At a pinch, a CD-ROM drive may still meet your needs.
- Mouse or equivalent point-and-click device: a mouse is a small hand-held tool you use to move the mouse pointer or "cursor" around the screen. Although not absolutely essential to use the Internet, a mouse will almost certainly speed up your viewing.
- Microsoft Windows-compatible keyboard.
- Sound card/sound capability: a sound card – also called a sound board – or built-in sound capability allows you to hear and record high quality sound from the Internet, Web pages, Web radio and TV stations, music download sites, videos, and so on. A sound card plugs into a spare PC expansion socket and needs configuring in your computer's operating system software. To hear sound, you'll also need loudspeakers.
- Loudspeakers: convert the signals from a sound card or sound chips into sound. Loudspeakers plug into a sound card or connector that links to the appropriate sound chips on the main computer board. Ideally choose compatible PC speakers that come with an amplifier built in to enhance the sound signals received from the sound chips.
- Microphone/headset: essential if you want to talk to others on the Internet. If you have some spare funds and want to get ahead of the game, consider getting a WebCam kit that combines with the above, to build in a kind of video phone capability.

Modems

A modem is another essential electronic hardware device most people need to use the Internet today. But modems come in a variety of types and specifications. This chapter provides information you need to know about choosing and using a modem.

What is a modem?

A modem enables a computer to share information with other computers using the standard phone lines, and as such, for most current Internet users, is probably their most important electronic component. The word "modem" is made up from the two words: MOdulator and DEModulator – which is another way of saying: "Code the information, send it, then decode it at the other end." Modems are available in three main forms:

- An external "box" that connects to a computer. An external modem can connect to the serial, parallel or USB sockets (discuss these options with your computer dealer when buying your modem).
  Benefits: you don't need to remove the computer's casing to install this type of modem. An external modem is often the best solution if you want to just get online quickly. You can also easily move an external modem to another computer. Indicator lights show the status or progress of a connection and if you have a communications problem, the condition of these lights can help point to where an error might lie.

Drawbacks: adds more cabling at the back of the computer. Requires some desk space and its own power supply adaptor. Usually more expensive than plug-in card modems for desktop computers.

- A plug-in card modem installs into a spare slot inside the computer electronic box containing the main circuit board (motherboard). Follow the maker's instructions. As a general guide, you'll need to disconnect the computer from the electrical mains supply first, fit an antistatic wristband, then remove the computer casing and carefully install the card. Ask your computer dealer for advice if unsure.
  Benefits: takes up no desk space, you don't need a separate power supply and this option doesn't add to the number of connection cables at the back of your computer.
  Drawbacks: you need to remove the computer cover and understand how to fit the card. Once the computer casing is removed, there's an

increased risk that electronic components may be damaged. Take care: electronic boards are fragile.

To ensure a modem can properly work with current modem speeds, make sure the computer/modem has a 16550 UART chip – ask your dealer if unsure. A UART electronic chip manages the information that flows into and out of a modem.

- For notebook computers, not desktops, a PC-Card – also known as PCMCIA – is a plug-in credit card-size module that installs into a special "expansion" slot on a computer's main electronic circuit board (motherboard). No need to remove the computer casing.
  Benefits: most PC-Card modems can work with most types of notebook computer; however, do check if any special restrictions apply. Get advice from your computer maker or dealer. Small and compact and don't need an external power supply.
  Drawbacks: usually more expensive to buy and cannot work with desktop computers. A PC Card must be installed into the correct slot otherwise permanent damage to the card and computer could result.

Why do we need a modem?

Information in a computer when broken down to its most basic parts is essentially made up of a series of ones and zeros and is termed digital information. Phone lines were of course originally designed only to handle a range of varying values (voice) not just ones and zeros. Therefore, to transfer computer information using the phone lines, a modem is needed to convert and prepare information correctly for sending through a phone line, and then reconverting and translating the incoming information to the digital format that a computer can understand.

 When buying a modem, you may still be offered an older, slower modem running at 33,600 bps (33.6Kbps). Buy the fastest modem you can afford that is compatible with the phone system in your country and avoid getting modems slower than 33.6Kbps. 56Kbps is the current standard.

Modems for networked computers

Most modems are designed to run on a single computer. However, if you have several computers linked together in a network, and want to provide Internet access to each computer, several options are possible:

- You could consider buying a network-compatible modem. A network modem installs on one machine but allows other computers in the network to use it as though it were connected to each networked computer. A network modem allows several different users in the network to access the Internet at the same time.
- Later versions of Microsoft Windows 9x/2000 operating systems that have Windows Networking installed allow a modem to be shared across a network. See your Windows 2000 guide (or "Windows 2000 Professional in easy steps") for more information.
- Users of Client/Server operating systems usually offer similar options. Check your documentation or speak to your computer dealer.

Modem speeds

Several years ago, once the value of modems became clear, many different modem manufacturers emerged across the world. To ensure modems could communicate properly with other modems, a set of standards became necessary so that all knew what was necessary. As a result, the "V" series of Standards has emerged.

How fast a modem operates tells us how fast information can be sent and received. The faster the modem, the less time you need to spend online to retrieve the information you want – so if you have to pay for every second while online, a faster modem saves you money. Modem speed is measured in bits per second (bps). Current modems ideally run at 56,000 bps – often written as 56Kbps (kilobits per second) or sometimes known as the V.90 standard. What this actually means is that a V.90 modem can receive information at up to 56Kbps and send information at a speed of up to 33.6Kbps. Note these are maximum speeds and in practice speeds are often somewhat lower. Why? Many modems still connect to the Internet using old copper-based phone lines – which were originally designed for voice communications, not computer data – even though a modem may be listed as 56Kbps speed, for most people, that level of speed is rarely reached.

The actual speed at which you connect depends largely on the "quality" of the telephone line. As an Internet and computer author, I obviously spend a lot of time online and use a 56Kbps modem often. Yet my connection speed averages at about 44Kbps which is acceptable for general surfing.

Modems that shake hands

Before two modems can "talk" to each other, they perform a kind of electronic handshaking routine. A few basic tests are carried out automatically to ensure they're "speaking" the same language. Essentially, that's what a "handshake" is: after a successful handshake, the two modems must "agree" that they're compatible and how they will exchange or transfer information.

The entire handshaking process usually takes place very quickly so you probably won't even be aware of it happening. Indeed for most purposes, you don't need to know how it works, just that when things are running properly, it's an event that simply happens every time you connect to the Internet.

For example, one aspect that two modems must "agree" on is the speed at which to communicate. If one "talks" faster than the other can handle, confusion would result. Handshaking ensures that they "talk" at the same speed or that a faster modem slows down to match the speed of a slower modem – that's one of the reasons why sometimes your Internet connection speed may vary.

Squeezing the lemon and compressing data

To speed up the rate at which your modem sends information to another modem, the data or information can be compressed – a little like squeezing a lemon – so that the information takes up less space and travels across the Internet faster.

At the other end, the receiving modem automatically decompresses the information to its original size. Some types of files compress better than others. For example: a text file compresses much better than, say, a picture file. All new modems should now use data compression techniques so if you're buying, make sure that your intended modem uses the latest data compression technology for your country.

Zapping those pesky errors

Just like people make mistakes from time to time, so do modems. However, modern modems use some clever techniques to check for and correct any errors that may occur in the information being sent. Modem error control technology is another measure that helps ensure that information sent arrives intact at the receiving end. The way error control works is to first break information into separate chunks or "packets" before sending the data.

US Robotics® Courier V.Everything modem - External/Internal

DATA SPEEDS
* x2 upgradeable*
* V.34+ at 33,600bps
* V.34 at 28,800bps
* V.FC at 28,800bps
* V.32terbo+ at 21,600bps
* V.32terbo at 19,200bps
* V.32bis at 14,400bps
* HST at 16,800bps

FAX SPEEDS
* ITU-T V.17 at 14,400bps
* V.29 at 9600bps
* V.27ter at 4800 bps
* EIA/TIA Class 1 and 2.0 with call selection
* Group III

ERROR CORRECTION & DATA COMPRESSION
* ITU-T V.42 / MNP levels 2-4 Error Correction
* ITU-T V.42bis / MNP5 Data Compression

FEATURES
* x2 upgradeable*
* Dial Back Security
* Flash Memory (upgradeable)
* Universal Connect (exclusive to U.S. Robotics)
* ASL (exclusive to U.S. Robotics)
* Auto Fax/Data selection
* QuickConnect (exclusive to U.S. Robotics)
* DOS/Windows software included
* Synchronous Dealing
* Voice/Data Switch (front-mounted selector)
* Help Screens
* BABT approved
* External and PC Internal Versions

At the other end, error control ensures that the receiving modem knows what the packets should contain and checks each one. If any damaged packets are detected, the receiving modem "asks" the transmitting modem to send another copy of the damaged packet. This process happens very fast and error control generally performs well.

A note about Call Waiting services

If you have a standard phone socket installed, you don't need a separate phone line for your modem: usually, you can connect your modem and standard telephone to the same phone line.

However, if you have a Call Waiting service set up on your phone system and your telephone and modem do share the same phone line, make sure that before using your modem, you turn off Call Waiting as these types of interactive services can cause connection problems. If in doubt, contact your telephone or Internet Service Provider for advice.

What else do I need to make my modem work?

Once you have your modem installed and connected to the phone line, every modem needs a software program to enable it to communicate with other modems and computers on the Internet and around the world.

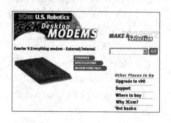

Usually, compatible software comes with a new modem, or you can buy from a range of suitable off-the-shelf software packages to find one that matches your needs.

What else can I do with a modem?

One really useful feature of a correctly installed modem is that while travelling or if you're located away from your home or office – say on holiday or on business abroad – you can dial into your home or office computer or company network and access your information, just as though you were actually working at your home or office computer! If you do this while on holiday: shame on you, why not take a break instead?

Sending and receiving faxes

Many modems can also send and receive fax messages so you may not even need a separate fax machine (and therefore rolls of fax paper). Often a basic fax

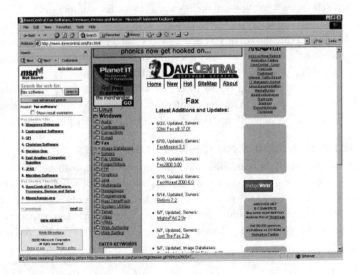

program may be included with a new modem but if you want more specific functions, upgrading to "Pro" versions is perhaps something to consider. If 24-hour fax capability is important to you, remember if you use a modem and PC, you may need to ensure your PC is either switched on permanently or can "wake up" on receiving a fax message. Excellent software tools like Microsoft Office may include all the fax software you need. For example, Microsoft Outlook 2000 includes a free version of fax software from Symantec that integrates perfectly with Microsoft Office and Outlook. Also, Windows 2000 now comes with a superb basic fax management package.

Then, when your computer receives a fax, the message is usually saved automatically. If you're working with some other software at the time of receiving a fax, often you can set your fax software to alert you to the fact that you are receiving a fax. You can then "switch" to the fax window and view the fax on-screen and optionally print it if you wish.

However remember that you usually can't edit a fax received in this way unless you have Optical Character Recognition (OCR) software installed and set up. Also, if you're using a separate computer display monitor, you don't need to have it switched on to receive a modem-faxed document as the information is already in the computer's main box – the monitor simply provides a way to view information stored on the computer's hard drive.

Internal modems for desktop computers

An internal "card" modem for a desktop computer is simply installed into a spare slot on the motherboard. Once installed and the case refitted, you'll be able to see the edge of the modem at the back of your computer (usually). If you're doing the job yourself, learn how to install a modem before attempting this sometimes-tricky task, as circuit boards in computers are fragile. You can learn more in "Upgrading Your PC in easy steps" from Computer Step (http://www.ineasysteps.com). Or speak to your computer dealer.

To install an internal modem in a desktop PC, follow the maker's instructions. However, as a general guide, consider the following:

1. Make sure your computer and modem are both switched off and disconnected from the electrical main supply.
2. Unplug your existing phone lead from the wall socket.
3. Fit an antistatic wristband to reduce the possibility that static electricity in your body may damage sensitive electronic components.
4. Remove your PC's outer case and find a compatible empty slot for your modem card. If necessary, remove the blanking plate covering the slot you want.

5. Carefully remove the modem card from its packaging and install into the desired slot. Secure the modem edge with the securing screw.

6. Then using the extra phone lead supplied, connect your modem to the wall phone socket.

7. Optionally, plug the lead from your existing phone into the correct socket on the modem card.

8. Carefully refit the PC case and reconnect your devices.

9. Switch on your PC. If you're using a later version of Microsoft Windows and the modem too is new, Windows should detect your modem and install the software it needs for you. Watch the screen closely and follow instructions.

10. Install any additional related software following the supplied instructions.

Modems for portable computers

Installing a modem in say a notebook PC is much easier than for a desktop model and you don't need to remove the outer case. Notebook PC modems are usually small, completely encased, credit-card-sized modules that you simply push into the correct socket.

Make sure however, that you use the correct slot: use the wrong slot and you could destroy the modem and the PC! Therefore, most importantly, follow the maker's instructions throughout installation and get advice from your dealer if unsure. Mistakes with portable PCs can be expensive to correct.

Working with external modems

An external modem usually connects to a special socket on the rear of a computer. External modems usually come with all the connecting leads and software you need to get up and running quickly, and so are usually easier to

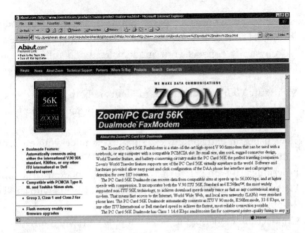

install when compared to fitting an internal modem. As a minimum, you'll have the connecting lead to the computer and the connecting lead that connects your modem to your phone socket.

Although an external modem can take up more room on your desk, usually a range of status indicator lights are present on the modem that can tell you what is happening while dialling your Internet Service Provider or when using the Internet. You might see the letters "RD", "SD", and "OH" to mean "Receiving Data", "Sending Data", and "Off Hook", to name but a few. When tackling Internet access problems that sometimes occur, your Internet Service Provider may ask about the condition of specific status lights, to quickly help determine where the problem lies. Also, you can easily move an external modem and connect it to another computer, whereas moving an internal card modem is more time-consuming and sometimes more tricky.

Remember, you don't need a separate phone line to use your modem and to make the job of connecting up even easier, most modems include a phone socket. To physically connect your modem, read and follow the maker's instructions. However as a general guide consider the following guidelines:

1. Make sure your computer and modem are both switched off.
2. Unplug your existing phone lead from its socket and simply plug this lead into the socket marked on the modem.
3. Then using the extra phone lead supplied, connect your modem to the wall phone socket.
4. Now plug in the larger lead that connects your modem to the computer. Usually, this lead will have moulded plugs each end with an 11-pin or 24-pin connector one end.
5. Connect the modem to its power supply and switch on.
6. Switch on your PC. If you're using a later version of Microsoft Windows and the modem too is new, Windows should detect your modem and install the software it needs for you. Watch the screen closely and follow instructions.
7. Install any additional related software following the supplied instructions.

ISDN Modem

Getting online

Once connected to the Internet, you can have a lot of fun, but probably the hardest part is successfully connecting for the first time. After all, if you're new to everything Internet, you don't know what to expect. However don't be put off; the software that you'll use to connect to the Net is designed for anyone to use – not computer geeks – so take your time. Usually, you'll only need to install the software once so that getting online is then only a few mouse clicks away.

Some of the most helpful people on the Internet are other Net users. For example, certain newsgroups are particularly valuable. Although this option is not much help until you're connected, if you do have a technical problem, perhaps you could ask a friend or colleague who already has Internet and newsgroup access to post your question and handle the replies.

Getting set up to go online is not that difficult, especially since software is generally getting easier to install and use. Also, in the never-ending battle for customers, many Internet Service Providers now provide added help to get you up and running as soon as possible. After all, they don't benefit until you're connected, so if you do get stuck, I'll bet there's a contact phone number in your pack that you can call to get direct one-to-one help. If not, think twice about using that Internet Service Provider. When you're new to the Internet, you want help, not hassle. Good ISPs understand this important point.

What do I need to get on the Net?

To gain access to and use of the Internet, here's what you'll need:

- An Internet-ready computer or other Internet access device: an Internet-ready television or mobile phone for example. Whichever electronic device you choose, remember that the Internet software you choose gets the results you want. Therefore, make sure that the electronic hardware is powerful enough to properly drive your chosen Internet software – Web browsers, Web design software, email and newsgroup programs. If you're buying new equipment, don't forget, true audio/video-based email may arrive sooner than we might think – and will probably make extra demands on your equipment – so try to think at least 1 year ahead to get maximum value for your money.

- Telephone or cable television connection: this must be physically close to your modem, computer or other Internet access device. Remember, however, that, although most users opt for a physical phone or cable line, a "wireless" (remote) connection to the Internet is now also available.
- Gateway connection to the Internet: currently, there are two main ways in which you can get connected to the Net: 1) With a Dial Up device like a modem or ISDN Terminal Adaptor, or 2) Using what is known as a leased line. A leased line is a fast permanent but expensive connection to the Internet – and therefore tailored to Internet-oriented businesses. Most people connect to the Net using a Dial Up service through either an Internet Service Provider – like Demon for example – or a commercial online service like CompuServe or America Online (AOL). With these services, each time you connect to the Internet it may only cost the equivalent of a local phone call, or less, or it may even be completely free of charge (eventually). Many choices are now available so we'll be examining ISPs in more depth a little later to help you choose the right one for you. See also pages 78 and 79.
- Internet software: necessary to perform various tasks on the Internet, like using email and surfing the Web. In addition, use up-to-date antivirus software to protect your computer while online. Software is available for both IBM-compatible PCs and Apple Mac computers. Most Internet access software is now available free of charge online. Or one of the best sources is your local magazine store: many computer and Internet magazines now include free CD-ROMs/DVD-ROMs that contain all the software you need to get started on the Internet. Once up and running, you can also download extra software or updates straight from the Internet.

Currently, computers or PCs offer the most popular way to access the Net. A typical Internet-ready computer is one that uses phone lines and an Internet Service Provider as described previously to connect to the Net. In practice, most types of modern computer can be used on the Net but older PCs will almost certainly struggle to properly display many current Web pages – especially those that contain animated components. Older slower computers usually have to work much harder to display complex Web pages, and generally put more strain on your computer's hard drive (a kind of semipermanent memory).

However, you can also use a growing variety of other Internet access devices including Web-compatible TVs (WebTV), Palmtop PCs, Psion Organisers and mobile phones. But times are changing quickly. Perhaps sooner than we might think, television is set to become the most popular way to access the Net.

Low-priced and free Internet access

Although much of what is available on the Internet may be free, unless you're connecting to the Net using work, University or library facilities, the chances are you'll probably have to pay some connection fees to an Internet Service Provider, local phone rate charges, and if using the faster ISDN, ADSL or cable connections, you may have further costs to pay. However, the cost of Internet access in many different countries looks set to keep falling: only time will tell whether a completely free system is sustainable.

In March 2000, Alta Vista started a new trend in the UK by announcing plans to offer low-cost access to the Internet for UK users through a freephone 0800 number for day-to-day use. Within hours of this announcement, NTL another well-established Internet provider and mobile phone chain Phones4U, also announced plans to offer completely free Internet access for UK subscribers. The battle for market share has only just begun as existing Internet providers will almost certainly announce plans to compete with these new services. At the time of writing this book, the well-known domestic electronics product maker Alba announced plans to provide a low-priced Internet-ready television. Almost certainly, many other manufacturers will follow soon with similar offerings. Developments like these are set to completely revolutionise the way we currently access and use the Internet and probably the best is yet to come!

Free/nearly free Internet access is a new concept in the UK and many other countries. Therefore, be a little cautious at least in the early days. If you sign up for low-cost access, do check the small print to determine whether any hidden charges might apply. If fast, reliable and regular access to the Internet is particularly important to you, do remember that during the early development stages of "free" Internet access, services may become swamped with a high number of new subscribers, which may in the short term affect connection quality and reliability until the providers are able to upgrade their services to properly cope with the new increased demands.

At the very least, make sure any Internet provider lets you connect at least at local telephone call rate or equivalent — ideally, check out free of charge packages.

With those Internet Service Providers that do charge outside of free access times, often the cost is the same as the local phone call rate, maybe even a little lower. However, some providers may charge more so do check your subscription small print to avoid getting large unexpected phone bills.

Modem roundup

Let's recap. Most people currently use an electronic device called a modem to access the Internet. A modem may come built-in to a computer or you can connect an external modem to your PC. Most new PCs being sold now do contain a modem either as a plug-in card or in the form of electronic chips built into the main circuit board (motherboard). Also, modem-like devices are likely to be used in the new generation of Internet-ready televisions and other Internet access devices currently being developed and soon to be on sale in the shops. Most PCs over 2 or 3 years old, however, probably didn't come with a modem as "standard." Add-on modems usually come either as a plug-in card that is inserted into a special slot in the computer or motherboard, or as an external box that you can simply connect to your computer with all the necessary wires and connectors provided. Modems are examined in depth in "Modems", page 55.

HP DeskJet 935C

Using a printer

Although a printer is not essential to access the Internet, sometimes you may need to print Internet or Web documents. Most printers today come in three main types: dot matrix, inkjet, or laser. If buying a printer, consider buying the best colour inkjet or laser printer you can afford. Dot matrix printers generally don't print graphics as clearly as an inkjet or laser printer. Whatever type of printer you decide to buy, do consider the running costs – especially printing ink or laser toner, as these can deliver some nasty shocks. Colour inkjet printers especially can use more ink than you might imagine – especially black which is necessary in order to create a wide range of coloured tints and shades in photographic-type images.

Remember to observe copyright, trademark and licensing laws when using or printing information and property "owned" by others – especially if used for commercial purposes.

Web TV: the future here now

Easy access to the Internet through television is almost certainly the way of the future for most Internet users. Using a special type of remote control handset, this approach allows you to view and "travel" around the Web on your television screen at the same time as watching television programs, perhaps in a smaller window. Switching between "television mode" and "Internet mode" is available with a single press of a button!

Popular in the USA at the time of writing, Internet-ready televisions are now becoming more widely available in the UK and other countries. So why has it taken so long? Well for a start, WebTV and computer display monitors use different display technologies.

Computer monitors use the Red-Green-Blue (RGB) system to create all the colours needed by mixing varying amounts of red, green and blue light. Televisions, however, need to receive and recreate a wide variety of colours and so use the more complex types of broadcast systems (the PAL system in the UK and NTSC in the USA, for example).

Computer monitors and WebTVs also have different viewing dimensions. For example, a display monitor may be described as 4:3; this means, if 4 units make up the screen width, 3 units make up the height. A modern television may use a 16:9 ratio. Therefore WebTV usually uses a special type of Web browser; one that is designed to reproduce Web pages for television rather than a computer. The electronic circuitry necessary to link a television to the Internet may be available in two main forms:

- As a separate add-on box placed near to the television.
- Components built in as part of a television's electronics.

Whichever method is used, most should be able to accept standard devices like printers, scanners and so on, in addition to standard telephone and cable TV connectors. But if you're buying, certainly check these facts.

Internet kiosks and terminals

If you want to explore the Internet but don't have your own PC, WebTV or other Internet access device, consider using somebody else's – with their permission of course! A growing list of options is becoming available. As ever-cheaper access to the Internet continues, all sorts of entry points to the Internet are expected to develop. In time, it's likely that you'll find Post Offices, shops, garages and even ferries may also provide email and Internet services as standard. Airports and train/bus terminals are also likely targets for more Internet terminals – in fact any place where people are likely to meet has potential for creating income from Internet services.

Cybercafés

If you live in or near many towns, you can escape from the office or home and visit your local cybercafé. There, you can enjoy light refreshments and optionally sit at a table that has a computer connected to the Internet. Often a great way to meet other users, perhaps enjoy a chat and have a fun time learning about the Net – especially if you're a new user. See also page 461.

Computer shops

Stores that sell computers often provide group demonstrations or presentations about using the Internet. Often, these kinds of promotion are likely to be biased towards the store's own products. However, you can learn much and perhaps get to try out those aspects of the Internet that interest you.

Public libraries and the Internet: perfect partners

Some public libraries in the know make Internet-ready computers available and even smaller local libraries can offer some free Internet access time. To use public library Internet computers, you'll probably need to reserve a time slot. The small public library in my own area – a suburb of one the UK's main cities – now provides free Internet access in prearranged 30 minute time slots; a wonderful way for anyone new to the Internet to experiment at their own pace.

Contact your local librarian for more information. Perhaps completely free Internet access will eventually become available, providing an entry point to the Internet for almost anyone. If you're completely new to the Internet, don't be afraid to ask for help; most library assistants are particularly helpful.

Don't forget trial Internet offers

If you're new to the Internet, reduced or free trial offers can be a great way to get started on the Net and try out different services. Most of the well-established Internet providers now offer a limited amount of Internet time free of charge. However, do check the conditions: until completely free Internet access becomes available, you may still have to pay the local rate phone charges for every minute you're online. Again, check the small print in your subscriber agreements. Often, you can find the software you need to get on the Net free of charge from the cover-mounted CD-ROMs that accompany popular computer and Internet magazines. Using these options, you can try out a particular Internet service for about a month, and if you like their offerings, sign up.

Introducing Internet Service Providers (ISPs)

An Internet Service Provider is an organisation that can provide you with access to the Internet in return for a monthly or yearly fee.

Popular Internet Service Providers in the UK, for example, include BT click, BT Internet, Demon, Freeserve (Dixons), FreeUK, Global Internet and Netcom to name but a few. Until recently, some ISPs provided a limited number of free access hours each day or month. An ever-growing group are starting to offer low-cost or completely free Internet access! Using the latest offers from some providers, you may only need to pay a small set-up or yearly subscription fee and use a freephone 0800 number to get on the Net.

For example, at the time of writing, BT Internet announced a welcome update to their Plan Unlimited package, providing completely free Internet access from 6pm - 8am every weekday in addition to their already free weekend access – that is, midnight Friday through to midnight Sunday. During other times, only local call charge rates apply. At the same time, they also reduced the yearly cost of Plan Unlimited by 15% to about £110 annually plus VAT.

Looking for fast, 24-hour 7-day Internet access?

For users who may need to spend quite a lot of time on the Net, some providers offer continuous 24-hour/7-days a week unlimited Internet access for a fixed fee. However, always check any such agreement for any possible hidden charges or special limitations. For example, at the time of writing, British Telecom also announced a new package offering 24-hour/7-day Internet access for a low monthly fee expected at that time to be around £30-£40/month – and available to businesses: see http://www.btopenworld.com/

Commercial online services

Commercial online services provide a range of their own information services and areas of special interest, like forum and Chat rooms, and access to the Internet. Examples include CompuServe, America Online (AOL) – who now own CompuServe – and the well-established and respected Computerlink

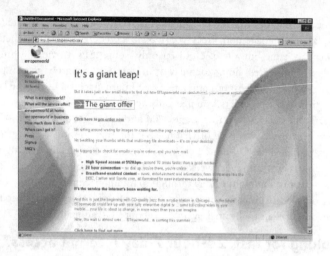

Information Exchange (CIX). CompuServe is popular with Business and, to a lesser extent, individual users, whereas AOL provides content that is arguably more oriented towards individual users and families. Often, commercial online services supply their own software or customised versions of existing software, to provide access to their services or to use the Internet.

If you're in business and looking for free or cheap Internet access, check subscriber application conditions carefully to make sure that as a business, you're not excluded or have to pay extra charges. Some new free Internet access plans at the time of writing apply to non-business customers only.

If after trying an online service for a while you then decide to switch to another Internet Service Provider, don't forget to cancel your subscription with your original online service provider – otherwise you may still have to pay for something
you're no longer using.

Some Internet Service Providers may offer unlimited Internet access in return for a fixed cost. Nevertheless, always check if any special restrictions or hidden charges may apply.

Although as subscribers, we obviously want to pay as little as possible, remember subscription costs are only one aspect to measure the value for money you receive from an Internet Service Provider. Depending on what you want from an ISP, other considerations may be just as important – especially for business users who might stand to lose much if their Internet access or Web presence is interrupted for any reason. In the following pages, we'll examine some desirable traits to look for in an ISP.

Online services like to promote the view that getting online is easier with them for new Internet users. Currently, like many Internet Service Providers, commercial online services usually allow you to try their service for free for a limited time, after which – if you decide to subscribe – you may have the option of a limited number of hours for free.

You may pay a fixed fee each month or year and outside of the free times you may only have to pay the equivalent of the cost of a local rate for each minute you're online. However, at the time of writing, some Internet Service providers have started offering low-cost or possibly free Internet access here in the UK. Similar moves may also start to affect other countries in Europe too. This trend may therefore soon change the nature and pricing of existing commercial online services in a variety of countries around the world.

Introducing domain names

In the same way a postal address ensures mail reaches a specific building, a domain name is an address of a computer somewhere on the Internet. Although sets of numbers are really used to indicate an Internet address, we humans much prefer words. For example, a full Web address might be: http://www.ineasysteps.com. The domain name for this Web address is ineasysteps.com. This is much better than trying to work with something like 267.43.97.84, for example. The four sets of numbers make up what is called the Internet Protocol (IP) address. When you choose an Internet Service Provider, your Web address and email address use their domain name.

Finding and choosing an Internet Service Provider

To gain access to the Internet, most people use an Internet Service Provider and connect using standard telephone lines or cable television services. Therefore, depending on your particular subscription package, you may have to pay for telephone charges or have other fixed or variable charges. Like the differences in people anywhere, Internet Service Providers are many and varied and can be found in many countries around the world.

Until recently, local ISPs or ISPs based in your own country would have generally offered the most cost-effective Internet access. However, where an ISP is located is now not necessarily the most important choice factor! For example, the well-known Californian company Alta Vista recently offered low-cost Internet access to residents of the UK.

So how do you find the best ISP? On page 411, we've listed some of the most popular Internet Service Providers from around the world. You can also find regular reviews of ISPs in popular computer and Internet magazines – usually offering an excellent source of up-to-date information. Often, magazines might list what they consider to be the Top 10 ISPs, so perhaps by making comparisons across several magazines, this approach can help you come to a quick and reliable decision.

Alternatively, you can do your own in-depth investigation. Below is a checklist to help you choose an Internet Service Provider that meets your needs. If this seems long and detailed to you, remember that a little extra knowledge gives you power – it's then unlikely that a poor Internet Service Provider can fob you off with excuses if they don't meet their obligations. Consider making a list of what you want from your ISP, then compare what's on offer from a range of ISPs. Discover the differences and weigh up the pros and cons of each provider.

- Dial-up cost: if you're paying for every minute of Internet access, the dial-up access number your Internet Service Provider provides is important. Ideally, choose one that uses a local dial-up number (for example 0345- and 0845- in the UK). Often, a completely free Internet Service Provider may offer a better choice if available.
- Internet Time: discover how much Internet time is available in the package you're considering. Some ISPs provide a fixed amount of free Internet time, beyond which local rate call charges may apply.

Other ISPs give 24-hour/7-day free access for a set monthly fee, or for a fixed yearly set-up charge.

- Range of services: covers the kinds of things an ISP provides – email, Internet access, newsgroups, FTP (page 321), Web space, mobile phone links, automatic virus scanning, and so on. Some provide full access to all services; others may limit certain aspects like the kinds of newsgroups you can visit. Some newsgroups, for example, contain material that is intended only for adult participation (for example: porn sites). If you have children, you may prefer to have only a limited number of newsgroups available: ask ISPs about their policy and what options are available for control in these areas.

- Connection options: although for many users modem access may be fine, some business users may need faster access through ISDN, ADSL or cable modem access (from page 193). With these more expensive connection options, compare and evaluate costs and benefits.

- Set-up Charges: some ISPs may still charge a "registration" or "set-up" fee to cover the cost of establishing your account. Others provide all you need for no extra cost. The cheapest options may not necessarily offer the best overall value when all terms are considered.

- Regular running costs: once your account is set up, discover if you have to pay any regular running costs and if so, what are typical costs.

- Modem-to-subscriber ratio: the greater the number of modems an ISP has available at any one time, the more subscribers can connect at the same time. If the modem-to-subscriber ratio is too low, you might have to endure irritating delays when trying to connect. A ratio of 20-30 users to 1 modem may be reasonable; 15:1 is better. An ideal minimum is 10:1 and a good ratio is about 5:1

- Internet software: the most well established Internet access software like Internet Explorer and Netscape Communicator/Navigator are now available free of charge. However, some providers may include their own customised software and charge a small fee on sign-up.
- Access speed: Internet access speed determines how fast you can view information and complete tasks on the Internet, so it makes sense to opt for the fastest speed you can afford. An Internet Service Provider determines overall access speed; therefore, choose an ISP that offers the fastest access speeds. Why? Even if you're using a standard 56Kbps modem but your ISP only supports speeds up to 33.6Kbps, your overall access speed slows down to match that of your ISP.

- Technical support: sometimes, you may need help to solve an Internet connection problem. If you're new to the Internet, it's not unreasonable to need extra help until you're more familiar with the Internet and getting connected. The better providers appreciate new users' needs and make email and phone support available to match. Email support is little help with an Internet problem if you can't get on the Internet in the first place, so 24-hour, 7-day, 365-days a year telephone support may be an important condition for you. Also, check at what phone rate technical support is charged: some provide freephone 0800 numbers, others charge local or even national call charge rates, and some charge more expensive Premium rates.
- Get testimonials: one of the best sources of information on an Internet Service Provider is its existing customers. Ask users of a service what they think about their Internet Service Provider. Visit support newsgroups (page 291) and read some posts.
- Additional services: some ISPs also provide extra services sometimes free, sometimes chargeable, which may interest you. For example, at the time of writing, BT Internet provides free fax services for their Plan Unlimited subscribers.

Web site hosting Internet Service Providers

If you plan to create your own Web site, consider the following guidelines to help get the best value for money:

1. Technical Support: 7-day, 24-hour email/live support with either reply in less than 24 hours – under 12 or less is better.
2. Contract duration: ideally, get a no-minimum contract deal so that you can cancel without penalty at any time if they don't live up the their promises or if you're not happy with the service.

To discourage you from cancelling, some providers may offer discounts if you sign up annually.

3. Mirroring and peering: applies particularly for those with Web sites hosted by an Internet Service Provider. Mirroring and peering ensure that your Web site provides the fastest connection speeds available.

4. Email addresses: you may think you'll want just one, but if you have a family, the chances are that at some stage everyone in the household might like an email address! Also, business Web site users may ideally need "unlimited" (or enough) email addresses or "aliases" to ensure you they can provide for services like:
   orders@mycompany.com, support@mycompany.com – and so on.

5. Autoresponders: an autoresponder provides an automatic reply when an email is sent to a specific email address. Ideal for businesses, for example, to handle general sales enquiries or provide some clearly defined information without the need for people to be on-hand. Business users should try to get "unlimited" autoresponders, as they are now an almost essential Internet marketing tool.

6. Downtime: for Web site owners particularly. During "downtime", your Web site is not visible. A good Web hosting company has 99% "uptime": 1% downtime is reasonable.

7. CGI-bin: no it's not an exotic dustbin, rather a CGI-bin provides special scripts and forms that Web businesses will probably need.

8. E-commerce compatibility, capability and support: essential for Web businesses that want to accept payments online 24 hours a day.

9. Check em' out live: visit some Web sites hosted by an Internet Service Provider to evaluate their claims. Check things like speed of access, loading time, how helpful they are, and so on.

A particularly good test is to call an Internet Service Provider's technical support line at peak times to evaluate their response under those conditions. The best ISPs plan ahead and make provision for changing conditions.

What happens when you connect to the Internet?

Once you have the necessary electronic hardware to connect to the Net, you'll need special software to do you want, for example: use email, browse the Web, visit newsgroups, copy and download files. We'll examine the software you need in each chapter that covers the topic. Before we cover how to install your Internet access software, to help you know what to expect when you do connect to the Internet, the following paragraphs outline what happens.

Most users who access the Internet currently use a modem and the services of an Internet Service Provider. The modem dials a special phone number provided by the Internet Service Provider. This type of access is sometimes referred to as a dial-up service. Here's the sequence of what happens:

1. You choose the command to dial your Internet Service Provider. The software you install uses a special program to dial and connect you to the Web.
2. Following the prompts that appear on screen, once connected, you may be asked to supply a user name and password – very often you can set up your software to remember this key information so that you don't have to keep entering these details every time you want to go on the Internet.
3. Once connected, you can use any of the various software applications to use the Internet. For example, you can answer email, browse the Web, take part in newsgroups, chat online, and so on.

Most email programs also allow you to set them up to dial-up, send and receive any emails and disconnect automatically, to save time and money if you have to pay for Internet access.

Although many email programs can be set up to automatically disconnect once all new email messages have been downloaded to your computer and you have sent your messages, usually however, you can change the default settings so that once connected to the Internet, even if you choose to close your email program, you can still remain connected – an ideal way to free up resources on your computer to browse the Web, visit newsgroups, chat online, and so on.

Connecting for the first time

If you've not installed Internet software before, don't worry if much of what follows in this chapter doesn't make much sense to you. Unfortunately, some jargon is unavoidable when discussing the options that get you linked to the Internet – the hardest part is connecting first time successfully. OK, let's get started. Before connecting to the Internet:

1. Always, always, always have installed an effective antivirus program that is kept up to date. Ideally, choose an antivirus program that scans email messages before downloading. For more information about antivirus programs, see also page 149.
2. Ideally, have your antivirus tables updated at least every 2 weeks especially if you use your computer often and reliability is critical to what you do.
3. Make regular backups of your data, ideally at least 2 copies, so that if a virus does get past your protection – no antivirus protection is 100%

effective – you always have a copy of your up-to-date information intact. You may lose some information but at least you'll still have most data available to reinstall once your system is "cleaned."

As a general rule, always follow the guidelines provided by your Internet Service Provider for getting connected first time. If you have Call Waiting active on the phone line you're using, usually you'll need to turn it off as Call Waiting can confuse a modem. You may not need to know some of the information provided in these paragraphs, so the process of getting connected should be easy. However, we've covered the business of getting connected for the first time in more detail here, just in case you come across problems and need to know a little more about what's going on.

Also, many Internet Service Providers include key information on their Web sites – not much help if you can't connect in the first place, I know, but in that event, maybe ask a friend who is already up and running to visit your Internet Service Provider's Web site and have a pen and paper handy. If you do come across problems, any Internet Service Provider worth doing business with wants you to get connected as soon as possible and as painlessly as possible. So if you're stuck, do give them a call: they are there to help.

CAUTION: Using the Internet increases the risk of picking up a computer virus or of someone breaking or "hacking" into your computer: see http://www.grc.com/ for more information. Although the virus threat is often over-hyped with many so-called viruses found later to be hoaxes or easily removed minor viruses that do little damage, the threat nevertheless is real. If your computer becomes infected with a virus, at worst you could lose your entire data store – possibly a devastating blow to anyone in business.

OK, let's examine the "nuts and bolts" of connecting to the Internet. Computers use two types of software to get up and running on the Internet:

- Internet access software: actually gets you connected to the Internet. In your Internet documentation that accompanies your Internet package or computer, you might see this labelled as Dialler, Winsock or TCP/IP stack software. Don't let the jargon worry you: in most instances, you don't need to know about the Winsock or TCP/IP Stack – just respond to the prompts your Internet software provides.
- Internet application software: lets you use the Internet once connected. Examples include Web browsers, email programs, newsreaders and online Chat software.

Once you've connected successfully, consider keeping a written record of user name, password, access phone number, and other details. Then, if you need these details later, you have them to hand. Caution: just make sure you keep your record in a secure place. With these details, anyone can gain access to your Internet Service Provider account. One solution: Password Keeper from Gregory Braun at Software Design: http://www.execpc.com/~sbd.

Internet access software: a closer look

Your Internet access software component must be properly installed and set up before you can access the Internet. Internet access software is itself made up of 2 components:

- Dialler software: dials the correct phone number at your Internet Service Provider, and provides information to verify to your ISP that you are an authorized user. Microsoft names this component Dial-up Networking (DUN) software.
- TCP/IP software: once the dialler software has enabled a valid connection, the TCP/IP software ensures that your Internet applications can communicate properly with other computers on the Internet.

Microsoft Windows 9x/2000/NT4, and current versions of the Apple Mac, include Internet access software either directly or as an easy add-on component. When you install Internet application software like email readers, Web browsers, and so on, usually you can set up the software so it automatically uses Dial-up Networking (DUN) to dial in to the Internet.

If you're new to the software procedure for setting up your Internet software, changing settings incorrectly can prevent you from getting access to the Internet temporarily – until the correct settings are reinstalled. A good guide is to write down original settings before making any changes so that, if the latest change causes problems, you can easily re-insert the original information.

Checking your Windows v9x TCP/IP settings

Most Internet access packs perform most of the set up for you. However, for Microsoft Windows 9x and later users, you can make sure you have TCP/IP active by performing the following steps.

1. On the desktop, right click the Network Neighborhood icon.
2. With the Configuration tab shown, check that "Client for Microsoft Networks" protocol is listed (installed).
3. Also check that "Dial-Up Adaptor" is also installed.
4. If both are listed, click the OK button to close the dialog box.
5. (Optional) If the items in steps 2 and 3 are not installed, click the "Add" button and install them one by one.
6. In the Primary Network Logon box, choose "Client for Microsoft Networks". The Illustration on the facing page shows the Windows 2000 settings.
7. Click the "File and Printer Sharing" button to clear it. If either check box contains a tick, click the box to erase the tick. The only time you won't want to clear these boxes is when you want to share your computer information with other users on the Internet – usually you'll want to protect your files, so this area is an obvious security risk.
8. Click OK to confirm your settings and close the dialog boxes.

9. Close down and re-start your computer to enable your settings.

Installing Internet software from an Internet Service Provider

Simply follow the instructions provided in the set-up software or Wizard and respond to the various prompts. You'll probably need your user name, password details, dial-up number, and various other pieces of information.

In most instances, wizard-based software provided by your Internet Service Provider should make installation straightforward, but you will need some key information they provided to create your account. When finished a few minutes later, the end result is that you can successfully connect to the Internet with just one or two mouse clicks.

If you choose different settings, you may not be able to connect properly to the Internet until the settings are correct for your particular Internet Service Provider.

Some common terms you may come across when establishing your Internet settings

Below are some settings that you may need to install or change sometimes, in their usual sequence:

TCP/IP settings: in Windows 95/98, if you connect to the Internet using a dial-up phone number and modem, each connection you set up is placed in your Dial-up Networking box. Here's how to get to it. First, on the Windows desktop, click the My Computer icon, followed by Dial-up Networking. Then in the Dial-up Networking box, you can make a new connection by choosing the Make New Connection icon to start the wizard and answering the questions it provides.

Or if you want to change or check the settings of an existing connection, right-click the icon you want and choose the Properties command. If you're using an Apple iMac, use the following sequence to get connected: on the Apple menu, open the Internet Access folder and choose Internet Setup Assistant, then follow the prompts.

Server Types: in Windows 95/98, you can view the Server type for a specific connection. Here's how. Click "My Computer", followed by "Dial-up Networking", then right-click on the desired connection and choose the "Properties" command. Click the "Server Types" tab. Now under the "Types of Dial-Up Server" category, you'll probably see a "PPP" connection. Typically this might read: "PPP, Internet, Windows NT Server, Windows 98". Therefore, unless your Internet Service Provider tells you otherwise, choose "PPP" as your connection method. Why? This option usually provides the fastest Internet speeds for modem-based connections. To help speed things along, under the advanced options if your Internet Service Provider instructions allow (check first), choose the following options:

- Disable (no tick mark in the box) "Log on to Network" (unless you're told otherwise by your Internet Service Provider).
- Enable (click to place a tick mark in the box) "Enable Software Compression."
- Disable Require encrypted password.

Under the "Allowed Network Protocols" category, for Internet access, you'll need to enable (place a tick mark in) the TCP/IP box.

Internet dialler software

When you sign up with an Internet Service Provider, they provide you with a user name and a password. Therefore, keep your user name and password details secure. Earlier in this chapter, I mentioned dialler software. In Windows 95/98, here's how to view, insert or change your dialler settings. On the Windows desktop, click "My Computer", followed by "Dial-up Networking". Right-click the connection you want and choose the "Connect" command. In the "Connect To" dialog box, you can enter or change your "User name", "Password", the "Phone number" you're using to dial your Internet Service Provider that gets you on to the Internet, and the "Dialling from" location.

Setting up your email and newsgroup software

The following settings need to be correct if you're to be able to send and receive email and visit newsgroups.

Don't share your user name and password especially. Otherwise, someone else can access all your email and use your Web account. If you only have a limited amount of free Web time, anything over and above this limit may be chargeable – to you. So if someone else is using your settings – and therefore your account – you'll get the bill!

Microsoft Outlook Express: Here's how you can view and change these settings. First open the "Tools" menu and choose the "Accounts" command. In the "Internet Accounts" dialog box, click the "Properties" button. In the "Properties" dialog box, under the "General" tab, you can specify your name, organisation (optional), your email address (for example: joe@mysite.com) and include a reply email address if you want replies to go to another address.

Click the "Servers" tab and you can enter or change other essential settings. Two main types of email system are usually available to handle all email sent to you (incoming mail): POP3 or IMAP. For our purposes now, we don't need to know how they work, just which one your Internet Service Provider uses. Most currently use POP3 but IMAP is growing in popularity.

To recap, a mail server is a powerful computer that handles email. You'll need to know the name of the server for incoming mail, outgoing mail and newsgroups:

* Incoming mail setting (POP3 or IMAP): to give you some idea of the pattern, here are two examples. If you're a BT Internet subscriber, the POP3 setting might be: mail.btinternet.com; or if you have a LineOne account: pop3.lineone.net (the illustration on the facing page uses a Norton 2000 antivirus protection setting, so is a little different).

- Outgoing mail setting (SMTP): again, here are a couple of examples. If you're a BT Internet subscriber, this might be: mail.btinternet.com Or if you have a LineOne account: smtp.lineone.net
- Newsgroup server (NNTP): to access newsgroups in Outlook Express, with the "Internet Accounts" dialog box displayed as described in the previous paragraphs, click the "News" tab followed by the "Properties" button. Using the "General" tab, you can set up your newsgroup access in a similar way to your email set-up. Click the "Server" tab to enter or change your newsgroup server. BT Internet subscribers for example, might enter: news.btinternet.com in the "Server name" box.

Setting up other Internet software

If you're using Netscape Messenger, you can gain access to similar settings as previously described for Outlook Express. In the main Netscape Messenger window, open the Edit menu and choose the "Preferences" command. Under the settings in the "Mail & Newsgroups" category, you can insert or change existing settings. For Eudora Pro, as a general guide, look under the "Special" menu and choose the 'Configuration' or 'Settings' command – depending on the version you're using. Other

Internet access software provides similar options to those discussed in this section, so you can follow the pattern.

Dialling the Internet

Here we really mean dialling your Internet Service Provider – which is the same thing. However, if successful, the result is the same: a connection to the Internet. OK, let's cover this topic. Usually, when you install the Internet access software provided by your Internet Service Provider, once you answer the prompts that ask for the essential information listed in the previous paragraphs of this section, when you dial the Internet you can connect. Now, the question you might ask is, how do I dial? In Microsoft Windows, usually, every time you start up your email program and choose the command to check your email box, the Internet dialler starts dialling automatically. Likewise, when you start up your Web browser, the Internet dialler can be set up to dial automatically. Also in Windows, you can:

1. Click on "My Computer".
2. Click "Dial-up Networking".
3. Then click on the dial-up icon you want in the Dial-up Networking box.
4. Finally click the "Connect" button.

To make things easier you could even create a shortcut of the desired Dial-up Networking icon and place this on your Windows desktop. So next time, you could avoid steps 1 and 2 above. Once you start dialling, if you have a sound card and speakers installed, or equivalent, you can hear the modem make some strange noises – a little like fax machine tones. As you're connecting, you should also see some small dialog boxes appear on the screen telling you what is happening.

Also, if you haven't set up your system for automatic user name and password identification, before you can connect properly to your Internet Service Provider, you'll need to enter the correct user name and password for the account your using.

Once connected, by default in Windows, you'll see a little icon appear in the lower right corner of the screen showing two computers connected or situated close together. You can double-click this icon at any time while online to view the speed at which you're connected, to see how long you've been online and there's an option to disconnect too. You can now check email, use the Web, read from your favourite newsgroups, and so on.

What if I can't connect using a dial-up modem?

Usually, modems are quite reliable: the problem is more likely to be related to basic software settings and physical connections you've established. So always check the simple things first like:

- Is the power on?
- Are the connecting leads installed properly?

But if you still have problems, let's go back a couple of steps and try to analyse what is going on. If you have sound capability on your computer or Internet access device, listening to the sounds that are made can tell you quite a lot about what is going on and if you use this option regularly, you'll get to know the sounds that should occur when your connection is successful.

Here's what I mean in more detail. Before dialling, switch on your speakers and turn up the volume, then try dialling again. Here's what happens when you dial in successfully: the first thing you should hear after you choose the Connect button or equivalent is a brief dialling tone which sounds exactly like the tones your hear when you pick up a phone before dialling a number. Soon after, you should hear the different phone number tones being dialled – this is the dialler software performing its role. Usually, these may sound clearer when connecting using PPP rather than the older, slower SLIP system. Now after the few dialling tones have completed, you'll hear some fax machine-type tones. What's happening here is your Internet Service Provider trying to recognize your account; this stage is sometimes called "handshaking". So at this time or soon after, you may be asked to enter your user name and password. If all is well, you'll get connected.

If you can't connect, considering the above sequence, try to discover where the problem might lie. Also, do remember, especially at busy times – certain times of the day and perhaps weekends – some Internet Service Providers may have too many users trying to dial in for their systems to cope with. However, you shouldn't come across this problem often. If you do, contact your Internet Service Provider and try to get a guarantee of improvement or consider changing providers. If you get a line-engaged tone, disconnect, and then try again a few seconds or minutes later. You may need to repeat this sequence several times at peak usage times. Here are some general suggestions if you still can't get connected:

1. Are you getting a dialling tone? If not, make sure that the modem phone lead is plugged into the computer or modem and the phone socket at the other end – and that your phone line is working of course.
2. Is your modem dialling? If not, if you're using an external modem, make sure that it is powered up and is in the "ready" state. One option to try is to turn off "Wait for dialling tone before dialling" in the modem settings. Here's how to get to it: Control Panel > Modems > General tab > Properties button > Connection tab. If the phone number does not appear to be answering or not responding properly, make sure you have the correct dial-up number. Try dialling a known voice phone

number with someone available to answer. With sound switched on in your PC, if the modem is dialling properly, when the recipient answers, you know the modem and dialler software are working correctly, so the problem lies elsewhere. If all the above are fine and you're using an internal modem that is not dialling, it's possible the modem may be faulty. Read your modem documentation and contact your Internet Service Provider for advice.

3. If you get a dialling tone and the modem dials, but the software rejects your user name and/or password, first make sure you have the correct details entered. If you misspell just one character, the "handshaking" sequence as explained earlier will fail – it's an easy mistake to make – after all, passwords are often designed to be difficult to copy and remember as an added security feature. If you know that your details are correct, contact your Internet Service Provider – if your account is new, perhaps it has not yet been made live or some sort of mix-up may have resulted.

4. If your telephone connection keeps breaking while online, first, check whether you have Call Waiting active on that phone line – if yes, then an incoming call will probably break your connection – the modem may think a disconnect command has been entered. One remedy is to disable Call Waiting. Other possible causes for dropped connections include poor telephone line quality (a crackling line), too many extensions from one phone line and other people using phones connected to the same line at the same time you're connected to the Internet. If necessary, consider checking the TCP/IP settings and Server settings as explained earlier in this section. To access the Internet remember, your modem must also be properly installed in your Microsoft Windows or other operating system.

To check your modem settings, open the Windows Control Panel and click the Modems icon. Click the Diagnostics tab, select the modem you want to check, then click the "More Info" button. After a few seconds, Windows tells you if any problems are detected here, otherwise the "port information" is displayed. If you can connect to the Internet but can't use one of your Internet programs, the settings in the software may be incorrect. You could try uninstalling the software and reinstalling once more or, if you're feeling really downtrodden, you might need the help of your Internet Service Provider.

Also make sure you have the correct modem driver and the latest version installed. The author found that an updated driver not only cured intermittent dropped connections but also boosted Internet access speed by about 25%! Speak to your Internet Service Provider or modem dealer.

Introducing Internet software to get things done

The Internet has many "faces" each fulfilling a different role. The software necessary to use these aspects of the Internet is often available free of charge. However, do check with the software owner or supplier on conditions of use, especially if being used for commercial purposes. To make full use of the Internet, you'll probably need the following kinds of software:

- Email: to send, receive and manage your email messages.
- Web browser: necessary to explore the Web.
- Newsreader: most Internet Service Providers allow access to thousands of newsgroups (see also "Internet newsgroups", page 291.)
- FTP: stands for File Transfer Protocol and enables you to upload and download files from the Internet.

- Web design: If you want to create your own Web pages, you'll need a Web design application and probably a basic graphics touch-up program like Paint Shop Pro. (See also "Software for creating Web pages", page 341.)

A simple trick to boost connection speed (sometimes)

Remember, the speed at which you connect to the Internet determines how fast you can send and receive email, how fast Web pages display and so on. For 56Kbps modems, typical Internet access speeds might reach 44Kbps or more. Once connected in Microsoft Windows, you can easily tell what speed you're connected at: by default, double-click the little icon of 2 connected computers that Windows places in the lowermost right corner of the screen when you're connected to the Net. In the small window that appears, view the connection speed.

If you think your connection speed is slower than it should be even though you're using the correct and most up-to-date software drivers for your modem, here's one option to consider: contact your phone line provider, tell them you're getting a slow connection to the Internet and ask them to increase the line gain. In the UK, British Telecom currently provides this service free of charge (dial 151). Then try restarting your computer and connecting again to see if you now have an improved connection speed.

Exploring the Web

So now you're up and running on the Web. Doesn't it feel great? Like over 145 million other Internet users worldwide, suddenly you have access to an awesome amount of free information from millions of Web pages located on tens of thousands of computers around the world! My guess is you're just going to love having the keys to a million new doors. OK, let's have some fun.

The Web (or if you like detailed explanations, the World Wide Web) is now one of the most important "faces" of the Internet. If the Internet is a large sprawling oak tree, the Web is one of its strongest, most important branches.

Web browsers: your window to the Web

To view the Web, you'll need Web browser software. You can then view Web pages and discover new Web sites. Several software producers have created Web browsers, including two of the most popular free of charge browsers today: Microsoft's Internet Explorer and Netscape Navigator. Currently, the more popular of the two is Microsoft's Internet Explorer, which is now included as part of the Microsoft Windows operating system and more recently sold with new Apple Mac computers.

Most Web browsers operate in a similar way to each other, using menus, toolbars (rows of buttons), dialog boxes and windows appearing on the screen at various times. Using a browser's commands, you can move around a Web page and navigate across a Web site or move to another Web site and start all over again. Or you can search the Web for specific information (see also "Finding what you want on the Net", page 158).

Both Microsoft Internet Explorer and Netscape Navigator are often included on free CD-ROMs that accompany many of the popular computer magazines. Or you can download the software from the Internet ready for installation later – however, be warned that larger software products can take a long time to download using a modem connection. Once you have a Web browser installed, whenever a new version becomes available, you can install the upgrade to keep in step with the latest Web developments. Microsoft Windows can make

You can have more than one Web browser installed – you'll just need to make one your default browser.

browser updating for Internet Explorer even easier through the Windows Update command provided on the Start menu.

What happens after I connect?

After you've installed the Internet access software usually provided by your Internet Service Provider, when you first connect to the Internet, your Web browser starts and you're usually automatically connected to your Internet Service Provider's Home or Index Web page. If you imagine you have just opened the front door to a large house, a Home or Index page is like the first room or floor space you see. The default Home page usually takes a few seconds to appear – but might take a while if, at the time you connect, the Internet is busy. Popular times include, of course, weekends.

A typical Web page contains text and images and is often designed like a printed magazine – except that, with a Web page, you "turn the pages" by clicking on special links. More on this later.

Your browser software usually contains commands that let you change which page appears as your default Home page. Hint: look under the program Options category in your Web browser software.

If, while navigating the Web, you feel lost, you can usually display your default Home/Index page easily: click the "Home" button on your main browser toolbar. You can identify what each button does simply by holding the mouse pointer steady on top of a button for a few seconds.

What can I do on the Web?

Once you are connected to the Web and have a Web browser available at your fingertips, you have access to an incredible range of choices. What's more, the Web is easy to use: just move your mouse pointer where you want to go and click. Here's just a taster of what you can do on the Web:

- Visit your favourite Web pages.
- Search for specific information.
- Beat the traffic and the queues: visit your bank and pay bills online.
- Visit your supermarket and do your grocery shopping.
- See what's on offer for a great holiday – and order your tickets online!
- Check out your investments online – and make some money!
- Watch your favourite TV show.
- Listen to radio.
- Play and download some music and video clips.
- Find a new job.
- Create your own Web pages.

How the Web works: a quick overview

The Web is made up of a huge number of documents called Web pages stored on millions of computers around the world and made available for people to access using a Web browser. These pages are either open for anyone to view or you'll need a password. A collection of interconnected Web pages at the same location can be considered to be a Web site.

Web pages can contain text, pictures, animations, sounds and both recorded and live video sequences. Individuals, companies, organisations, schools, colleges, universities, research institutions, governments, the military and, in fact, just about anyone can set up a web site with just a little knowledge and some know-how – and this book can show you what you need to know.

Physical distance or location is not really relevant on the Web in terms of navigation, so you probably won't know if the page you're viewing is located on a computer a few blocks away or half way around the world. But the point is, it doesn't matter where the original Web page is located.

The Web offers easy, low-cost (and more commonly now, free) access to an incredible ever-growing variety of information! One of the great things about the Web – and the key to its amazing rate of growth – is that it is so easy to use. Users don't need to know much about computers – that's the Web's great advantage. You simply get online and in your Web browser, either:

- Enter the Web address you want in the "Address" box or "Go to" box above the main browser window pane, and click the Enter key or…
- Move your mouse pointer to a Web page link you want and click it. In seconds – usually – your desired Web page is displayed on your screen, providing the Web address you choose exists and is available online. More on this later.

Although the Web is not owned by anyone, key organisations help it develop and improve, to meet ever-growing demands from users. One of the most important steering bodies is the World Wide Web Consortium (W3C) – a group of companies and organisations that help develop new standards for the Web. The W3C is actually run by the Laboratory for Computer Science at the Massachusetts Institute of Technology (MIT).

Introducing hyperlinks: the invisible thread that binds the Web

The single most important component that makes the Web so powerful is the link to other pages. Links are sometimes known by other names, for example: hyperlinks, hypertext and hot-links (but let's use the word links).

A link can be made up of text, a picture or another object and can easily be identified. Some text links are shown highlighted in bright blue and underlined. With another type of link, when you place your mouse pointer over it, the link changes colour.

With some text links and all graphically-based links, the mouse pointer symbol usually changes to a pointing hand as soon as you place the mouse pointer on a link object. Also with most browsers, while your mouse pointer is placed on a link, the Web page address to which the link points is also shown in the display bar at the bottom of your browser window. If you click on a link shown on a Web page, the contents of the Web browser window changes to display the contents of the page you chose. In this way, you have moved from one Web page to another position on the same Web page or to an entirely different Web page. To recap, a Web page link can point to another:

- Position on the current Web page.
- Web page at the same Web site.
- Web page stored on a separate computer (Web server) at another Web site – which may be local to you or situated on the other side of the world! Remember, distance doesn't really matter on the Web!

More on the Home or Index page

When you first reach a Web site, you know one of the first pages you usually see is the Home or Index page. Traditionally, non-business oriented Web sites usually refer to their main entry page as the Home page. Business Web sites often prefer the more formal Index page. Some mainly business-oriented Web sites use an introductory page that is displayed before the main Index page appears. An introductory page links only to the Home/Index page either automatically after a pre-set time delay, or when a visitor clicks the only link on the page. From the Home/Index page, you can usually gain access to all other pages on the Web site – although some pages may require a password.

If you want to start your Web browser without being prompted whether you want to connect to the Internet, you can change your default Start-up page to a blank page rather than any particular Web address. In Internet Explorer v5.0x, you can choose the Internet Options command in the Tools menu to display the Internet Options dialog box, and with the General tab displayed, click the Use Blank button, followed by OK to have a blank page displayed when the browser starts.

How do I change my Home/Start page?

You can change the Home page that usually appears first every time you connect to the Internet. Do remember, however, that your default Home page probably contains information that is useful and helpful to new users especially. However, before changing the Home page, it's worth making a note of its Web address, so that if you change your mind, you can always re-install your original Home page easily.

Here's what to do. Get a pen and paper and look in the Address box usually just above the main Web browser window. Here's an example of a Web address – also called a URL: http://www.ineasysteps.com (To build in more impact, this domain name could also be promoted as: http://www.InEasySteps.com – Web browsers treat them exactly the same.) So write down the address of your default Internet Service Provider's Home page. Every Web page on the Internet has a Web address. For more information see the facing page.

In Internet Explorer, the Web page address is placed in the box immediately to the right of the word Address. In Netscape Navigator, the Address box is usually labelled either "Location" or "Netsite" when a Web address is present. If the box is blank, Netscape changes the box label to "Go to". Alternatively, you can just save your original Home page. Internet Explorer calls a Web address that is saved for access later a Favorite, while Netscape uses the term Bookmark. See page 132 for more information on working with Bookmarks and Favorites.

Introducing the HyperText Markup Language

HyperText Markup Language or HTML is the basic computer language used to create Web pages. However, HTML has already been available for several years with at least three revisions to-date: v2, v3.2 and v4. The latest advances have resulted in the development of Dynamic HTML (DHTML) to provide a much richer and more animated Web environment. Dynamic HTML allows self-running programs on a Web page to operate in various ways even after a Web page has fully downloaded. In a HTML-based page, once the page has downloaded, usually what you see is what you get. Entirely new changes only happen when the user clicks a link or performs an action on the page. However, sometimes "richer" Web pages may take longer to download and some visitors may not be prepared to wait.

In a DHTML page, an animated component, for example, can "play" even after a page has fully downloaded into a Web browser. DHTML is not just a single development but rather several technologies combined that allow events to happen without needing to communicate with the Web server (the computer that makes a Web page available to anyone) or have a user perform any steps to complete the action. JavaScript – another basic computer language – is one of these key technologies used in DHTML. However, to "view" JavaScript components, your Web browser must have this option turned on.

What you need to know about URLs

Each Web page needs to have a unique address and in fact a more formal name for a Web address is a Uniform Resource Locator (URL). A URL can also tell us quite a lot about that particular page. Here's an example of a Web address (URL): http://www.ineasysteps.com. This Web address points to Computer

While downloading software and information from the Web, long download times may be acceptable if you have lots of free or low-cost access to the Net, but probably completely impractical if you have to pay for every second while online. In that event, check whether any free CD-ROMs from computer magazines may contain what you want.

Step's Home or Index page – the full address might be: http://www.ineasysteps.com/index.html – however, most Web servers nowadays are set up to need only the basic Web address. In most modern Web browsers, you don't usually even need to enter the "http://" component if you're entering a Web address. For example "www.ineasysteps.com" is usually enough. Also, most current browsers assume the Web address you're entering ends in ".com", unless you enter another type of ending address (like ".co.uk", for example). Therefore, continuing the example above, most current Web browsers need only: ineasysteps.com to find this Web site.

Don't worry if this makes Web addresses look confusing: they're really no harder to understand than a postal address, just a little different. So let's recap and take a closer look at what's actually in a Web address in more detail:

- Traditionally, Web addresses are written using lower case letters, but most Web browsers now accept upper or lower case letters.

- Every Web page contains the first part "http://" which stands for HyperText Transfer Protocol. The colon (:) and two forward slashes form the last essential part of the protocol. If you omit http:// when entering a Web address, most browsers are now intuitive enough to include it automatically, so usually, you won't need to enter http://

- The following three letters: "www" stand for World Wide Web. Most Web pages also will have "www" included. A full stop always follows

Web browsers are clever little critters! Often you may not even need to type any Web address, instead just click the links you want on a page to move around a Web site and around the Web. The point is, where a Web page is located is not usually relevant to your Web browsing session.

"www". If the Web address you're looking for ends in ".com" (and sometimes .org and .edu), again, with most modern browsers, you may not even need to enter "www". For example, to find Computer Step at http://www.ineasysteps.com, often you only need enter: ineasysteps.com – as we use the default .com domain name extension.

Key point: this is one reason why dotcoms are currently considered the most valuable domain names and perhaps why currently there's a shortage of good cheap dotcom names.

- The third part of a Web address is the host name of the particular Web site or page, often referred to as the domain. In our example above "ineasysteps.com" is the domain name that points any Web browser to the first page in the Computer Step Web site. Host names can use upper or lower case characters, so "ineasysteps.com" and "InEasySteps.com" are considered to be the same. Note that no spaces are allowed here and a full stop is always placed between the host name and the domain name extension (".com" in this example).

- Finally, the last component – the domain name extension – identifies the kind of Web site to which the page belongs. In our example, ".com" stands for a company or other commercial organisation. Here are the most popular current choices:

Academic institutions: .... ac
Company or commercial organisation: .... com
Same for a UK or New Zealand company: .... co
Educational institution: .... edu
Government establishment: .... gov
Military body: .... mil
Internet-based organisation: .... net
Non-profit organisation: .... org

Individual Web page names usually end with .htm, .html or .shtml. However, some newer database-driven Web sites may use other filename extensions, like .asp and others.

Some new domain extensions like ".firm", ".banc" and ".eu" are currently being discussed and promoted, but it's too early to tell whether these will become established or popular. You can also mix and match extra codes here to indicate your Web site's country of origin if desired. For example, "co.uk", "org.uk", ".ltd.uk", and ".uk.com" can be used for UK-based companies and non-profit organisations respectively. Below is a sample of the main countries:

Australia: .... au
Canada: .... ca
Germany: .... de
Spain: .... es
France: .... fr
Japan: .... jp
The Netherlands: .... nl
New Zealand .... nz
Norway: .... no
United Kingdom: .... uk
Taiwan: .... tw

Note: the USA is omitted as any domain lacking an individual country identifier suggests that the Web organisation may be US-based. However, in practice ".com", ".net". and ".org" can also suggest an international organisation.

Finding a Web page quickly

Often, if you know the full Web address of a specific page, you can enter it into your Web browser Address box instead of navigating to the Home/Index page and clicking on the various links to arrive at your desired page. For example, imagine I wanted to move to a page at Computer Step's Web site that described a book on Web page design, I need only enter the following in my browser: "www.ineasysteps.com/ineasysteps/web-page-design.html". Quite a lot to remember. However, there's an easier way. This imaginary example shows that a Web page named "web-page-design.html" is stored in a Web folder called "ineasysteps" that is accessible from "ineasysteps.com". Once you have found a page you want in this way, you can save it for easy access later as a favorite in Internet Explorer or as a bookmark in Netscape Navigator. Then, next time you want to return to this page, you won't need to enter the full Web address; simply click the favorite or bookmark link.

Working with non-Web based URLs

To gain access to parts of the Internet other than the Web, you'll need to change the first part of a URL (http://) and replace it with something else:

- "ftp://" followed by the remaining part of the address, points to a File Transfer Protocol (FTP) site. For example:
  ftp://ftp.computerstep.com/books/pdf/wpd/chapter1.txt
  You may not even need to enter ftp:// as most browsers today know that what follows is an ftp-related address (for FTP, see also page 321).
- "news:" is used to access newsgroups. Note, you don't need to include the two forward slashes (//) – only the colon (:) – to enter a newsgroup name. For example, if I wanted to go to a gardening newsgroup on orchids, I only need enter "news:rec.gardens.orchids"

Web portals: information magnets

During the 1990s, lots of new buzz-words began to appear about various aspects of the Internet: Web portals, Web communities and hubs are three of the more popular labels for example. A Web portal is really a fancy name for a Web site that offers a doorway to information about a specific topic – not necessarily the Internet either – although a portal can form an ideal starting point to discover all about the Internet.

By grouping information topics together in this way, Web site providers can make things easier for Web users – and anything that does this always get attention, doesn't it? The idea is to provide quick access points to the popular themes. Many also offer extra features, for example:

- Free Web-based email services, so that wherever you are in the world, providing you can gain access to the Web, you can use email.
- The ability to customise your own portal Home page so that you can work with only the kinds of things that interest you every time you switch on your computer and log on to the Web.
- Chat services enable you to talk with other subscribers from around the world live (sometimes referred to as "real-time") on topics that interest you!
- Key information like national and world general news and sports news, and finance information to help you closely monitor financial markets, track your favourite shares, etc., and generally see what's happening around the world.

Web portals, search engines and directories have much in common as most Web portals also provide fast search facilities. Popular examples include Yahoo – http://www.yahoo.com (and .co.uk), MSN – http://www.msn.com, Excite – http://www.excite.com and Netscape – http://www.netscape.com

Streaming multimedia fun on the Web

We live in a world that is dominated by our five senses with colour, movement and sound playing a central role. On the Web, designers can entertain or entice through the effective use of text, pictures, sounds, animation and moving video images. The combination of any or all of these components is what we call multimedia.

Business Web sites especially sometimes like to use multimedia to help sell their products and services – after all, video can be highly enticing can't it? Or you can hear simple sound clips or sound sequences on a Web page or listen to your favourite pop, rock and classical works.

If you need a lift, why not visit the movies: hear your favourite movie sound tracks and gripping video clips. With streaming live multimedia, perhaps you can still see that "must have" concert or sports event for which you just couldn't get the tickets this time. Discover what's going on in the world: watch your favourite news program on the Web or play back video sequences of your favourite celebrities.

To play streaming multimedia, you'll probably need an Add-on program if it doesn't come with your browser. Two of the most popular are RealPlayer from RealNetworks (http://www.real.com) and NetShow from Microsoft (http://www.microsoft.com/netshow/vxtreme/plugin.htm).

A closer look at Web browsers

Your Web browser is your own powerful doorway into the amazing World Wide Web and other parts of the Internet. Today, although several types of Web browser are available, the vast majority of Internet users choose either Microsoft Internet Explorer or Netscape Communicator/Navigator. So in this chapter we'll mainly examine these browsers in more depth.

At the time of writing, Microsoft Internet Explorer is by far the more popular of the two. Internet Explorer is considered by many to be closely linked with the Microsoft Windows operating system, and like Netscape Communicator/Navigator, Internet Explorer (IE) is available free of charge, so perhaps this too has been a major factor in its amazing growth take-up.

Modern Web browsers are amazingly powerful tools and like powerful software everywhere can sometimes be confusing to use. However, don't forget lots of online Help is usually available through the Help menus and at the Web sites of the various Web browser providers.

However, bucking the trend for ever-larger memory demands is Opera, a slick Web browser, email program and newsreader suite from Norway that makes surprisingly light demands on a computer – unlike the two generally larger heavyweights Microsoft Internet Explorer and Netscape Navigator. Although Opera is not free, it is reasonably priced and you can install a trial

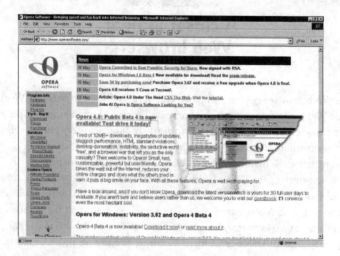

copy from http://www.operasoftware.com However, earlier versions of Opera might have problems handling some JavaScript in some Web sites: check the relevant documentation.

What's in Microsoft Internet Explorer?

Internet Explorer allows you to not only browse the Web but can also closely integrate with your Microsoft Windows Desktop and help manage a company network if required. Both Internet Explorer and Netscape Navigator have grown from a single product (Web browser), but which now includes several other add-on programs that handle: email, newsgroups, Web page creation, Internet telephony, online Chat and various multimedia enhancements including:

- Microsoft Outlook Express: one of the most popular email programs and Newsreaders (For information on newsgroups, see page 291).
- NetMeeting: a program that allows you to communicate live with another person on the Internet. For more information about Microsoft NetMeeting, see page 314.
- Microsoft FrontPage Express: a basic Web page creation program. For more information about Web design, see pages 341 and 359.
- Windows Media Player: ideal for playing many popular video and audio clips that are included on many Web sites – including of course, Microsoft's own streaming media files.

Internet Explorer includes some helpful additional features including IntelliSense, which can "remember" various settings and complete common entries for you. For example, with IntelliSense turned on, when you enter a user name a second time, IntelliSense can automatically insert the accompanying password for you in the relevant box.

The standard Copy and Paste commands are usually available in browsers if you want to copy information into another program. However, do remember copyright and laws that may apply.

Identifying your Internet Explorer version number

Web browsers are usually updated at regular intervals. You can usually identify the version of your current browser from the "About…" command often available on the Help menu. Also any particular version might have a build number to cover particular varieties.

The table below lists some common build numbers for current versions of Internet Explorer 5.0 and 5.5:

IE5.0: .... 5.00.2014.0216.
IE5 in Office 2000: .... 5.00.2314.1003.
IE5 for Windows 98 Second Edition: .... 5.00.2614.3500.
IE5.01: .... 5.00.2919.6307.
IE5.5 Developer Preview (beta): .... 5.50.3825.1300.
IE5.5 with Internet Tools beta edition: .... 5.50.4030.2400.

So by looking at the build number, you can identify your particular version more accurately – which is sometimes useful for problem solving: your Internet Service Provider may ask for this information. At the time of writing, Internet Explorer has reached v5.5 moving up from v5.01. If you're using versions earlier than 4.0, your browser may struggle to properly display many of the Web pages today.

My advice is to upgrade to the latest version as soon as you can. Internet Explorer v5.0 and later versions also make fewer demands on the operating system of a computer and so are arguably more stable, although a few strange quirks have been identified in the different "builds" (v5.00.2919.63071C, v5.01…, etc). Nevertheless, the general development trend is that newer browsers can be more demanding, so if you're using an older computer, your Web browsing sessions may perform better with an older browser.

Tuning in to your own channel on the Web

A striking feature of Internet Explorer is that you can also view "channels" covering a wide range of information topics. A "channel" Web site can automatically deliver only information that you're interested in at specific times. You simply "subscribe" to a specific channel and set the times you want.

Channels can cover a wide range of topics, for example: travel, business, news, finance, stocks and shares, entertainment, computing, Internet, movies, etc.

Checking Internet Explorer browser security

Although recent versions of Internet Explorer have included additional security updates to further protect users when buying online, some browser weak points have also been identified. The latest updates and patches are usually available from the Microsoft Update Web site. For more information and access to the latest upgrades, bug fixes and updates, see:
http://www.microsoft.com/ie/

You can also use the "Windows Update" command. If your version of Windows followed the standard installation route, click the Windows Start button and Windows Update should be installed on your Start menu. Alternatively, in the Internet Explorer v5.0x main window, Windows Update is also available in the Tools menu. However, do remember that Web browser software can now take up megabytes of hard drive space, so downloading and performing updates while online can take quite a while. Unless you have uninterrupted cheap 24-hour Internet access, a better option might be to use update options that are often available on a CD-ROM or DVD.

What's in Netscape Communicator/Navigator?

Both Internet Explorer and Netscape Navigator have grown from a single product (Web browser) several years ago, to now include several other add-on programs which handle: email, newsgroups, Web page creation, Internet telephony, online Chat and various multimedia enhancements. Amazingly, most essential Internet and Web software is now available free of charge today! Netscape Communicator is the name used to describe a suite of programs that include the Web browser Netscape Navigator. Netscape Communicator includes:

- Messenger: a powerful email program and newsreader.
- Composer: a basic Web page editor.
- AOL Instant Messenger: a live/instant Internet Chat program.
- RealPlayer: plays live streaming audio/video clips and other formats.
- NetWatch: a tool that is now also included as part of the Netscape Communicator package and is available if you want to block access to certain Web sites. However, unlike a similar option in Internet Explorer, to turn on NetWatch you'll have to log on to the Internet first and then choose the NetWatch command from the Help menu.

Once you disconnect from the Internet, when you re-connect again, your browser doesn't remember the previous Forward/ Back sequence. The Forward/Back buttons work only for the current session.

For more information and access to the latest upgrades, bug fixes and updates, see: http://www.netscape.com Also, whenever you're connected to

the Internet, you can use the Software Update command in the Help menu and follow onscreen instructions. However again, do remember that downloading and performing updates while online can take quite a while. Unless you have uninterrupted cheap 24-hour Internet access, a better option might be to use update options on a CD-ROM or DVD.

Earlier versions of Netscape Navigator

At the time of writing, the latest version 6.0 has just been released. However, as this version is a beta copy, currently it has not been tested widely, so don't install this version if you want maximum stability and no unpleasant surprises. Earlier versions worth mentioning include: 4.6, 4.5x, 4.08, 3.x and 2.1. If you have an older version installed, consider upgrading as soon as possible to the latest stable version Web browser, as earlier versions may not be able to handle some current Web pages properly. However do remember, modern Web browsers usually include several other add-on programs and therefore may need a surprising amount of storage space on your computer.

Web browsers: the menu bar

With the main Web browser window visible, at the top of the window just underneath the Title bar is the browser menu bar. Here all the commands you need to set up your browser and surf the Internet are available.

Toolbars and buttons

The commands you'll probably use most while using the Internet are easily available in the form of buttons usually placed just below the menu bar. So instead of having to open the menu you want and choose your command, you can instead simply click the button you want. Usually, you can quickly discover the name or purpose of a button simply by placing the mouse pointer on the button you want briefly – the program then shows a text description next to the button which disappears when you move the mouse.

Forward and Back buttons

The Forward and Back buttons usually allow you to navigate to pages you have visited while online during the current browsing session. To go back to a previously visited page, simply click the Back button, as many times as necessary until you see the page you want. Likewise, you can move forward through a sequence using the Forward button.

The Home button

Whenever you want to return to your browser Home/Index or Start-up page, click the Home button – which in both main browsers can easily be identified with a house symbol/icon.

Stop and Refresh/Reload buttons

Sometimes after you click a link to move to another page, the page you want may not appear, display too slowly, have errors, and so on. Or you may change your mind and decide to visit another page. The Stop button allows you to cancel an action. The Refresh or Reload button allows you to re-display a page with the most up-to-date information. Example: some pages contain information updated every few seconds; Refresh lets you see the latest display.

Refresh actually causes an older version of a page that may be stored in your browser's cache memory, to be replaced by the most recent version. Also, Refresh is sometimes useful if a page fails to load properly.

The Address or Go to box

The Address or Go to box holds the Web address of a Web page. You can enter a Web address in this box or if you click a link on a Web page, your browser software places the destination Web address of the page you want in the Address or Go to box. Internet Explorer v5.0 (and later) uses IntelliSense – a software tool that, when turned on, attempts to guess what you're entering as you type a Web address into the Address box. IntelliSense examines your History list and Favorites as you type, so you may not even have to enter a full Web address before IntelliSense finishes it for you. Netscape Navigator versions also use a similar approach by looking at your browser's History list.

The right mouse button short-cuts

IBM-compatible PCs can make use of an extra set of menu command short-cuts only available when you press the right mouse button – by default. The actual commands presented depend on which part of the browser window your mouse pointer is on when you click the right mouse button. For example, in Internet Explorer, using the right mouse button commands you can quickly choose the Add to Favorites command. Or you can place the mouse pointer on an image and choose the Save Picture As command.

Bookmarks and Favorites

Web addresses or URLs are not the easiest of entries to type: enter one character incorrectly or insert a space where there shouldn't be one and the Web address will be incorrect – probably forcing an error page to be displayed instead of the page you want. To help make the task of entering Web addresses easier, Web browsers let you save the Web addresses of the Web sites you like best or want to visit frequently so you won't have to enter an address next time. Internet Explorer calls these Favorites – note the US spelling convention is used here. Netscape Navigator uses the term Bookmarks, but both names essentially fulfil the same purpose.

In Internet Explorer, the Favorites command is available as a button on the main toolbar or from the Favorites menu. When you opt to save a Web site as a Favorite in Internet Explorer version 5.0x, you can also choose the "Make Available Offline" check box, to save the desired Web site and those pages linked to it, so you can browse the site content offline.

Also, at specific intervals, you can set up Internet Explorer to check for any changes and update the copy stored on your computer to match. You can also rearrange Favorites using the Organize Favorites command on the Favorites menu.

In Netscape Navigator, you can find the Bookmarks button on the Location toolbar usually directly under the main Navigation toolbar; or the Bookmarks commands are available from the Communicator menu. Netscape Navigator provides the Edit Bookmarks command from the Bookmarks command or the button on the Location toolbar to rearrange bookmarks. Also, Update Bookmarks from the Edit Bookmarks command allows you to check for bookmarked sites that have changed since you last saved them.

The History list

As you move from page to page while browsing the Web, sometimes you may want to return to a Web page that you visited some time ago. The best Web browsers record the Web sites you visit and make these available in the History list. You can then easily gain access to the History list using the History button or its equivalent command. Although in some instances, you can use the Forward and Back buttons to find a page you visited previously, the History list is much more powerful. In Internet Explorer, the History command is available from the History button, and in older versions as a command in the File menu. In Netscape Navigator, open the Communicator menu, followed by the Tools menu.

Even though a History list can be really useful, the best way of recording a Web address for easy revisiting later is to save the page as a Bookmark or Favorite. Why? From time to time, you'll probably want to flush out old, no longer required Web addresses and files that may slow down your browsing and this action usually means deleting the current History list.

If your History list gets too large, your Web browsing may become slower. Use the Clear History command in Internet Options (Internet Explorer) or Preferences (Netscape Navigator) to empty your History list. You can also change the default number of days when History clearing automatically occurs.

Cleaning out your Web browser cache

For Web browsers especially, regular housekeeping is a worthwhile activity to perform to help Web pages display more quickly and for your browser to perform more efficiently. Both Microsoft Internet Explorer and Netscape

Navigator provide commands to empty the cache using the Internet Options (IE) and Preferences (Netscape Navigator) dialog boxes.

Weaving an easier Web with AutoComplete

Internet Explorer versions 5.0x and later include AutoComplete that can remember essential but boring information for you like user names, passwords, Web addresses and Web forms. So if you regularly access a password-protected Web site, with AutoComplete turned on you won't need to repeatedly enter your passwords, etc.

Usually, you can turn AutoComplete on or off using the Internet Options command in the Tools menu and check either the General tab or the Content tab – depending on your particular version.

Saving a Web page

You can save a Web page using the Save As command from the browser File menu and in the Save dialog box you can usually choose whether to save the page as plain text or HTML format. If you choose plain text, you can view and work on the page text in any text editor. Although you can't save the images using this option, you can still save individual images separately (see the following page). If you choose to save in HTML, you can view the page later in any Web browser – saving both text and images.

Internet Explorer v5.0x goes one step further and allows you to save an entire Web page complete or as a single Web archive file. A Web page complete option saves the page images into a different folder from the main page. A Web archive single file option saves everything on the Web page into a single folder – great if you want to share the Web page contents with friends or colleagues – but they'll also need Internet Explorer v5.0x or later to view a page saved in this way.

Saving a Web page as a desktop short-cut

In Internet Explorer, with some free desktop space visible and the page you want shown in the main browser window in the Address bar, drag the page icon immediately to the left of the Web address onto the Windows desktop. In Netscape Navigator, in the same way, drag the icon on the Location toolbar (placed immediately to the left of the word Location or Netsite) on to the desktop and drop it where you want it.

Saving parts of a Web page

Often, you won't want to save an entire Web page, just one of its components: say an image or some text. To save an image, click the image you want using the right mouse button to display a floating menu, then choose the Save Picture As or Save Image As command. Windows 9x and later Web browsers also allow you to save an image as desktop wallpaper. Click the right mouse button on an image and look for the Set As... or Save As Wallpaper command. You can also save sound, music/video clips via the Save Link As or Save Target As commands.

Printing a Web page

With the Web page you want on view, simply choose the Print command from the File menu (or the Print toolbar icon) and choose the options you want then click OK or Print.

Changing your browser default options

When you first install and set up your browser, the software enters some default settings to enable your browser to work. However, once you become more familiar with how to use your browser, you may want to change some settings. So here's how: in Internet Explorer, look for the Internet Options command in the View or Tools menu. You can also change Internet Explorer options by right-clicking the Internet Explorer program icon on the Windows desktop and choosing the Properties command, or using the Internet or Internet Options icon in the Windows Control Panel. In Netscape Navigator you can change the default options using the Preferences command usually found in the Edit menu.

Typical categories in Internet Explorer include General, Security, Content, Connections, Programs and Advanced. Netscape Navigator typically includes: Appearance, Navigator, Mail & Newsgroups, Roaming Access, Composer, Offline and Advanced. In Internet Explorer Internet Options dialog box, if you use a newsreader other than Outlook express or Internet Mail & News, remember you'll need to enter its name in the correct box usually found in the

Programs category options. You can also change entries for your default HTML editor (Web design), email program, and others.

Turning images off and on

Why might you want to elect not to see images? Well, one reason is that pictures and other images can take a while to display in your Web browser. If you have a slower Internet connection, an older computer, or if you're only interested in the text content of Web sites you're currently visiting, then one powerful way of speeding up your browsing is to change the default settings to turn off images. You can easily change them back again later. This command option is usually found under the browser Options category. In Internet Explorer v5.0x, choose Internet Options from the Tools menu and click the Advanced tab. Under the Multimedia category, click the box to clear a tick mark from the

Show Pictures command. Once images are turned off, every time you move to a Web page that contains images, a bounding box with a thin perimeter line appears to show where the image would have appeared. Also, if a Web page has been designed properly, within these bounding boxes, you should see some text briefly describing what the image is about. More on this surprisingly important point later in the chapters about designing your Web pages.

With images turned off, if you want to view an image, place the mouse pointer on the image you want, and in Internet Explorer, right-click to display the floating menu and choose the Show Image command. In Netscape Navigator, choose the Show Images command from the View menu. When finished, you can turn all images back on again, by reversing the commands, closing the browser and then re-starting it.

Plug-ins and Helper applications

Web pages nowadays can be made up of more than just words and pictures. Lots of sophisticated Web pages contain special types of files, and most modern Web browsers can automatically display a wide range of file types. However, sometimes you may need to install a special program to display or use a particular file embedded in a Web page. A plug-in is a computer program that makes itself available to your Web browser when needed. An ActiveX control is another type of program that works with your Web browser.

Usually, the Web site provider includes a link that installs the plug-in or Helper application you need, or links to another Web site that makes what you need available. You just follow the onscreen instructions to install the plug-in or Helper application. Sometimes you may be asked to accept a software Certificate – if you trust the Certificate source completely you can click OK, if not refuse to accept the Certificate.

The reason I suggest caution here is that anything which directly interacts with your computer from the Internet is an obvious security risk: viruses, hoaxes, etc. So you need to be sure that the Certificate provider is trustworthy.

Java, JavaScript and ActiveX

There's a never-ending demand for interesting animated and colourful ways to make a Web page more attractive, compelling and interesting. Java is a programming language used to create highly animated and interactive Web pages. However, for a Java component – sometimes called an applet – to work, it must first be downloaded fully and run in the Web browser.

JavaScript, a much simpler language than Java – and arguably now more popular – is also a Web language that can be used to create attractive and powerful Web pages. JavaScript is also part of the latest variety of Web language used to create Web pages: DHTML (see also page 343). The main difference between Java and JavaScript however, is that JavaScript information is understood by current Web browsers directly. Popular JavaScript examples include animated images, fade-ins and fade-outs and scrolling messages.

AcitveX is a Microsoft development designed to make using Web pages easier and to provide more flexibility in design options. ActiveX controls are modules that are installed to work with a browser, for example: RealPlayer (examined later in this chapter).

Downloading files from the Net

One of the great benefits of using an up-to-date Web browser is that often you can start the operation to download a file simply by clicking a link on a Web page. For example, you might want to download a software upgrade, an ebook (electronic book) or even an entire software program. Internet Explorer and Netscape Navigator both include the tools you need to download files in the background while still using the Web. So even though you may be downloading, you can still perform other Web tasks. However, if you have too many Web tasks running at the same time, instability may result or the speed at which a file downloads may fall. And when you download a file, you'll usually be prompted to enter the location you want to download the file to and to provide a name for the download.

Downloading files using a Web browser may work OK for smaller files, but if the item you want is a large file size, you're usually better off using a dedicated FTP program to download the file for you. For more information about FTP, see page 321. The main benefit of using a dedicated FTP program is that if you lose your Internet connection while the download is in progress, most FTP programs can reconnect and continue downloading the remaining part of the file. While using a browser however, usually you'll have to start the entire download again! Not a fun way to spend an afternoon!

Viewing and listening to multimedia content

Many Web sites provide popular sound and video clips including many tracks available in the popular MP3 audio format. Internet Explorer comes with Media Player – this can interpret many types of new media formats. However, often better players are available. For example, to view and listen to lots of sound and video clips on the Internet today, you'll almost certainly need the RealPlayer ActiveX/Plug-in installed. RealPlayer is a software tool that allows you to play RealVideo and RealAudio clips.

If your browser does not already have the RealPlayer installed, you'll probably find a link on a Web site that already provides RealPlayer content or if not, visit: http://www.real.com. The big benefit of RealAudio is that it offers a way to provide music clips, both recorded and live, that can start playing while downloading to your Web browser – a much better option when compared to the older type of discrete audio clips that had to be downloaded completely before they could start to play. In fact, lots of radio stations from around the world are now broadcasting on the Internet using this "streaming" technology. For example, if you're into relaxing classical music, take a look at: http://www.classicfm.com/

Microsoft too have also realised the scope for radio on the Internet. To discover more, in Internet Explorer v5.0x, right-click anywhere on the main toolbar then choose the Radio command. A new Radio toolbar then appears just below the main toolbar. When you next go online, you can click the Radio Stations button > Radio Station Guide to see what's available and check it out.

To discover more, consider visiting:

- http://www.mp3.com
- http://www.msn.com
- http://www.microsoft.com

Viewing special effects and animated content

More and more stunning animation routines are becoming commonplace on sophisticated Web sites. Many of these now use fast-loading cutting-edge animation clips that employ ShockWave and Flash technology. Shockwave and Flash animations can be likened (in a basic way) to self-running television advertisements. However, the real key to their obvious success is that they're quick to download and play at average connection speeds. To view these kinds of compelling sequences, you'll need to have the correct Shockwave and Flash ActiveX/plug-ins or "players" installed in your Web browser. Currently, the Shockwave and Flash players are free for anyone to download. Usually, they're made available from reputable Web sites that include this kind of content in their Web designs. Or you can get more information from: http://www.shockwave.com

Computer cookies

The best ones are superb biscuits that perhaps bring back colourful childhood memories – just one more from the cookie jar! However, sorry to burst your bubble but in this context we're really discussing something with a less crunchy nature. The cookies we're interested in here are small computer files that are often copied to a visitor's computer when they first visit a Web site. Then, when a user re-visits the Web site that originally copied the cookie, this Web site can identify the Web browser used at the time the visit was made.

A cookie can only really identify a Web browser, not a person – unless you decide to provide extra information like your name, email address, and so on.

A popular application for a cookie is to personalise a Web visit, so that when a visitor returns to a Web site, a message like: "Welcome back John/Jane…" appears. So that when we revisit a Web site three months later, we're suitably impressed that these nice people have remembered our first names. Not quite right: Web pages don't remember us, but a cookie can remember some key information and so help Web site providers identify some basic characteristics about their customers, for example:

- Types of Web browser being used.
- Which pages are visited.
- Where customers are located.
- The URL of the Web site visited immediately before the current one.

And so on... Sometimes Web site providers may ask for more detailed information about you to help you and them next time you visit. If you decide to provide this extra information, the Web site provider can build up a more accurate picture of what you want from their site and this information helps them provide the most appropriate kind of advertising, and so on.

Viewing Web page Source code

If you're interested in Web page design, you can usually view the HTML code that helps make up a page. Viewing the source code of a Web page can help you understand how the page works so that you learn more about Web design. In Internet Explorer, with the Web page you want on display, choose the Source command from the View menu, or right-click somewhere on the page you want and choose the View Source command. In Netscape Navigator, choose the Page Source command from the View menu or right-click somewhere on the page and choose the View Source command.

Viewing Web pages offline

If you have to pay for every minute spent online, one way to save money is to first go online and visit each Web page you want. Wait until each entire Web page has fully displayed, then choose the Work Offline command usually found in your browser's File menu. When you view Web pages in this way, once a Web page has fully displayed all its contents are stored in a temporary area of your computer's memory, called:

- Temporary Internet files in Internet Explorer.
- Cache memory in Netscape Navigator.

Once you've visited the pages you want and you've disconnected from the Internet, you can then usually use the Forward, Back and History buttons to visit the pages again to examine the content at your own pace without worrying about online charges. Next time you go online and visit the same page, usually your Web browser first chooses the "cached" version, unless the page has been changed or updated. (The new version usually overwrites the old version in the cache memory area.)

You can change the rules of how your browser treats cached Web pages using the Internet Options command in the Tools menu, followed by clicking the Temporary Internet Files Settings button. In Netscape Navigator, choose Preferences from the Edit menu, followed by Advanced, then the Cache command. Then enter the changes you want in the boxes.

Key Web browser Tips

Let's recap and look at some ways to enhance your Web viewing:

- If your time is precious or you have to pay for every minute spent online, if possible plan your Internet sessions in advance. If you know what you want before going online, you'll save money and time.
- Depending on how busy the Web is when you go online, you may meet delays when trying to access some Web pages. Rather than wait for each page to display fully, if you have other tasks to complete like answering or sending email, use your computer's power to perform those tasks while waiting for the page you want to display.

- If you're browsing the Web for text-based information only, you can speed up your browsing by turning off images in your Internet Options (Internet Explorer) dialog box, usually from the Advanced tab – multimedia content too – or Preferences (Netscape Navigator).
- The more Windows you have open and the more programs you're using concurrently, the greater the demands on your computer. Therefore, before Web browsing, ideally save any open documents and close any programs that you don't need.
- If your computer becomes unstable while several large programs are active, the chances are that your computer is getting low on memory or resources. Save open documents immediately and close any unused open program windows – if you're unlucky, you may even have to close down and re-start your computer to cure the problem.

In the author's experience, Windows 2000/NT is much better at handling memory and resources, compared to earlier versions of Microsoft Windows.

- If you find Web browsing slow and sluggish, consider flushing out your Cache memory or Temporary Internet Files and History lists.
- If a Web page is not displaying fast enough for you, click the Stop button, then re-click the link but – this time – choose the command to open the page in a new window. Then at least while the page is being displayed you can continue to work with your original Web page.

Maintaining your security online

The Internet is essentially a vast network of computers connected together and this fact has created enormous opportunities for those few people who want to create havoc and steal information. Let's examine a few simple steps you can take to defend your online activities from attack.

Dealing with Internet pests

Once you get an email address and optionally a Web address, take part in newsgroups, online chat and discussion lists, your online "identity" becomes available to anyone with an Internet connection. Sometimes, interaction with others can result in being pestered or harassed by inconsiderate Internet users. So what can you do to stop this kind of unwelcome activity? Consider the following guidelines:

1. If possible, try to ignore any email messages you receive from unknown sources. Most pests are seeking a reaction. Don't give it to them.

2. Keep all email messages received from a pest in a separate folder – just in case your harasser doesn't stop. In extreme situations, you can then provide these as evidence in a court of law – every email contains code that can be traced to a computer somewhere on the Internet, so in the worst of circumstances, a harasser can probably be traced even if they try to cover their tracks!

3. If ignoring the pestering doesn't appear to be working, contact your Internet Service Provider and send copies of the emails you have

received. Internet Service Providers usually don't want Internet troublemakers working from their servers and so, in mild cases, may send a warning to the originator, or if the offence is more serious may simply close down the perpetrator's account without warning, or even take more serious legal action.

Be careful if playing Internet pranks: what you may consider a joke may be interpreted by others in an entirely different light. An email death threat sent to US President Bill Clinton resulted in a jail sentence for the originator!

Avoiding hoaxes and scams on the Net

Occasionally, someone sends a false message to many people on the Net, with instructions to pass the message on to as many people as possible. These hoaxes and chain letters can include the usual drivel; for example:

- How to make "free money": of course we know that nothing is ever really free; a price has to be paid by someone somewhere. Usually, these kinds of emails are targeting people who genuinely could use some extra cash quickly. However, like some envelope addressing scams, the offer is often not genuine. Sending out these kinds of bulk email broadcasts is also a great way for scamsters to harvest new

If you think an offer is too good to be true, you're probably right and it probably is. This is your intuition trying to warn you. However, if you do want to follow up, check them out; get independent opinions; do some research before signing up. Here's a common warning sign: most scamsters don't like to include a genuine phone, fax and mailing address on their Web site. But don't assume that because they do include these verifiable details, they're genuine. This may still form an elaborate con trick.

genuine email addresses, which then get sold as part of a "new" email list. So my advice is simply not to reply to this kind of rubbish, just delete the message. Or expect to get a lot of junk email in the future.

- Dire warnings about opening emails: especially if they contain specific words or phrases in the Subject box.
- The lowest of the low: sending out urgent appeals to raise money for a child dying of cancer.

However, genuine appeals for help are made, so don't automatically assume all such emails are false. You can do a lot to check if an email is genuine. To discover the latest hoaxes and scams, visit your antivirus program's Web site: many include information about hoaxes in addition to genuine computer viruses. Or you can check out renowned independent sources like:

- http://www.fsa.gov.uk/ (The UK Financial Services Authority)
- http://www.fraud.org/ (The Fraud Information Centre)
- http://www.scambusters.com (Scambusters)
- http://www.urban-myths.com/
- http://www.kumite.com/myths/
- http://www.scamfreezone.com/
- http://www.onelist.com/subscribe/net-alert (email newsletter)

Computer viruses

To some people, the entire topic of computer viruses has been over-hyped by the media. Others consider viruses a real threat exacerbated by widespread Internet use. There's some truth in both of these views. The Internet is an absolute dream for virus writers. However, this real threat has made most people more security conscious, so that you're more likely to catch a virus working on a company/organisation/university network than from the Internet.

Nevertheless, always use antivirus software with up-to-date virus tables installed – ideally updated at least every 2 weeks – whether you use the Internet or not, and run virus scans regularly. Remember, you can still catch a virus from sources other than the Internet – friends and colleagues for example.

How to catch a virus

Unfortunately, computer viruses are an ever-present threat to computer and Internet access users everywhere. Once we connect a computer to others to form a network, a virus can spread more easily. As the Internet is the ultimate network, the potential for virus infection is much increased. For Internet users, a virus can be caught from various sources. The risk is dramatically increased if you're unprepared, or do not use up-to-date antivirus software. For example, consider: common virus sources include the following:

- An attachment to an email message (high risk). Until you're 100% sure, consider all Microsoft Excel/Word/Access documents sent to you with caution, especially if they contain macros, a perfect home for viruses.

The above approach may seem extreme, but a computer virus can be devastating! It's not a bad idea to assume all macro-based documents DO contain a virus – until you're proved wrong! Next, don't accept any macros from anyone unless you know and trust them and they have assured you that the document has been virus scanned before sending to you. Then, still use your own up-to-date virus scanner to check it anyway.

- Downloading an unknown program from a newsgroup (high risk).
- A routine embedded in a Web site (lower risk – but higher if you're using an older Web browser). Most Web sites want to keep customers, not kill any chance of doing business, and so in practice most Web sites and Internet Service Providers provide high levels of protection.

Email viruses: a special threat

Most email viruses come as attachments to plain text email messages. Providing you don't "open" or run an infected attachment, you probably won't catch a virus. Remember, in most email programs you only need click an attachment to open it, so beware. However, recent virus scares that don't involve attachments have been shown to exploit weaknesses in certain email programs confusing the issue still further to many. So what do you do? First, don't accept any email attachments from someone you don't know. I choose to immediately delete all attachments I receive from any unknown source, period! Friends and colleagues are often the most common way to spread a virus – they may not even know their system is infected. So again beware.

An email virus still currently circulating the Internet is a Trojan Horse virus called Happy99.exe. A Trojan Horse is a program with another program hidden inside – and often the one inside is out to cause trouble. A Trojan Horse can't do any harm until you open the attachment and run the little critter. If you receive an email with this program (or any other Trojan Horse) attached and if your antivirus software has not already picked it up, DO NOT OPEN THE ATTACHMENT, simply delete it. Then reply to the sender and let them know that their computer has been infected with this virus.

Recently, a new kind of email worm-type virus has emerged that at first glance appears to be activated as soon as a plain text message is read. Bubbleboy was the first example of this new strain of havoc. What really happens, however, is that a script file is embedded into the email message that can write a file to the recipient's hard drive if:

- They're using certain types of email programs, and...
- Those email programs have not been updated with a patch to fix the security "hole" or bug. For example, some versions of Microsoft Outlook may still not have received the patch to fix this error even though it is freely available from Microsoft.

Get into the habit of not opening any attachments until you have scanned them using an up-to-date antivirus program. And even if your software does not find a virus, an attachment can still be infected: the software may only detect those viruses that it knows about. So keep your antivirus program up-to-date: regularly download updates from your antivirus provider's Web site.

If the worm file does get written to the hard drive, providing the virus file is immediately deleted, the problem may be solved. However, if the worm file remains, when the computer is next switched on or re-booted, the virus can again run unhindered to cause havoc. At the time of writing, the Loveletter/Love Bug virus, classified as VBS/LoveLetter.A by Symantic (http://www.symantic.com/) also emerged around the world with unexpected amazing speed. However, a fix became available within hours from Symantic: hats off to them! The following paragraphs include some pointers to help you avoid catching a computer virus and action to consider if you do.

Are HTML emails safe?

No, absolutely not! Remember HTML is the language used to build Web pages. An HTML email can contain malicious virus components that can overload a computer. Nevertheless, HTML-derived viruses do not appear to have presented a major threat (yet). Just remember, vigilance and an active up-to-date antivirus program are your best defence against any computer virus.

Antivirus software on the Net

Some of the more popular and well established antivirus programs are:

- InnoculateIT from Computer Associates is available free for personal users and home businesses at: http://antivirus.cai.com/
- Norman Virus Control: http://www.norman.no
- McAfee: http://www.mcafee.com/
- Norton 2000 Antivirus: (free trial) from: http://www.symantecstore.com/Pages/TBYB/index.html
- The AntiViral Toolkit (free trial software): http://www.avp.ch/
- Panda Antivirus: http://www.pandasoftware.com/
- Sophos Antivirus: http://www.sophos.com/

- F-Secure from Data Fellows is designed for corporate use or large computer networks: http://www.datafellows.com/
- For Mac users, consider Norton Antivirus Mac at: http://www.symantec.com/nav/nav_mac/

Avoiding virus infections

To minimise the chances of catching a computer virus, let's group the most important antivirus points in this chapter. Consider the following powerful guidelines to help keep your computer virus-free:

1. Always have installed an effective antivirus program that is regularly updated. My own Norton Antivirus 2000 (from http://www.symantec.com/) is automatically regularly updated at least every 2 weeks online to cover the latest virus threats. Lots of free antivirus programs are available online (for example: http://antivirus.cai.com/ Or consider shareware or full-blown retail copies from well established companies like McAfee and Symantec.

2. Never, repeat never open any email attachments that you're not already expecting – especially if received from friends, family or work colleagues. If in doubt, contact the source and confirm that they did indeed send it to you, then virus scan it anyway. If in doubt, simply delete it.

3. Back up your essential files regularly – if all else fails, this step alone can "save the day" – and your sanity! You can use tapes, zip disks and Jaz disks, recordable CDs or at a push even floppy disks.

4. Question whether using a popular email program is justified – to create maximum impact and spread a virus quickly, virus creators often target the most popular software like Outlook Express. Only you can decide what is best for you, but alternatives can be viewed at popular download sites like: http://www.download.com/

Virus infection and what to do about it

Sometimes, even the best laid plans are still not enough to prevent infection. Therefore, if you do catch a computer virus, consider the following steps:

1. Don't panic! Easy to say, I know, but it's crucial that you remain as calm as possible. If you're still able to use your computer, don't send any email messages to anyone; don't copy or send information on floppy diskettes, zip disks, Jaz disks, backup tapes or CD/DVD-ROMs until you're sure the virus has been deleted.

2. At this point, what you don't do can be more important than what action you do take. In other words, don't make any changes unless you know what you're doing and why you're doing it.

3. If you have antivirus software installed and have kept it up to date, there's a good chance that the software has detected the little nasty. So, your antivirus software may have a remedy or offer suggestions. Follow the prompts and instructions carefully.

4. If your antivirus program cannot offer a cure, read the user guide and program Help file to better understand what action you should take.

5. Ask a friend or colleague if you can use their (virus-free) computer to access the newsgroup "alt.comp.virus" to get (usually) quick and helpful feedback and advice – possibly by people who may also have been infected so who know exactly what you're going through. Key point: online folks can be amazingly helpful when you're in trouble.

6. If you can still get online, some antivirus program providers make antivirus detection software available online for use in emergencies. For example: check out HouseCall at: http://www.housecall. antivirus.com/ or the McAfee Online Clinic at: http://www.mcafee.com/ can help check for viruses live on your computer.

7. If the virus problem remains, your data is valuable and you haven't got any backup copies, consider contacting reputable professional experts to recover your data and clean your system.

8. In extreme circumstances, the only option may mean completely wiping your computer's hard drive and re-installing the operating system, software applications and data (if available). After which, scan all other disks that you have or use to make sure the virus has not been transferred.

Protecting your PC from hackers

Use the generous free tools and guidelines provided by Steve Gibson's superb "Shields Up" site at http://www.grc.com/ to test online just how vulnerable your computer is to hackers. If you use Microsoft Windows, believe me, surprises and shocks are almost guaranteed! Plus, you can get lots of superb information about how to prevent the uninvited from trying to gain access to your computer. To provide maximum security, install a good "firewall" program like Zone-Alarm v2.x from http://www.zonelabs.com/which is free for personal use and costs only about US $19 for a single business licence! A good firewall is, I believe, an essential defence product for active Internet users everywhere.

Finding what you want
on the Net

The Internet is like a huge library in which some books move around, others disappear without warning and new ones are continually born seemingly out of nothing and without pause. A vast collection of information on almost every topic imaginable is emerging that grows ever larger every second of every day – and this pace of growth is still increasing! Today in the 21st century, we're seeing only the first shoots of an enormous tree that one day will truly cover the entire earth and probably far beyond!

But until then, how do we mere mortals find what we want on the Internet today under these ever-changing conditions? Answer, we do what anyone does when travelling in a strange land: we use maps and guides – or to be more precise, search tools. Today, most are still free of charge – although as Internet growth starts to settle down into a more predictable rhythm, that may change.

The Internet is rich in the variety and number of free tools that you can use to search for information. Some tools however, stand out more than others in their awesome power and flexibility. The Web in particular contains many superb search tools – also known as search engines and Web directories – and it's mainly these little beauties that we want to cover in this chapter.

Types of Web search tools

Specific tools on the Web are used to collect, store and logically arrange key information about Web pages around the world to make the job of finding specific information easier. The most important search tools available today include search engines and Web directories and their various spin-offs. So what's the difference? Essentially, search engines are computer-run, whereas a human operator usually compiles information made available in a directory. Below is a list of the most popular and most important search engines, directories and Agents available on the Internet today. In fact, most searches come from the most important search engines and directories including:

- About.com: http://www.about.com
- AltaVista: http://www.altavista.com or http://www.av.com
- Ask Jeeves: http://www.askjeeves.com
- Copernic: http://www.copernic.com
- Dogpile: http://www.dogpile.com
- Direct Hit: http://www.directhit.com
- DMOZ Open Directory Project: http://www.dmoz.org
- Excite: http://www.excite.com and http://www.excite.co.uk
- Google: http://www.google.com (see the tip on the facing page)
- GoTo: http://www.go.com or http://www.goto.com
- HotBot: http://www.hotbot.com
- InfoSeek: http://www.infoseek.com
- Iwon: http://www.iwon.com
- LookSmart: http://www.looksmart.com

- Lycos: http://www.lycos.com
- Magellan: http://www.mckinley.com
- MSN: http://www.msn.com
- Netscape: http://www.netscape.com
- Northern Light: http://www.northernlight.com
- Snap: http://www.snap.com
- WebCrawler: http://www.webcrawler.com
- UK Plus: http://www.ukplus.co.uk
- Yahoo UK/Ireland: http://www.yahoo.co.uk or http://www.yahoo.com

Google is a new kid on the block dreamed up by some rather clever folks at Stanford University and probably set to be a big player! Why? Google uses robot programs to scan and explore the entire Web – just like many other search engines. However, results returned for any particular site are determined by the quality of each resulting link to that site and the quality of the other sites that link back to it. In Google, the only way a Web site can improve its ranking is to have more good quality Web sites linked to it. A superb idea that helps improve the quality of the Internet for all of us.

How search engines work

Some search engines – also known as spiders or Web crawlers – automatically and regularly send out search agents – amazingly clever software applications – to continually scan the Web and report back the information. Intelligent Agents or "bots" (from the word robot) continually roam the Web in search of information, log what they find and report the information back to their source. Remember, this sequence happens very fast and is a continuous non-stop activity.

So most search engines have three main components:

- One or more intelligent Agents or "bots".
- A database to hold information received from the intelligent Agents.
- A search tool that allows users to search their database of Web sites.

In this way, search engines try to map the Web. I say "try" because the amazing pace of change and relentless growth and unpredictable nature of the Web have defeated all attempts at cataloguing every single Web page! The task is probably impossible. However, intelligent agents or "bots" never stop trying. Search engines also collect key information when someone has published a Web page or Web site and submitted details manually to a search engine. Some search engines automatically record every word on a Web page; others may record only basic information like Web page titles. You can learn about submitting a Web site to search engines and directories in "Internet marketing secrets revealed", on page 401. Because individual search engines work differently, they return different results. Some concentrate more on Web site titles, others use the first few sentences; others use keyword density, and so on. Often, the method a search engine uses to map a Web site also changes without warning to keep fair play for everyone. Also, several search engines use the same tools themselves. For example, the Inktomi system is currently used by GoTo, HotBot, MSN and Snap; therefore, entering the same word or phrase into these search engines will probably return similar results.

Some search engines like Metacrawler, Dogpile and Copernic, are especially powerful and can search the databases of multiple search engines all in the same session.

Searching for what you want in a search engine

To find specific Web sites, you'll need to enter a word or short phrase into the search box and click the Submit or Go button. (Search engines usually treat upper case or lower case text in the same way, so you don't have to be concerned with entering capital letters.) Before you do so, however, note down several different key words or brief phrases covering the topic you want.

For example, let's assume you want to search for Web sites covering classic cars. If you enter "classic cars", your search might result in all Web sites containing the words "classic" and "cars" – which could amount to hundreds or even thousands of Web pages! You might even end up with irrelevant pages about classic history, classic jokes, classic novels, and so on.

If your search returns hundreds or thousands of pages, then clearly, checking each Web address manually is simply not worth the time and effort. Most people may only examine the first 10 – 30 Web sites listed anyway. Therefore, one workable solution is to fine-tune your search so that only the Web sites you really want are returned.

Whatever tool or method you choose to use, plan what you want to do in advance before starting your search tool. Read the quick guides usually provided on each search tool: as search tools get better, how best to use them changes. Consider using several search engines/directories for detailed results, and try performing several searches using different words on your search topic/theme.

Examine the search rules and options for the particular search engine you're using. The better search engines however, let you at least specify whether to search for any word, specific sequence of words or an exact phrase. Various methods might be called for. As a general guide though, consider the following examples and relate these to your own searches. To search for Web sites:

- On Australian wines, enter:
  +Australian +Wine
- About any types of wine except Australian wines, enter :
  -Australian +wine
- Containing the word "Australian" or "wine", enter:
  Australian OR wine
- Some search engines accept anything in quotes as the search phrase, so: "high tech investments" or "high-tech investments" would theoretically return only those Web sites relevant to high-tech investments.

When entering search words and phrases, consider the different ways a word might be spelt by people in different countries, for example: "organization" or "organisation".

In the search examples on the facing page, note, the use of the capital letters OR. In search engine terms, essentially, OR means one or the other; AND means this one plus the others.

A new more specialised breed of Internet shopping-related search engines is emerging, that can find and compare prices and availability for various products. For example, take a look at Shopper.com on http://www.shopper.com.

Making sense of Search results

Once you've entered your search requirements and clicked the button, if your topic is rare you might get just a few Web pages listed. However, for many topics, you'll get hundreds or thousands of Web page "hits" returned. Usually each hit lists some basic details about a Web page or Web site.

For example, in AltaVista, Computer Step appears as:

----

1. in easy steps computer books by computer step
Computer Step, top British publisher of computer books. Our in easy steps series uses concise language and has an easy to follow layout....

URL: www.computerstep.com/
Last modified on: 12-Apr-2000 - 30K bytes - in English (Win-1252)
[Translate] [Related pages]

Or, from InfoSeek:

----

1. Computerstep competition
Computer Step is the leading British publisher of quality computer books. In concise language, easy-to-follow layout and in easy steps, this series explains all that's important for everyday use - and more! ...
Relevance: 100% Date: 29 Oct 1999, Size 13.7K,
http://www.computerstep.com/millennium.html
Find similar pages | Translate this page

The first line usually shows the name or title of the Web site, followed by a description. Usually the description is extracted from information that the Web site designers provide, or the search engine may attempt to form its own description from the Web page contents.

The following line contains a percentage score figure that indicates how relevant a Web page is to the search word or phrase entered. The higher the percentage figure, the closer

When you decide to visit a Web site found from your list of search "hits", whatever search tool you decide to use, rather than just click the relevant link, right-click the link you want and choose the command to open the destination site in a new window. This way, you always have your original list of search results handy in the original window. Then, if the latest search result proves not to be relevant, close the second window and repeat the tactic to visit each relevant Web page listed in your search results.

the search engine considers the Web page matches what you want. You can also see the date this page is found, its file size, and a full link to the site.

Web directories

Search engines can return a list of Web sites based on what you ask them to search for. Web directories work differently: they store Web information under relevant categories and sub-categories. These categories might have headings like: Business, Arts, Science, Language, Internet, Computers, and so on. Under each main category is usually a list of sub-categories. Under each

If you're really into Web searching, you could consider making your favourite search engine's start page as your Web browser's Home page. That way, as soon as you connect to the Web, your search page automatically displays ready for searching. On your Search engine entry page, look for a link that says something like: "Make this my Home page", or change your browser settings yourself (hint: look for the Options dialog box).

entry in a sub-category, there may be a further list of categories, and so on. In this way, a Web page or Web site is placed into the most logical location.

Finding what you want in a directory

The best directories provide a search box in which you can usually enter the word/phrase you want to find. You could start at the "top" (main entry page) and navigate "down" through the relevant categories until you find the group/single category you want. That's where your desired Web pages should lie.

Finding a lost Web page

Imagine some time back you saved a particular Web page "deep" within a large Web site. For example, imagine the link you saved pointed to:

http://www.ineasysteps.com/books/ineasysteps/miniguides/uti.html

Two months later, you connect to the Internet and want to find that same page. But when you click the bookmarked link, you get a "File Not Found" error message page. As the Web is continually being updated, these dead links are a continual problem; however, sometimes a few minutes' investigation may be all that is needed to find what you want. If a Web site provides a search engine to help find the product or page you want, then usually that offers the best search option. If not, one sometimes-quick remedy is to simply edit the Web address provided in the Web browser Address bar. Using our example above, we start by removing the last one or two components to display:

http://www.ineasysteps.com/books/ineasysteps/miniguides/

From that resulting location, we may find the new link that points to the page we want. If not, we edit some more:

http://www.ineasysteps.com/books/ineasysteps/

Then, if necessary, edit further still to display: http://www.ineasysteps.com/ books/ And so on. These steps take only a few minutes but if you're still left empty handed simply email the Web site and ask for what you want – this can be a good way to check out how helpful they are and how fast they respond.

Email address locators

Finding the email address of someone on the Internet is a little like performing some detective work. The most obvious places to look in include email address directories – providing the person you want has agreed to have their email address listed in a public directory. Also, if necessary, check out options for finding individuals in the Web search engines and directories. Direct links to various email directories are available from the Address Book command in Outlook Express and Netscape Messenger. In Outlook Express v5.0x, click Tools > Address Book, then click the Find People button. In the Find People dialog box, under the Look In drop-down list, you can gain access to various email locators. Choose an option and enter your search details. The most popular email address locators include:

- Bigfoot: http://www.bigfoot.com
- WhoWhere: http://www.whowhere.com
- Yahoo PeopleSearch Directory: http://people.yahoo.com

Internet search tips

1. When you find pages that interest you, save a copy of the page on your computer, so that when you disconnect from the Internet, you can access the information when you want.

2. After performing a search, you may be given a list of hundreds of Web sites. Rather than just clicking the relevant links to examine some of these, instead choose the command to open each link in a separate window – so you'll always have the original search page handy. In Internet Explorer and Netscape Navigator, you can right-click a link and choose the command: "Open in New Window", from the floating menu that appears.

3. Often, during a search, if you're really only interested in text information, consider turning off graphics in your browser. Remember, by default, when you visit a page your browser attempts to show everything on the page. Turning off graphics speeds up browsing as only a bounding box and some associated text may be displayed.

4. If you pay for every second while connected to the Internet, you can often save money by connecting at off-peak periods – in the evenings or at weekends – with some payment plans.

5. If the Web site you're visiting is based in another country and the site is particularly busy – you may have access delays or Internet "traffic" jams. Consider coming offline and re-connecting again during the night hours of the relevant country: access speeds may then improve if fewer people are using resources relating to that part of the Internet.

6. When using Internet search tools regularly, consider briefly noting down the best and worst times to use specific search engines or directories.

7. Save each of your favourite search engines as a Bookmark or Favorite, for quick and easy access later (for more information about Bookmarks and Favorites, see page 132).

8. Don't forget some great printed Internet directories and month-by-month guides are also available, for example: The Internet Directory or magazines like .net. These can provide an ideal start especially if you're new to the Internet. Do remember, however, that as the Net is continually changing information in a printed Internet directory is probably out of date as soon it's published!

9. If you're not quite sure what you want but merely want to find out more about a topic or theme, here's a neat strategy to consider. If you enter "FAQ" (without the quotes) as the word to search for in your favourite search engine, you'll get many topics returned all about Frequently Asked Questions. You can fine-tune your FAQ search by entering one or two more words about what you want. For example, "FAQ dogs" would return all listed entries that contain a Frequently Asked Question file on dogs. Spend some time experimenting to locate the best way to find what you want, so that the next time you want to search for a different topic you'll know the best way to proceed.

Shopping online

A recent Durlacher report suggests that about half of all UK Internet users believe the Internet will change how they shop within 2 years. Online shoppers can save money, have more choice and don't have to brave the traffic jams, fight for a parking space and spend ages queuing in one form or another. But like any new system, there are teething problems, risks and drawbacks. So let's take a closer look at what's possible when you shop on the Net.

Why shop online?

The main value of being able to shop on the Internet is that you can choose and pay for products and services using your computer or other Internet access device and suddenly have a much wider choice of where to buy your goods and services. However remember, you can also pick up some superb last minute bargains on the Net! You no longer need to accept what stores in your local or national shops provide and if you don't like queuing or getting stuck in traffic jams, maybe online shopping – at least some of the time – might be for you.

What's more, an Internet shop or store often doesn't need an expensive high street building with all the incredible extra costs that are associated with providing a public access resource. Therefore, as costs are cheaper, Internet businesses can often afford to sell their products and services for less – potentially saving you money. Already in the UK, at the time of writing, there's been much talk in the media about the amazing savings car buyers can get simply through buying online (or from mainland Europe), for example:

- http://www.carbusters.com

- http://www.enterprisecity.co.uk
- http://www.bizweb.com
- http://www.shoppingsearch.com

Is it safe to shop online?

Any company or organisation that is serious about doing business on the Internet must take into account the security of your credit card details while online. Currently, the most popular way the best companies protect your sensitive details while online is to use an encryption technology called Secure Sockets Layer (SSL) with several additional levels of security being considered. Breaking into an SSL secure transaction is extremely difficult and requires a huge amount of computing power.

All the best security systems work by simply deterring criminals and, in essence, this is the strength of SSL: for those who are bent on crime, there are simply easier ways. As a result, millions of shoppers now accept that online transactions performed in this way address their concerns. This new confidence is demonstrated by the massively increasing amounts of money changing hands online around the globe in the last year – a trend set to continue.

Some things to check before buying online

On the Internet, in theory, it may not matter where you live, right? After all, let's say your want to buy a DVD or CD-ROM product online from a company based in the USA, and which is designed for the UK market. The product may essentially be the same item that you buy from your local computer store.

However, by buying online, if we compare the value of the UK pound against the US dollar, we would currently expect to save money. However, in practice, the transaction may not be quite so straightforward. For example, always check out delivery costs and whether you may need to pay VAT and import duty when the goods arrive in the UK – these costs coupled with any extra hassle can make the entire experience simply not worth the trouble; you could even end up losing money!

Therefore, if buying goods online that are to be imported, first check your country's policy for handling online purchases. UK users can find more information at HM Customs Web site: http://www.hmce.gov.uk/ Currently, goods costing more than £18 may have VAT and import duty added. However be warned, the rules and guidelines vary for similar products and can be confusing. Also, you can look for Which?, the Consumers' Association Web Trader logo. To display this logo, Internet shops are investigated by lawyers from the Consumers' Association and Web site members must follow the Web Trader code of practice – which covers important things like following consumer laws, displaying prices clearly with no hidden extras, delivery obligations, dealing with complaints properly, and so on. For more information, see: http://www.which.ent/webtrader

Here's one strategy that might save UK buyers money when buying online. Whenever appropriate, buy products in bulk online from sellers in your own country to get the best prices. If you want to import products you buy online that are worth more than £18 (currently), ask the supplier about delivery and import charges. If you wish to continue, first buy a single product and wait until the product arrives to check if any extra charges apply on that product.

Consider the following 10 key guidelines to help you shop online safely:

1. When you pay for something online using your credit card, make sure you're using a "secure" payment page – look for a closed padlock icon somewhere in your Web browser payment window, or a Web address that starts with "https://" instead of "http://".
2. Don't send any sensitive financial information using ordinary email. Web forms that use "https://" are much more secure.
3. Never provide credit card details online as proof of age or identity.
4. Never reveal your Personal Identification Number (PIN) number to anyone (both online or offline).
5. Don't ever give out your credit card details in Chat rooms, newsgroups or discussion forums (also known as bulletin boards).
6. Get suppliers to confirm delivery and guarantee details by email.

7. Discover refund and goods return policies before buying.
8. Keep copies of all email communications used in Internet transactions.
9. When you receive your credit card invoice, if you see any transactions listed that you did not make, contact the online retailer and your credit card company immediately. If you do get conned, most banks now limit your liability to about £50, but do check these terms.
10. In my opinion, genuine "etailers" should display a real mailing address (not a Post Office box) and include contact phone and fax numbers. If you don't see these, be especially cautious.

What can I buy?

Thousands of different items from smaller products like music CDs, books and videos to a growing range of larger goods. You can also buy or use a wide range of services on the Internet: house and car insurance, holidays, business services, online banking and property buying and selling to name but a few. You can get an idea of what's available by viewing the Web sites listed in our Web directory on page 421. If you want to make the online shopping experience even easier, you may prefer to do your shopping all from one location on the Web using a shopping mall in which a range of different companies offer their products and services all conveniently in one place. Web shopping malls are particularly popular in the USA with a growing trend now becoming evident in other parts of the world including the UK.

How do I buy online?

Often, smaller Web sites may use basic Web forms in which you enter product details or make a selection, and in which you add your name, address and payment details. When ready, you click the "Send" or "Submit" button and the form information is almost immediately emailed to the company or organisation.

Sites that have many different items, sizes or varieties for sale usually use a more sophisticated shopping cart system in which you can search categories of products and choose the ones you want as you shop by clicking the "Add to basket" button or equivalent. When finished, usually you'll go to the "Checkout", confirm and optionally change any entries. The Shopping cart software then usually calculates your total order and optionally adds any sales tax, handling and delivery charges. At some stage in the Checkout stage, you'll need to enter payment information – the favourite usually being credit card details. When you are satisfied, you'll click the button to complete the order. Once payment is cleared you should receive a receipt or invoice by email.

Internet banking and online trading

The cost of completing a commercial transaction using a walk-in high street bank in the UK is currently about 50p; online it's about 0.5p. So it's not difficult to see why the major banks are investing millions in development costs to create secure ways of doing business on the Internet. Soon we can probably expect further banking savings, as banks will probably start to transfer credit card statements and other similar financial documents to customers using the Internet.

Children
and the Internet

Although the Internet is, without doubt, an amazing development offering enormous opportunities, possibilities, remedies and solutions in many forms to millions of users, it can also be a wild "land." Freedom always carries with it a high price and the uncontrollable nature of the Internet can bring additional problems. Parents therefore, naturally want to protect their children from unsuitable parts of the Internet.

If you're a new Internet user with a sensitive nature, if you go on a random voyage of discovery around the Web, be prepared for some shocks! At some stage, you'll almost certainly come across introductory pages to sex sites or porn banner adverts in other Web sites in an attempt to get you to click. OK, let's tell it like it is: the plain truth is that more money is made from the sex industry on the Internet than from any other single source!

If you do not want to see any of that side of the Internet, you'll need to know in advance the Web address of where you want to visit each time you use your Web browser, or consider installing and setting up Web filtering software. However, filtering software is not a perfect solution and tends to err on the side of caution, so may block sites that might be perfectly acceptable to you.

Nevertheless, those who do break their country's decency laws – even on the Internet – stand to get caught, as some have already discovered to their cost. With the right equipment, almost anything is traceable – and the tools are getting better and more sophisticated every day. A key question is, will staying anonymous on the Internet become a thing of the past soon?

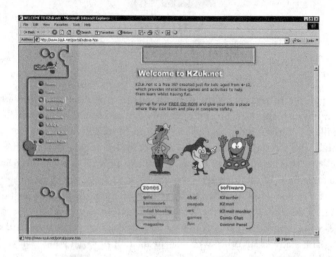

Although a variety of filtering tools and methods are available as covered later in this chapter, probably none are completely 100% reliable. The only sure method for protecting children 100% while they use the Internet is for a parent to be with them 100% of the time while online – a clearly impractical option for most parents today – or not to use the Internet at all.

Identify the key danger categories

Arguably, the Web, Internet newsgroups and FTP download sites probably rank highest as the most controversial areas of the Internet, especially for parents. However also remember that there may be other areas to which your child could gain access. These may contain material that at one end of the scale parents might consider mildly inappropriate or others areas that are absolutely off-limits to minors! For example, parts of the Web contain pictures, text and video information that are intended only for adult viewing. The most responsible Web site providers of these materials ensure that adult verification procedures are in place to stop children gaining access. However, these systems may not be adequate in every instance to stop under age users accessing these sites, and often such Web sites may include "sample" material on their "introductory" pages anyway – clearly irresponsible! So why do they do it?

For many Web businesses, an important way to earn extra income from advertising starts with being able to demonstrate high numbers of visits. As a result, the largely unregulated nature of the Internet means that some Web site providers are simply not concerned about who accesses their site.

What about porn, drugs and other dangers?

Older children especially are naturally curious and can be exceptionally resourceful. Anything with the slightest hint of "no, you shouldn't go there", and we've got their attention: their minds are already working out "HOW TO go there." I suspect readers like myself who have children especially understand the strong urge for the new, the curious and the driving force for independence as our children start to grow into young adults.

Here's a startling statistic: probably about a third of all Web sites that make up the Internet include some adult sex-related content! Without filtering software in place, children can easily access sex sites and other Web sites of "questionable intent". However, even with filtering software in place, resourceful children may still work out how to "beat the system."

The problem does not end with access to pictures, sound and video clips intended only for adult use. All sorts of documents can be made freely available on the Web to anyone who wants to read them. For example, some extreme Web pages may show how to make poisons and home-made guns, and so forth.

Others may show how to just play relatively harmless but possibly expensive pranks. Those that show how to make atomic bombs and so forth hardly present a problem as, in practice, the process is almost totally impossible for anyone who does not have access to all the right components, which is why the same information is probably already available in many other higher educational establishments in one form or another around the world.

As the Internet is essentially an information store, children can find out about drugs if they're persistent enough. They can also see lots of instances of how abuse of drugs has ruined the lives of other people and of course there's no access to drugs simply by viewing on the Internet. Those who do "push" drugs, usually prefer the up-close, one-to-one, in-the-shadows contact, rather than the anonymous and "open" Internet in which anyone can be traced.

So what's the answer? Well unfortunately, there is no easy, simple quick-fix answer. What may work for one parent may not be appropriate for others and different people have different levels of tolerance. However, the following paragraphs can help you develop a strategy for minimising Internet dangers and helping your child get the best from the Internet.

Getting involved

For parents who have children with access to the Internet, the most basic essential piece of advice I can offer is to get involved. If computers are new to you, why not put some time aside to learn – ideally side-by-side with your child – about computers and the Internet, if only for their sake? It's a perfect opportunity. You can learn from each other but, in the crucial early stages of your Internet experiences, you're present and can monitor what your child is viewing immediately. To help learn more about the Internet, you can read books, magazines, take evening classes and so on. Lots of options are available; somewhere there is probably an ideal solution to suit your particular situation.

Ideas for creating boundaries and rules

As a parent of two teenage children myself, I appreciate that it's not always possible – or desirable – to be with your children all the time while they are using the Internet. They too need to learn independence and responsibility. And of course, as children get older, most let their parents and guardians know in plain English about their need to do their "own thing."

Some parents may not want to tightly control their children's use of the Internet. Parents may consider they have a trusting relationship with their child and so are quite happy to work out a system on that basis. This is the route our family follows and it works well in practice for us. You pay the phone bill and your Internet Service Provider's fees and you probably provided the computer or WebTV, so you can set the rules. Therefore, as a start, consider the guidelines below:

1. If you have to pay for your Internet connection, agree times for your child to use the Internet and put a strict time limit for use. The animated nature of the Internet can become addictive.
2. No visiting X-rated or adult-themed Web sites. Period.
3. No intentionally visiting sites containing bad language or including material that your children know you don't approve of.

4. No giving out their (or your) personal information, email address, phone numbers, mailing address, personal photos, and so on, to anyone you don't personally approve of, especially in "live" areas like Chat rooms. Put a big "No" on this one – permanently!

5. Get agreement on the kinds of newsgroups your child can visit. Certain "alt..." newsgroups again contain material that deals with adult themes and some material may be highly illegal in your country.

6. Explain to your child that they should not send emails to anyone that you don't know or of whom you don't approve. On the Internet, someone with paedophilic intentions can easily assume the identity of another child who is also keen to meet others on the Net.

You can also explain to your child that, whatever they do on the Internet, a record is stored on the PC or at your Internet Service Provider and that you as the parent may be held accountable – or that, in the case of older children, they may to have to answer questions they might prefer not to answer ever!

Discuss content control and filtering options with your Internet Service Provider

If you're concerned about what your child may access on the Internet, consider seeking an Internet Service Provider that promotes a child-friendly policy and includes appropriate options.

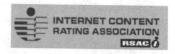

Some provide added security with downloadable free blocking software tools. Some providers can ensure that access to certain newsgroups is refused; for example: alt.sex..., alt.binaries... and so on. In combination with other methods like Web blocking software, this approach could provide a lot of protection from much of the pornography on the Internet.

Changing your Web browser settings

The best Web browsers include options that allow you to change or restrict the kinds of Web sites that a user can visit. Both Microsoft Internet Explorer and Netscape Navigator can let users control access by using a rating system. This approach offers one way to restrict the kind of information your child can access on the Internet. This approach can work with the ratings labels that may be installed on certain Web sites by responsible providers as outlined in the following paragraphs.

The PICS system

A group called the Platform for Internet Content Selection (PICS) have established a set of standards that can classify the content of a Web site into different categories. Any compatible Web browser – like Internet Explorer, Netscape Navigator, and

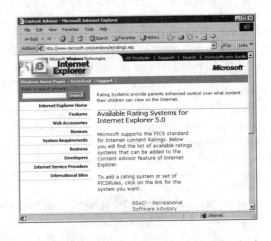

other compatible software – can then be configured to use the PICS standard as a guide to Internet content. Any or all the categories of language, nudity, sex and violence (from mild to extreme in each category) can be set. In Internet Explorer v5.0x, you can set your preferences using the Internet Options command in the Tools menu. Then in the Internet Options dialog box, click the Content tab and examine options in the Content Advisor. In Netscape Navigator v4.5x, go online then choose the Netwatch command in the Help menu to make your changes.

This approach offers a great way to protect children from accessing inappropriate Web sites, or to block out certain categories of Web site – for example, some companies and organisations may not want employees accessing information that is not relevant to their industry during working hours.

However, PICS and other similar blocking systems are arguably far from perfect. Within a PICS-enabled Web browser, perfectly "acceptable" Web sites may get blocked simply because the software detects a word that is used out of context or if a Web site does not have any rating label, as indeed many perfectly reasonable sites don't. Also, as content controlling software has to first examine a Web site, usually browsing speed overall slows down and so Web pages may take longer to fully appear compared to a browser with no filtering active.

RSACi

Many responsible Web site providers rate their Web sites in a similar way to that which is done for television and videos. Several methods exist and one of most well known is the RSACi system. RSACi-rated sites should include the RASCi logo somewhere on the Home or Index page.

Web filtering and blocking software

In addition to built-in Web browser tools for controlling access to the Internet, you can also buy software that can detect a Web site's content and block access to it if necessary. Filtering software can use a combination of tactics.

- Examine in advance Web page wording and block those pages that contain suspect words.

- Block known sites.
- Ban other sites.

However, Web filtering and blocking software usually does slow down browsing – there's usually a time delay while a Web site's content is being "checked."

So using the full options in blocking software can result in frustration. However, this is an issue that only you and your child

can resolve. Some of the most popular filtering and blocking software include Net Nanny, Cybersitter and CyberPatrol. Most blocking programs include regularly updated lists of Web sites considered unsuitable for children to visit. Popular filtering programs include:

- CyberNanny: http://www.cybernanny.net/
- CyberPatrol: http://www.cyberpatrol.com or www.cyberpatrol.co.uk
- Cybersitter: http://www.cybersitter.com/
- Cyber Snoop: http://www.pearlsw.com/
- Net Nanny: http://www.netnanny.com or http://www.netnanny.co.uk/
- SurfWatch: http://www.surfwatch.com/
- Some ISPs – BT Internet for example – provide free Web filtering software to help parents set up safer Web viewing for their children. Customised blocking software providers like, for example, CompuServe, AOL and Prodigy provide their own tools for blocking access to certain Web sites or other dubious Internet content.

Using the Internet for homework and adult research projects

The Internet can be an incredible aid to children in completing their school homework and indeed just making homework more enjoyable. If a child can access and use the Internet to help with homework projects, they have the tools available to enrich their contribution.

The well-known Encyclopaedia Britannica has been available online for some time. However, recently http://www.britannica.co.uk took the brave decision to make their entire information store available free for anyone to access on the Net. A wonderfully generous and indeed smart marketing move – a

great benefit for anyone doing research, school projects or homework. Lots of other encyclopaedias are also available online.

You can see lots of interesting Web sites for children and adults in our Web directory starting on page 421.

On the road and
using the Net

Ahh... A laptop and an open road winding around a stunning Mediterranean coastline. Not a care in the world. The wind rustling through your hair on a fine summer's day. OK, enough... I just wanted to get your attention and dream a little myself. People across the world are moving around now more than any other time in history. It's perhaps not surprising, is it, when we consider all the modern gadgets, tools and different kinds of vehicles that are now commonplace in many countries?

You can also access the Internet from almost any country in the world, but once you move away from your base, you need to plan in advance and be prepared for the unexpected to minimise disruption.

With all this movement, people still need Internet access or to at least use email and a growing number need access to the Web

If you live a highly mobile life and want to use the Internet regularly, get an Internet Service Provider that allows you to gain free access to your email accounts from the Web. This approach ensures that wherever your are located, providing you can gain access the to the Web – and that usually means a phone line connection – you can also use email.

while on the move in order to perform their work tasks or just to have fun. To use email anywhere in the world, you only need a phone line – just start up your Web browser and log on to your Web-based email box.

Choosing and using a portable computer

The pace of development of computers is simply amazing and perhaps even more so with portable computers that have to perform the same kinds of tasks as their desktop counterparts and yet occupy a fraction of the physical space. Often when price comparisons are made, equivalent mobile computers are not as powerful as their desktop cousins. Obvious essential features include:

- Weight: as light as possible but balanced with what you want. Sizes range from laptops, notebooks, sub-notebooks, down to palmtops – or you may need only something like a Psion Organizer, Personal Digital Assistant (PDA) or even an Internet-compatible mobile phone to use email and basic Web facilities.
- Superb warranty: consider what might happen if you're in Afghanistan and your notebook PC dies. If, under those conditions, a replacement computer can be sent to you within say 48 hours, you'll have a good chance of keeping your sanity!

- Power supply: ensure the computer can be used on electricity mains supplies ranging from 100 - 240 volts at 50 - 60 Hertz.
- Modem: ideally, include a 56Kbps modem or equivalent modem components built in that can also link in to a cellphone – even if you don't think cellphone compatibility is important now, the chances are it will be in a few months time. If not, you can usually obtain a compatible equivalent plug-in card modem (PC-Card/PCMCIA). Also, ideally find a modem that includes a digital line guard protector in case you try to connect to an incompatible phone system.
- Battery power: include batteries that keep a working charge for as long as possible – ideally 4 hours or more. A well-thought out design nowadays can provide up to about 7 - 9 hours. Usually, lithium-ion batteries currently offer the longest charge times and battery life.
- Phone connectors and adaptors: before leaving for far off places, make sure you have a "universal connection kit" that includes the various phone connectors and adaptors you may need, so that, whatever country you're located in, you can physically connect your computer to the phone system. The number of different phone systems around the world is mind-boggling. Thankfully, the US RJ11 phone connector is emerging as a world standard.
- Networking: finally, if your work involves connecting regularly to your company network (LAN), you'll probably want to include a network card or network capability in your list of desirable features.

The great thing about email is that once you have a Web-based email address, unlike you mailing address, people can stay in contact with you wherever you're currently located – for a growing number of people in the next few years, an email address may become just about as important as their mailing address! However, whenever you're on the move, usually you'll want to set your Web mail program to "leave Mail on Server" and make sure that for each message you send to someone, you also send a copy to yourself using the CC (Carbon Copy) field in your mail program. Then, when you return home, you'll have a copy of all emails you sent while on the road.

Preventing random phone line disconnections

If, while using the Internet abroad, you keep getting disconnected, here are few ideas to help prevent line disconnections or "dropout":

- Turn Call Waiting off on the line you're using. Call

Waiting usually sends a series of beeps down the phone line and modems can misinterpret these beeps as a command to disconnect.

- Some countries usually send pulses down the phone line at regular intervals to calculate call times, for example: Germany, Spain and Switzerland. Therefore, unless you're using a modem that is compatible with the phone system of the country you're in, or you're not using a modem that can filter these pulses, you'll probably lose the connection. A third option is to install a filter between the modem and the phone socket. For more information, speak to your computer dealer.

- Try unplugging any other phones that share the same phone line – each additional phone on a phone line can reduce the overall current level.

Mobile phones

The Internet and mobile phones are natural partners as demonstrated in the latest models that usually provide Internet access. Also, mobile phone screen sizes are expected to increase to provide a better "window" onto the Net. Eventually, built-in cameras too are expected to complete the video link – possibly leading to the first true global low-cost video wireless connection system. International videophone calls at low-cost Internet prices? Only time will tell but fierce global competition for business should benefit customers.

Unwired on foreign shores without a computer!

Sometimes when travelling abroad, through force of circumstances – or through personal choice – you may not have access to the Internet or email, but unexpectedly wish you had! So what are your options? A growing list of countries now includes WebTV access or equivalent, so you may find that you don't even need to venture out of your hotel room. Also public places like airports, rail and bus stations, ferry terminals and shopping arcades or malls are set to include more Internet terminals or Net booths in addition to conventional telephones and fax machines. Other possible options might include Cybercafés – shops, bars and other public access areas that contain Internet access terminals from which you can rent Internet time and enjoy a beverage and light refreshments. For more information about Cybercafés around the world, see: http://www.cyberactive.com/ or http://eyesite.simplenet.com/eurocybercafes/

Working with fax while on the move

Yes you can send and receive faxes on the Internet too – using computers and mobile phones. Many Internet Service Providers and other companies now allow you set up a phone number from which any faxes sent to the number are converted to email message format and can therefore be sent to your email address. For example, my own ISP BT Internet provide this service. In the first instance, speak to your ISP – you may find a fax-to-email service is free for the asking.

Also, see Jfax at http://www.jfax. com – their service can also include converting voicemail messages to a small computer audio file format which can then be emailed to you as attachments.

For a currently free fax-to-email service, you can find more information at: Efax at http://www.efax.com and http://www.plus.net/

Speeding up your Internet connection

Although many people use a modem to connect to the Internet, other faster options are usually available. In this section, we'll examine these topics to help you decide if the fast-track approach is for you.

For example, BT Internet offers their BT Home Highway service that essentially provides an extra telephone line purely for Internet access. Faster connections are also available with other ISDN- and ADSL-based services.

Do remember, though, that services which provide faster connections to the Internet than are currently available using the standard telephone system, usually have significantly higher running costs.

Free software tools to track your Net connection

If you're getting a continuously slow connection to the Internet, consider examining the VisualRoute utility at: http://www.visualroute.com/ or using some free tools to help identify where the problem lies. If results point to your Internet Service Provider, you can contact them armed with the evidence.

Ping is a software tool that is included with Microsoft Windows 98. Ping sends a beep to another computer somewhere on the Internet and measures how long it takes to reach its destination and return. Here's an example of how to use Ping in Windows 9x/2000:

1. Go online.
2. Click the Windows start button.
3. Choose the Run command.

4. In the Run dialog box, type the word ping followed by a Web address; for example: ping ineasysteps.com (or ping www. ineasysteps.com)

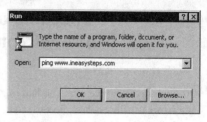

5. Copy and paste the results into a word-processed document or text editor and save. You can then present these to your Internet Service Provider to help them identify where the problem may lie.

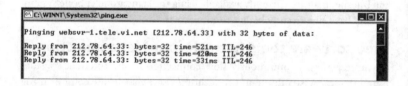

Trace Route (sometimes called Tracert or TracerRoute) is a program that is included with Windows 95/98. Remember, information on the Internet hops from one main server to another to reach its destination. Trace Route traces the route and follows the number of hops taken from your Internet Service Provider to the Web address – in our example, ineasysteps.com.

If any delays or stoppages are found, you can identify where the delays are – for example, at your Internet Service Provider's computers – from the "time-out" indicators. With this new-found information, you can show your Internet Service Provider the results of your test – select all and copy and paste into a word processor document and save. Here's how to use it:

1. Repeat Steps 1, 2, and 3 as listed on page 193.
2. Type: tracert followed by the Web location you want to trace into the box. For example: tracert ineasysteps.com
   (or tracert www.ineasysteps.com). If necessary, check your operating system Help file for the exact method.

Using your ISP's proxy server

Remember, Web pages are stored on powerful computers permanently connected to the Internet called servers. Some Internet Service Providers make available a proxy server to help speed up access to the Web. A proxy server is a system that includes a special storage area called a Web cache that can help speed up access to the Web by storing copies of certain Web sites situated on distant servers – which therefore, are likely to take longer to display in your browser. Some Internet Service Providers even rely totally on use of a proxy server, so may form part of the set-up routine for an Internet Service Provider.

To use a proxy server, contact your Internet Service Provider and if available follow their instructions to install the correct Web address for your browser to use. In Internet Explorer, you can install a proxy server Web address, using the Internet Options command in the Tools menu, then click the Connections tab in the Internet Options dialog box and click the Settings button to see the proxy server box.

Avoiding Internet traffic jams

As the popularity of the Internet increases, so it becomes busier – especially the Web. Just like on our roads and motorways, increased use of the Internet can sometimes result in Internet "traffic" jams! This can happen particularly on popular Web sites, when simply too many people are trying to access the same information for the networks to cope with properly. When Internet traffic jams occur, users at those Web sites can experience delays. A Web page may take much longer to display, or when you click on a link to another page you may not be immediately moved to the new page, and so on. In this event, sometimes the best remedy is to simply try again later.

ISDN & ISDN2

ISDN – or if you're feeling brave, Integrated Services Digital Network (ISDN) – is one option for people who want to have a faster access to the Net, or to an office network when working from home or on the road. In the UK alone, many companies provide ISDN services, including both British Telecom and Cable and Wireless. Typical ISDN connection speeds between a user and an ISP are 56Kbps or 128Kbps depending on how your particular service is set up – up to 4 times the speed of a typical conventional modem speed of around 33Kbps! And usually, a connection is made almost immediately!

LINXPEED
ISDN Modem

HERMSTEDT
Communication Products

Plus an ISDN line can handle two calls at the same time. So you can talk on the phone while sending computer data – however, you'll probably get two separate call charges under that kind of system. Even so, the pace

Leonardo SL

of technological development has a habit of outdating ideas of just a few years old. The advantages of ISDN and the more advanced ISDN2 are now being outweighed by developments in DSL, ADSL and cable technology as discussed in the following paragraphs. Nevertheless, to use ISDN, you'll need:

- A special modem also called a Terminal Adaptor or Terminal Modem.
- An ISDN telephone link: discuss this option with your ISP.

You'll also probably need to install key files to update your computer's operating system. You can discover more information about how to prepare Microsoft Windows for ISDN at: http://www.microsoft.com/windows/getisdn/ For Apple Mac computers, go to: http://www.apple.com/ Therefore, check your computer documentation or discuss the steps you need to take with your Internet Service Provider.

ADSL: just what the doctor ordered!

In recent years, one of the main challenges for telecommunications companies was to devise a system that could provide a fast Internet connection yet which could use existing telephone technology.

ADSL or more formally, Asymmetric Digital Subscriber Line, looks like it could provide an ideal solution! Essentially, ADSL can provide a very fast link to the Internet using the well-established conventional (copper wire) phone lines, so the need for any necessary upgrade or conversion work at telephone exchanges is minimised. Let's take a closer look at the main benefits of ADSL:

- Typically, a home-based user can receive information from an Internet Service Provider at an incredible rate of around 512Kbps rising up to 2Mbps and eventually 6 - 8Mbps. Data coming in this direction is sometimes referred to as the data in or downlink speed.

- Information can be sent (data out or uplink) at about 64 - 256Kbps but is typically 128Kbps! Compare that to a conventional 56Kbps modem that most of us use today and which might typically connect at about 30 - 45Kbps – then you can appreciate what all the excitement is about! ADSL looks set to be the preferred connection method in many countries including Britain.

- Users do not have to share a phone link with other users, unlike cable. The overall speed of connection with ADSL is a combination of both

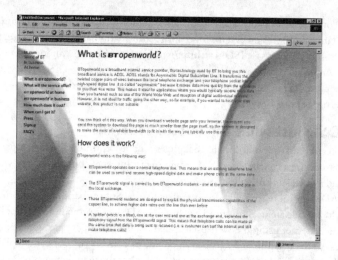

the data in and data out values, leading to a much faster connection, with little upgrading to the phone superstructure being needed!

- ADSL also has an ace card: you can explore the Internet while talking on a conventional phone with both computer and phone connected to the same phone line.

Perhaps it comes as no surprise that ADSL promises some incredible benefits to Internet users and we suspect that many of the best Internet Service Providers in many countries – including Britain – will probably adopt the system sooner rather than later.

Where ADSL is new, currently prices tend to be higher but as the technology comes into the mainstream, prices usually drop, helping to provide a cheap, fast and reliable Internet infrastructure.

Currently, in Britain at least, ADSL looks like a much better option compared to say an ISDN-based Internet link. However, discuss options with your Internet Service Provider and phone company to arrive at the best choice in relation to your own particular circumstances. For more information about ADSL options from British Telecom, see http://www.btopenworld.com/

Using cable modems

A cable modem allows you to connect to the Internet using the same cable used to receive cable television programmes, providing that Internet access is supported by your cable provider – and most do. The big advantage is speed and low cost: cable modems can move information from an Internet Service Provider to a home-based modem hundreds of times faster than a conventional phone-based (copper wire) modem. Incredibly, cable modems speed can reach 8,000 - 10,000Kbps (8 - 10Mbps) – if you're lucky. In practice, rates are often lower, but still in the Mbps range.

Actual connection speed depends mainly on where you live and the number of other users currently sharing the connection. In some countries – like the USA – the ability of a cable modem to offer a fast, reliable connection to the Internet and television programmes has made cable a popular choice. Cable TV companies in the UK and other countries are now offering Internet access in addition to their standard cable TV subscriptions; a trend almost certainly set to continue.

Are you ready for the UK's first commercial cable modem service? Do want speedy connection, at a cost-effective monthly fee - with no additional online charges? Then welcome to ntlworld via cable modem...

flat rate charge

For just £40 a month you get unlimited Internet access and no additional online call charges. You can download information at up to a blistering 512Kbps - that's four times faster than your average ISDN line and can upload at up to 128Kbps.

Satellite connections

Companies that are providing television information through direct-broadcast satellites can also adapt their systems to provide fast Internet access. You'll need a special TV-type satellite dish to receive information (data in), while you send information (data out) using land-based phone lines either through a Dial-up or leased line connection. Typical transfer speeds from the satellite Internet Service Provider to a home-based modem (data in) are usually between 200 - 400Kbps. However, transmitting inform-ation from your modem to your Internet Service Provider (data out) is typically at a much slower rate: 33.6Kbps or a maximum of 56Kbps using a modem.

Nevertheless, overall speed is a combination of the two, so typical satellite connections speeds are very fast compared with a 56Kbps modem. Satellite connections are ideal for companies or organisations wanting a fast, "permanent" Internet connection or for individuals whose geographical layout means that using a conventional modem is simply not possible.

Using leased lines

Commercial users who want fast, permanent access to the Internet may opt to have a leased line installed. However, this option is expensive, really expensive! Leased lines are probably more suited to mid to larger-sized companies and organisations who do much business on the Internet.

Part II
Using Email

Getting started with email

Just like the Pony Express, the telegraph, telephone and fax, email has changed – and still is changing – the world in which we live, work and play providing yet another reliable communications option – and the show has only just begun: video mail is just around the corner! However today, let's explore how to get up and running with email.

Introducing email

Electronic mail or email refers to the activity of sending and receiving electronic messages or documents across the Internet or a computer network. Most of these documents use plain text but you can also work with lots of different types of files and documents. Email is perhaps one of the oldest and most well established

"faces" of the Internet and, although still largely text-based, voice- and video-based email systems are set to dominate in the coming years. An email message travels at electronic speeds and should therefore take only seconds to arrive at its destination, wherever a recipient may live – providing all the "links in the chain" are in place and working normally. When you send an email, the message first needs to reach your Internet Service Provider's computer that deals with outgoing email and which examines the email address, to identify where to send the email first, then sends the email to the most appropriate computer for handling email sent to that particular address.

The next computer in the chain repeats this exercise and continues to route your email message to the following computer in the "chain." And so on across the Internet until your message reaches the Internet Service Provider (ISP) or the particular computer that provides the email "box" of your recipient. Remember, "box" for our purposes is not really a box, rather think of it as a special storage area on a computer reserved for email messages for a single person only.

The one big benefit is that email messages can take just seconds to travel anywhere across the globe for only a small cost outlay.

Sometimes, the computers that handle and process email may stop working for a while (become overloaded) or work incorrectly in some way. However, these events that happen from time to time usually do not last for more than a few hours. Email is therefore considerably more reliable than conventional mail. Furthermore, many Courts of Law around the world now accept an email message as documentary proof or evidence of a communication.

You can create an email document using software in a computer, mobile phone, WebTV, and a growing range of other electronic devices. Email is a great way to communicate with family, friends and work colleagues whether they live close to you or are located thousands of miles away in another country. Two key characteristics have helped email to thrive: it's simple to use and it offers a low cost way to communicate. So how do we use email? Once your email software is properly set up – we'll cover this important topic a little later – here's what you do:

1. Type your message and address it to someone else on the Internet – that is, someone who also has an email address (the Internet equivalent of a postal address).
2. Click the Send button to connect to the Internet, then sit back and watch the magic happen. Most email programs can send and receive email automatically during the same session.

Not used email before? No problem, when you really do start using it, you'll soon see the benefits and probably use the phone and fax less. Email is an informal, direct way of communicating so you can leave out any unnecessary words and just state your message plainly and simply. As a bonus, you'll probably get things done quicker, and so have more free time – just don't become addicted to email. If, like me, you're always looking for ways to save time and get more done with less, email will help you do just that and regain some quality time in your life!

To send and receive faxes and emails on a PC, your computer needs to have a compatible modem correctly installed (Internet ready). ISDN users need a special type of modem more popularly known as a Terminal Adaptor.

How do I work with email?

Currently, the most common tool for using email is a computer – desktop or portable – but that may change to mobile phones and television soon. You can send and receive email in two main ways:

- Using email software installed on your computer or other Internet access device. Popular examples include: Microsoft Outlook Express, Netscape Messenger, Pegasus and Eudora Pro.
- Through the use of email facilities already established on a Web site: this approach is popularly known as Web mail.

Many people – especially those who travel or are away from their home or office often, use a combination of both methods above to ensure they can access their email system at any time and in almost any location.

To ensure that both Web- and discrete software-based methods of working with email are in place takes only a little extra work. Then you're guaranteed at least one other way to always have access your email box if for some unexpected reason, your usual method fails or is unavailable at any time.

Email benefits v. drawbacks

Email has a lot going for it; perhaps that's why it is now one of the most important ways to communicate around the world with millions of messages whizzing across the globe daily. Let's explore some reasons why the rapidly growing use of email is causing many changes to the way we communicate. Benefits include:

- Email is fast: it takes only seconds to send and receive an email and it operates 24 hours/day, 365 days/year.
- A recipient does not have to be present to receive an email.
- Email is cheap to use, much cheaper than phone or fax in which cost can vary depending on where you're calling or faxing to. Many Internet Service Providers (ISPs) now include free email accounts with their standard Internet access accounts. Often, your only cost, other than the time it takes to learn how to use email, may include only the cost of a local phone call irrespective of where an email is sent. New "free" Internet access deals starting to develop at the time of writing promise to reduce the cost of email even further. In the UK, BT Internet for

example has also started to follow this approach by offering free
Internet Access through an 0800 number from 6 pm - 8 am weekdays
and from midnight Friday to midnight Sunday. Other organisations
are also proposing various free Internet Access deals. However, check
the small print: hidden charges may still hit your wallet.

- The use of email generally means less paper is used saving some trees
  and helping reduce the amount of waste and resulting pollution! This
  has just got to be a great move, hasn't it? However, in practice, much
  depends on whether we print our email messages. With regular
  computer data backup routines in place, the need to have hard copies
  printed is often no longer a serious issue. So, why not pick out your
  imaginary tree in some precious part of the world and adopt it.

  If you're in business, however, the use of computers has probably
  escalated the amount of printed material and the law in some countries
  requires that certain documents must still be kept in printed form.

- An email is an original document and many organisations – particularly
  some legal bodies – now recognise this fact. However, if this aspect is
  important to what you do, variations do exist so you may need to check
  what is valid with legal representatives in your country.

- To send and receive email, you don't need to be concerned with
  stationery, stamps, envelopes, mailing labels, DTP design or printing
  costs. A big saving for some!

- Email allows you to concentrate on the content of your message rather
  than spend time working with fonts, paper, logos, layout and design.

- Duplication of text or Web information is simple with email. Like
  most software, Copy, Move and Paste commands are only a click away.
  Plus you can use the powerful Carbon Copy (Cc) and Blind Carbon
  Copy (Bcc) commands, to route a message to hundreds or even

thousands of additional recipients. However, to reduce the number of bulk emailing complaints, many Internet Service Providers now put limits on how many messages you can send at any one time.

- Email is a superb way to communicate across different time zones and so avoid the "red eye": email can be read when the addressee is ready. You can also attach a special "This message is important" marker to urgent emails to help ensure the addressee is alerted quickly.

- Compared to many other computer-based routines, email is a simple, proven, well-established and reliable system.

- "Smiley" characters are often used in plain text to put over emotion, special meaning or simply just to have fun. Smiley examples include:

  :-)   (smile)
  :-((frown)
  :-D   (laughing)

  and so on. For more information on Smileys, see page 249.

- With email slang or the use of abbreviations you can reduce the amount of typing required. Of course this approach is only useful if all parties involved understand the slang. Common examples include: BTW (By The Way), HTH (Hope That Helps) and FYI (For Your Information). See also pages 249-250.

- The simplicity of email helps develop quick, to-the-point communications saving time for all concerned.

- At the end of each email message, you can automatically include a "signature"– a few lines of text about you, your company, contact details, special offer, etc., without having to re-enter this information every time you send an email. You can often create several email signatures to use for a variety of different purposes and simply call the one you want when you want it.

- You can send email messages in plain text (no formatting, colours, etc.) or if you want precise control about how an email looks, use different colours, etc. You can create an HTML-based email – HTML is essentially the language that is used to create Web pages. Just make sure your recipient can also receive HTML email messages first though.

- A permanent record of what is being discussed can also be available with email, as opposed to phone or direct meeting communications.
- No need for large filing cabinets to store paper files that become a little more worn every time you examine them.
- Specific email records can be searched for quickly using powerful Search and Find commands.
- You can add other types of files to an email message as "attachments" – which can be made up of text, pictures, sounds, video files, database files, spreadsheet files and software programs.
- Email is an ideal way to communicate with someone who is usually busy, uses a phone often, or is on the road away from their office.

- You can literally have fun with email! Lots of folks play games, chess, etc., using email. Or if you want to send a special type of greetings card, the chances are the one you want is available to be sent by email. For example, if you celebrate Valentine's Day, maybe that special person might appreciate a smouldering email containing a Web link that they simply click to fire up their Web browser and see the eCard design you chose with perhaps a favourite tune playing in the background. Valentine's day may never be the same again!
- A powerful feature of email is that you can send or forward a single email message to multiple recipients with a single command! However, as discussed elsewhere in this book, use multiple email tools with consideration and care – otherwise, you could get yourself into quite a lot of trouble. Bulk email refers to sending the same email to many recipients at once and can annoy people intensely – especially if they didn't ask for your message in the first place!
- You can use email to take part in Internet discussion groups and newsgroups covering the thousands of different topics available – or even start your own discussion group/newsgroup. However remember, subscribing to discussion groups or mailing lists is one of the quickest ways to suddenly start receiving a lot of email!
- Using email regularly can help you compile better communications and learn to type quicker.
- The beauty of text-based email is that it's simple – and it works!
- Pure text-based email messages take up little storage space in a computer's memory, and therefore don't make large demands. Plus, of course, you don't need filing cabinets, folders, paper, etc. – however, do get into the habit of backing up your computer data regularly. Superb as email is, it has drawbacks – see the next page.

- For an email message to be received, the specific email address has to be correct: any spelling or syntax errors and the message is "bounced" back to the sender. Some email addresses can be challenging to enter at the keyboard or keypad. Upper case and lower case characters may be considered different. Simply put, you need to know the exact email address before sending a message. However, often you can then store an email address in a special address book for easy retrieval next time.

- Email is only useful if used regularly and all parties concerned know how to use their email systems.

- Even though sending an email is fast, the speed advantage is only realised if the person at the other end checks their email box often.

- You need to have access to a computer, mobile phone, WebTV or other Internet Access device and know how to use them.

- Currently, most of us still need to use a keyboard to create an email message or understand the symbol systems that are used with a specific mobile phone.

- If you're completely new to email, like any new activity, it takes time to learn and get accustomed to new methods of communicating.

- To keep credibility when creating text-based emails means that users could benefit from ensuring messages are clear, concise and accurate often demanding extra time input.

- Arguably, putting over emotion is difficult in an email and open to misinterpretation. However, once the communicating parties become familiar with email, accepted methods and symbols have been developed which can help bridge the gap (see page 249 on "Smileys").

- The power of email can trap the unwary. Sending email to large amounts of people who have not asked for it – often referred to as bulk email spamming – is a sensitive issue to many. Most Internet Service

Providers take a tough line with spammers – you can have your email and Web accounts closed without notice and even receive a bill for their extra "clean up" time. Apologising to thousands of email subscribers is expensive in terms of time and resources.

- Email, like the Internet, can become addictive and so may reduce, not enhance, the quality of life for some people. As with any addiction, treatment is available and often the best guidelines are available online – the very place email and Internet addicts go.

- Although you can record messages and attach sound files to an email, arguably these systems have not yet gained wide use as several other factors need to be taken into account, and computers at both ends must be compatible and set up to deal with these more complex types of files.

What do I need to use email?

Usually, the following components are needed to send and receive email:

- The electronic hardware: computer, mobile phone, WebTV, one of the superb new Internet-compatible microwave ovens, and so on.
- A phone line or equivalent connection to the Internet.
- An email account: for example, with an Internet Service Provider.
- Email software: to send, receive and organise email messages.

Popular email programs include Microsoft Outlook Express – comes with Microsoft's Internet Explorer Web browser and is currently free. Outlook Express also supports Microsoft's free Hotmail Web-based email system, so you can literally get an email account within minutes – look for the command to set up a Hotmail account on the Tools menu (usually). Others include Eudora Pro from Qualcomm: http://www.eudora.com and Pegasus Mail: http://www.pegasus.com. Netscape Messenger is another fine email program that comes free with Netscape Communicator/Navigator Web browser – which you'll need to have installed first before you can use Messenger.

In fact, lots of different email programs and enhancements are available on the Internet. So if those above don't fit your needs or if you're curious, take a look at the list on page 222. Even some of the latest refrigerators and microwave cookers allow you to send and receive email and more and more household electronic devices may well include some sort of email capability in the next few years. So if you're in the mood to create a really spicy or exotic culinary masterpiece but can't quite remember the instructions to that superb meal you had last month at Roberto's, you can simply cheat: just tap in what you want to know on the fridge door and away you go!

How does email work?

In the editing window of your email software, remember, you enter the email address of the person you want to send your email to, type your message, then you might want to check it for spelling mistakes, etc., and click the Send button when ready. Now depending on your email program and how it is configured, your email software may send your message immediately or move it to the "Outbox" for sending later when you're ready or when you next connect to the Internet. Once your email message is sent, it is usually stored in a special area on a powerful computer that is part of your recipient's Internet Service Provider network.

Alternatively, if the organisation to which you're sending your email has their own direct connection to the Internet, the relevant email is stored somewhere on their own dedicated PC, often also known as a mail server, email server, mail client, mail host, or other similar-sounding label. Each email message then gets re-routed to the correct person internally. On a mail server computer, the storage space for holding email messages is actually divided into

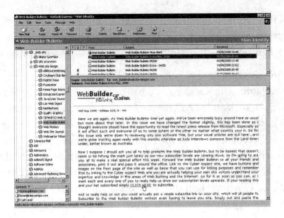

numerous, smaller, separate areas each with a unique address and called an email box.

When a recipient decides they want to "open" their email box, they connect to the Internet (or company network) and choose the command to check or retrieve their email messages. A user name and password may need to be entered at this time to identify the authorised user unless the software has been previously set up to check email automatically. Then any email messages present in the email "box" are sent to the computer authorised to retrieve it. Although we have examined the email process in some detail, in practice, checking for email usually takes only a few seconds. Furthermore, in most email systems currently you can send and receive email in two main formats:

- Plain text: includes no formatting, bold, italic, font styles, colours, etc, just plain text. The main benefit is that any recipient should be able to display your message without problems.

- HTML format: here lots of design flexibility is built in, with similar options as available for Web pages – text, hyperlinks, different backgrounds, pictures, different font styles and animations, etc.

If you use this much more colourful and possibly animated format to send email, make sure your recipient's email software can handle HTML-type messages. Even so, if an HTML message is sent to an address that is not set up to handle it, the message can still be read providing the recipient is using an HTML email-compatible program. In this event, Outlook Express for example, ensures a recipient receives a plain text version of the message and the HTML version is included as an attachment. However, some email software might only send the HTML version and therefore would display as a mass of hard to read characters in a non-compatible email reader.

What's an email address?

For newcomers to email, it's not a street address in Cyberspace city; rather, an email address is a unique name so that only the email addressee can receive their email messages. Here are some imaginary and real e -mail addresses:

billgates@mycompany.com
scully@xfiles.co.uk
mulder@TheTruthIsOutThere.com
president@whitehouse.gov
primeminister@number10.gov

Currently, an email address is made up of two parts separated by an @ symbol to ensure they do not become mixed. Full stops are used to separate the various address components. Let's examine the structure of an email in detail:

- The first part of an email address is simply the name given to the addressee – not necessarily an individual's personal name, although that may be possible providing no one else in the same organisation or Internet Service Provider is using that name. Or you can use a shorthand version, a nickname, or simply something unique. However often, a "User Name" provided by an Internet Service Provider forms this first part of an email address, so you may not have a totally free choice. In the fun examples above, this part includes: "billgates", "scully", "mulder", "president" and "primeminster".

- Characters that follow the @ symbol and precede the full stop make up the address of the recipient's Internet Service Provider or a Web domain name (see also page 115). For example, in the Web address: http://www.ineasysteps.com, this part is "ineasysteps".

- At the end of an email address, the characters after the full stop usually denote the organisation type. The most popular (with their expanded meanings in brackets) include, for international uses:

- .com (commercial company)
- .org   (non-profit organisation)
- .net   (Internet-based company or organisation)
- .edu (education establishment)
- .gov (government)
- .mil   (military)

Country-specific addresses can also be used, if preferred e.g.:

- .co.uk (UK-based company or organisation)
- .ltd.uk and .uk.com (example newer variations that are emerging)
- .co.au (Australian-based company or organisation), and so on.

So using our previous imaginary example "billgates@mycompany.com" translates to really mean: "Bill Gates at My Company.com."

Are there any characters I can't use?

Currently, not all characters available on your keyboard can be used in an email address. Some characters like a forward slash (/), etc. will almost certainly have a special, reserved meaning in your computer's operating system. Full stops also have special meaning and as we have seen can only be used in a specific way in an email address. The full list of these "illegal" characters depends on computer operating systems (for example: Microsoft Windows 95/98/2000/NT, Apple MacOS, UNIX, Linux, etc).

However, most Internet connection standards allow you to use letters, both upper case and lower case, numbers, dashes and full stops as described in the previous paragraphs. Usually, using upper case or lowercase letters doesn't make any difference: both are considered the same. To discover your precise options, check with your Internet Service Provider. You can also learn more about what you can and can't use in an email address in your computer's email software or operating system software.

Autoresponders: tireless workers on the Net

Here's another type of email address: info@mysite.com It's an address that does not "point" to an individual, rather it uses the word info and suggests that when someone sends an email to that address, they're asking for some kind of information in return.

This information may be sent manually, however our relentless desire for instant results means that usually these types of email address are set up so that the desired information is automatically sent back to the sender, often within seconds using an autoresponder system – a kind of Internet fax-back tool.

One of the big benefits of using an autoresponder is that once it is set up, no one need be present to enable the autoresponder to work. For example, every time someone sends an email to the (imaginary) autoresponder info33@mysite.com, the autoresponder could automatically reply with an email message containing the desired information. The autoresponder message content need only be created once and stored on the Web mail server computer as part of that particular autoresponder. You can set up autoresponders for all sorts of purposes, for example to provide:

- Basic information.
- Your latest newsletter.
- A report on a particular topic or theme.
- A Help file.
- A Frequently Asked Questions document.

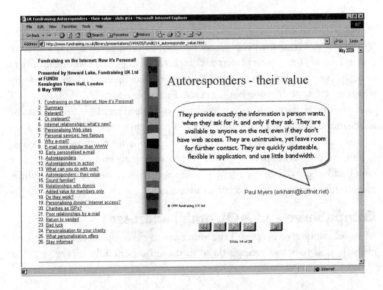

Creating an email address

An email address must be unique to ensure that email intended for that address can be received. For best results and if you have a choice, try to make your email address short and easy to remember. The more complex an address is, the more likely people are to get it wrong, make typing mistakes and become frustrated – and if you're in business, this can have serious consequences.

Generic email addresses (like info@companyname.com and report1@companyname.co.uk) can also be used as autoresponders.

For personal email addresses, obviously your name is probably the best option. However, many people have similar sounding names; so if someone else has already taken your preferred choice, consider perhaps adding numbers or dashes or providing some other variation. For example, let's light-heartedly imagine that your Internet Service Provider is called "custard"; if john.smith@custard.com is not available, consider j.smith@custard.com or john.smith2@custard.com and so on. Or if you're in business, you might want to use job titles or service names like: publisher@mycompany.com, help@mycompany.com or special.offer@mycompany.com. To set up a new email address, make a list of your preferred choices before going online. Experiment and try out different combinations.

CompuServe and AOL email addresses

Many CompuServe users still use numbers to make up their email address even though they can change these to more user-friendly nicknames. For example, I think you'll agree 13579,864 is arguably not as friendly as John_Doe@compuserve.com. CompuServe users can also exchange email using a comma instead of a full stop to separate the key components as shown in the above example. However, this approach does not work on the Internet.

To convert this kind of CompuServe email address for use on the Internet just replace the comma with a full stop and add @compuserve.com. Therefore, after we convert our example CompuServe email address above, it now becomes 13579.864@compuserve.com. AOL users can in a similar way convert their internal email address for use on the Internet by adding @aol.com to the end of their email name. For example: John_Doe@aol.com.

Getting an email account

To use standard email, you'll need access to the Internet. For most people, this means using the services of an Internet Service Provider and, usually, a wide range of choices are available. An Internet Service Provider makes available at least one email box and some provide several – ideal if you have other family members. Other providers like BT Internet with their yearly Plan Unlimited package allow you to have an unlimited number of email boxes – a great option if you want to use different addresses for different purposes, for example:

- sales-smith@btinternet.com
- help-smith@btinternet.com
- and so on.

One of the main benefits of using the services of an Internet Service Provider is that, usually, the same configuration and settings used to enable your access to the Internet can also be used to make email services available to you. So overleaf, let's examine the two kinds of Internet email accounts that are available through Internet Service Providers:

- Those that create their own standards and therefore use customised software; examples in this category include: AOL and CompuServe – which is now part of AOL anyway. Usually, they provide their own software or customised versions of popular email and Web software. A possible drawback with this approach is that sometimes communication with "open" Internet can lead to problems or be overly complex. However, this approach is often popular with new Net users.
- Providers that use open standards, protocols and software: examples here include: HotMail, FreeServe and BT Internet. With this option, usually, you can use any standard email and Web software to communicate with others on the Internet. Arguably, software available with "open" providers is easier to install and use.

Storage space for your emails

For storing your emails, usually a provider allocates a few megabytes of space on their mail server. For most people, this is more than enough; however, checking your email box(es) regularly is a good habit to develop to avoid losing any email. Regular email checking is especially important if you expect to receive emails with large attachments.

Finding an email provider

Computer magazines also often carry out surveys of the best Internet Service Providers and so include essential contact details. The table below lists some currently popular providers:

- AOL (America OnLine): http://www.aol.com/
- BT Click: http://www.btclick.com/
- BT Internet: http://www.btinternet.com/
- CompuServe (CIX): http://www.compuserve.com/

- Excite Mail: http://www.mailexcite.com/
- Dixons Freeserve: http://www.freeserve.com/
- iName: http://www.iname.com/
- LineOne (British Telecom): http://www.lineOne.net/
- HotMail: (Microsoft): http://www.hotmail.com/
- Yahoo: http://www.yahoo.com or http://www.yahoo.co.uk/
- Geocities: http://www.geocities.com/

Free email accounts

Many organisations now offer free email accounts. In combination with CD-ROMs that often accompany popular computer magazines, you can have all the software you need to get online quickly. Or if you already have access to the Internet, you can go online and easily sign up for a free email account.

Most free mainstream Internet Service Providers now provide some free Web space and at least one free email account. For personal use and for most purposes, a free email address is ideal – hey, it's free and does the job. However for businesses, some caution is needed: credibility is at stake! How you appear online says a lot about you and your approach to business. An email address linked to a true Web site address arguably puts over a more professional image.

Billg@microsoft.com obviously means Bill is part of Microsoft.com, whereas john.smith@hotmail.com and jane.smith@compuserve.com immediately show that like many others, John Smith uses a free Microsoft Hotmail email box and Jane Smith uses a CompuServe email box. Convenient, easy and cost-effective to use? Yes absolutely! However a potential new customer might seriously question both John and Jane's business credibility with thoughts like: "If they have to use a free email box, or aren't even using their own domain name, maybe they're not as successful as they suggest." Ouch! A bad start before a new sale is even made.

Working with Web email

Many free Internet Service Providers allow you to set up your email accounts on the Web first, and then provide you with the know-how to have your email re-routed to your email software should you choose that option. In fact, you don't need to have dedicated email software installed on a computer to send and receive email! Equivalent 100% Web-based options are available. Also many Internet Service Providers now provide free Web mail accounts as part of their basic subscription package.

However, most people who pay for every minute while online currently prefer to access their email using dedicated email software like Outlook Express or Eudora Pro, to connect to the Internet, send and retrieve email then disconnect. Working with Web-based email can arguably be more time consuming so may be more expensive for business users, but is usually much easier to work with while travelling away from your base and some would argue even essential.

Web-based access is ideal if you're on the road or travel abroad often and most Web email accounts also allow you to redirect mail to another email box if you prefer.

Installing and setting up your email software

Working in partnership with your Internet Service Providers, email software allows you to create, edit, send, receive, view and manage all email messages with which you work. Lots of email programs are available, however some packages have become especially popular, including:

- Microsoft Outlook Express: probably by far the most popular email software in use today; also includes a fine basic newsgroup reader and currently comes free with Internet Explorer Web browser: http://www.microsoft.com/
- Netscape Messenger: also includes a newsgroup reader; is currently free with Netscape Communicator Internet suite and Web browser: http://www.netscape.com/
- Microsoft Outlook: a Microsoft "heavyweight" and a superb Personal Information Manager (PIM) and powerful email management program; available as a standalone product that is also part of the Microsoft Office suite: http://www.microsoft.com/office
- Eudora Pro: from Qualcomm, this popular, powerful and well established email program is available for both the PC and the Apple Mac. Currently, a free version is available if you allow banner advertisements to display while you're using the software. If you don't like seeing the banner ads, a chargeable version is also available: http://www.eudora.com/
- Pegasus Mail: another powerful emailer that is currently free: http://www.usa.pegasus.com/

To use your new email account, you'll probably need to know several pieces of key information as described in the following paragraphs. Usually however, most of the information you need to get up and running quickly is provided by your Internet Service Provider. Furthermore, wizard-based installation software often available from good Internet Service Providers automatically covers much of what is listed in the following paragraphs – so you may not even need to know the details to at least get up and running.

However, if you perform a manual installation at any time, you will need the specific information listed in the following paragraphs that applies to your account. Anything that you're not sure of you can check with your Internet Service Provider. So let's cover the basics:

- Internet Service Provider's telephone access number: in the UK, make sure your dial-up number uses either a local dialling code or preferably an 0800 free phone number. Some providers are now developing 24-hour fixed rate Internet access that uses a free phone number for dial-up.
- User Name or Account Name: often this is taken from the first part of your email address and so you may not have a choice. For example, in the following imaginary email address: fox.mulder@ TheyWontGetMe.com, the first part, "fox.mulder" or even just "fox" might form the User Name for this imaginary account.
- A password: this component is usually made up of letters/numbers and optionally some other special characters. The key point is, your password needs to be unique and known only to you or other trusted parties. While your email user name is public knowledge, your password should be kept private. Within the set-up dialog boxes, a password should appear as a series of asterisks (★★★★★) for security reasons.

Anyone who knows your password could gain unauthorised access to your email box. Therefore keep this information private. Usually you can set up your software to "remember" a log-on password – a useful option to consider if other people do not have direct access to your computer.

- Your email address: as agreed with your Internet Service Provider.

- Return email address: usually only needed if you want replies to be sent to an email address other than your default address. For example, if working from home, you may prefer to have any replies sent to your office or work-based email address.
- Your Incoming Mail (POP3) address: to recap, a protocol is nothing more than a set of rules. Post Office Protocol (POP) 3 ensures that all email addressed to you is stored and routed to your email box. If you're not using POP3, you can use IMAP below. For BT Internet or BT Click customers, POP3 examples include: mail.btinternet.com or pop3.lineone.net respectively.
- Your IMAP address (usually optional): Internet Messaging Access Protocol (IMAP) is essentially a more sophisticated version of POP3 described in the previous paragraph. To establish whether you can use the advanced features of IMAP, check with your Internet Service Provider.
- Your Outgoing Mail (SMTP) address: Simple Mail Transfer Protocol (SMTP) handles all email messages you send to other people – hence "outgoing." Usually, you can use your own ISP's outgoing email server. For BT Internet or BT Click customers, examples here include: mail.btinternet.com or smtp.lineone.net respectively.
- And finally your name.

Armed with the previous information, to start a new email account in Outlook Express, first choose the Accounts command from the Tools menu, followed by the Add Mail command in the dialog box. Then to complete the set-up of your new account, simply answer the questions the wizard asks.

When you first install Netscape Communicator v4.6 which includes Netscape's email program, Netscape Messenger, the Mail & Newsgroups

Setup Program starts. This wizard approach also asks for information similar to that listed earlier, so make sure you have the key information provided by your Internet Service Provider handy. If you want to make changes later, in the Netscape Navigator Web browser choose the Preferences command from the Edit menu, and in the dialog box, click on the Mail & Newsgroups category to gain access to the essential email settings.

From my own experience with software and hard disk crashes that may occur from time to time (oh what joy!), even though you may think you don't need to keep a written record of the email settings like those above, do it anyway. You never know when you'll need it. But remember to keep your record in a secure safe place away from prying eyes.

A word about email security

"Normal" email is not a secure system: anyone with the correct equipment can tap into the entire contents of your email box or peer into your PC while online. And yes, there are bogies out there – or more precisely unscrupulous people who use email scanners in an attempt to discover key information. So what can you do to keep these people out?

If you're particularly concerned about your email privacy, take a look at encryption methods as discussed on page 264. But remember that even so-called unbreakable encryption systems may be "hackable" for someone with the right equipment and know-how. Pages 147-156 also examine Internet security in a more general sense. However, for those of us who have no plans for world domination, or not to pay our taxes, or to do anything else that we know we shouldn't be doing, for most purposes, simple email is probably fine and works wonderfully well.

A peek at Microsoft Outlook Express

Outlook Express enables you to send and receive email messages on the Internet, and you can also set up multiple dial-up email accounts. So, for example, you can set up one account for John so he can work with his email; another account for Jane, so she can do the same, and another account for Jim, and so on. In this way, providing each "account" holder has different email settings, user names and passwords, etc., each can work with only their own email messages without affecting others. Also optionally, email messages can be adorned with images, animation and multimedia clips but more on this later.

Currently free of charge, Outlook Express is perhaps not surprisingly one of the most popular email programs available. The following paragraphs outline how to use the program. Most email programs have similar ways of operation and once you're familiar with a popular product like Outlook Express, if you choose to switch to another email program – say like Netscape Messenger or perhaps Eudora Pro – you'll probably be up and running sooner than you might think.

With Outlook Express correctly installed and set up, when you start the program, you'll probably see the main screen made up of at least 2 main panes, as shown overleaf. Towards the top of the screen, Outlook Express provides the essential drop-down menus, commands and convenient buttons to provide quick access to the most popular tasks. To see a brief tip about the purpose of a button, place the mouse pointer stationary on top of the button you want.

In the left column, you can see the various mail "boxes" you've created and are using, whether any waiting or unread email is present, and, at the bottom, a list of any newsgroups to which you subscribed. The main Outlook Express window provides quick and easy access to the most important activities, in which you can:

- Read and download mail.
- Compose a message.
- Use your email Address book.
- Work with newsgroups.
- Find people.

To read your mail, you simply click the small Read Mail text link or picture icon in the large pane or click the Inbox folder in the left pane. The Outlook Express main window, by default, then changes to a 3-pane arrangement as shown in the example on page 231. Remember, the left pane shows the list of folders available. If you select a folder in the left pane, if any email messages are present in that folder, their message headers are shown listed in the top pane. When you click a message header in the top pane, the lower pane displays the actual contents of the message. When you first install Outlook Express, you'll probably find one or two messages by default already installed in your Inbox.

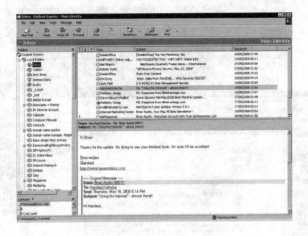

You can learn much simply by opening, closing, moving and copying these messages, but read them first: they may contain important new information.

Ideally, why not make a copy of one message and practice the various common commands and tasks on your message copy, rather than use the original. To get more familiar with your new email program, why not create a new message, send it to a colleague who is experienced with email and ask them to reply. And don't forget, many of the commands listed in the menus are available quickly through selecting an item, then clicking the right mouse button and choosing the command you want from the floating menu.

Sending and receiving email messages

The guidelines provided in this chapter assume that you already have an Internet connection and that you successfully installed and configured your email software as outlined in previous chapters. Now you're ready to really get to grips with email! In fact, email is simple to use; essentially, there are only four main email activities:

- Receiving and downloading email messages sent to you.
- Creating email messages.
- Sending your email messages.
- Organising your email messages.

The email header

When you send or receive an email message, some important information is recorded in an area of the email message called the email header. So where is the email header? In Outlook Express, if you double-click a particular email message in the top Outlook Express pane, a new, independent window opens showing the chosen email. The upper pane of this window contains the email header information. The most essential details are then made immediately visible, for example:

- Who it is from (double-click to view full contact information).
- Who the email is for (double-click to view full contact information.)
- Who else it was sent to (optional).
- The time and date when the email was sent.

- A short description of what the email is about in the "Subject" line.

The "To" and "From" lines may contain nicknames that your email program may use. To view the true email addresses and optionally other contact information, simply double-click the line you want. To view full Internet header information in Outlook Express, choose the Properties command on the File menu.

When replying to an email, you can help save time for your recipient: consider deleting all unnecessary information from the original email and quote only the part that is relevant.

You don't need to have your computer, mobile phone or "whiz-bang" super microwave cooker switched on – and doing what they do best – in order to receive an email message! You can receive email messages any time (whether you're present or not while an email is being sent) once your email account is set up and running. Your Internet Service Provider stores your email messages until you're ready to receive them (within reason).

Check your email box regularly in order to possibly avoid losing email messages caused by an overflowing email box. Usually, once an email box is examined, the queued messages are downloaded to the caller's computer. This approach can ensure the amount of space reserved for an email account is never used up.

If you have to pay for every minute of Internet access, here's how you can save money. Set up your email software so that, once the program has sent and retrieved any email, your email program automatically disconnects from the Internet and hangs up the phone line. You can then read and organise your email messages without having to be concerned about excessive phone costs. When replying to an email message, you can queue your replies in the "Outbox" and, when ready, again send and receive in a single session.

'You've got mail': receiving an email

When you receive an email message, usually your email software causes a beep to sound; however, if this arrangement irritates, check the options available – you can probably turn the beep off. Other "You've got mail" indicators include messages displayed on the screen and highlighted icons in your email program – so you can instantly identify new messages from those that have already been read.

Although an Internet Service Provider stores all your messages until you need them, do check your particular email box usage conditions with your provider: some only keep a limited number of messages for a finite time and if messages are not retrieved before the limit, they may be deleted.

Reading your email messages

In order to know which messages are new and therefore unread, your email program has to identify each new message. In Outlook Express, new emails that you have just downloaded and have not read are shown in darker lettering (boldface). So at a glance, you know which messages are new and unexamined.

You can read mail in two main ways:

- To read a new email, in the top pane simply select the message you want and its contents appear in the lower preview pane. After a few seconds of previewing, the darker lettering style of the selected message in the top pane changes to a normal (lighter) colour to indicate this email has been examined.

- If you want more control and do not want to be distracted by other items on the screen, in the top pane simply double-click the message you want to read. Outlook Express then creates another independent window that you can maximise to fill the screen or adjust to the size you want.

Sometimes, it's easy to unintentionally select a message in the top pane, or when you're not really ready to read the message: selecting a message for only a few seconds is sometimes enough for Outlook Express to think you've read it. Remedy: simply don't change or move the current selection or click another message until you're ready to read the next message.

At the top of the independent window, Outlook Express provides a toolbar that lets you easily work with your messages – in particular the 'Previous' and 'Next' buttons enable you to step through each message quickly and easily.

Also, the time you receive an email from someone new is the ideal time to consider adding that person to your Address Book. You can do this manually; however, you can usually set up your software so that anyone you reply to is automatically added to your Address book – a great time-saver!

Designing reader-friendly email messages

In Outlook Express, when creating an email or deciding what to put in it, you can import text from other locations and use the standard Cut, Copy and Paste commands; doing this saves time when you are moving information around. If you've got a lot to say, you can enter over 60,000 characters into one email message – not something I would recommend unless your recipient knows they're going to be receiving your condensed version of Tolstoy's War and Peace.

Although Outlook Express (and other great email programs) make a lot of power available at your fingertips, usually email programs leave the layout and formatting to the user. After all, as individuals most of us have our own way of doing things. However, it's easy to get carried away with all the superb features now available with most good email programs and this is something to watch carefully, especially if you want your message to be understood quickly by a large number of people. Therefore, let's look at some simple ways to help you create great emails every time.

1. Developing a compelling email writing style

Here's an obvious but often overlooked fact about email: as people (usually) cannot see you, they make judgements about you by what you write, how you write it and how it appears to them. With email, often your credibility is at stake. Also remember, the text-based nature of email means that a permanent record of what you've said may always be available – so don't say anything that you wouldn't mind your mother hearing or a judge sitting on the bench!

So let's look at some simple ways you can ensure your email creates a favourable impression, whether you're sending a simple message to a friend, family member, or perhaps sending a regular email newsletter to 7,000 keen subscribers eager for money-saving hints, tips and insights from your latest brain dump!

2. Which do I use: plain text- or HTML-based email?

Plain text format – sometimes referred to as ASCII (American Standard Code for Information Interchange) – offers a way to ensure that anyone who can receive email can read and see your email message properly. You can also send an email in HTML format – that is, using the same codes and tags that are used to create Web pages – like the example shown on the facing page. Using HTML-formatted email, you can send exotic-looking email messages: formatted text, pictures, and so on. You can even create a Web page newsletter in your favourite Web design software, then use Copy and Paste to transfer a copy into your email program. For more information on how to create HTML (Web email messages), see pages 341, 348 and 359.

However, for your recipients to be able to view your email exactly as you intend, their email software must be compatible and be set up to properly detect HTML-based emails. Often you won't know which email programs your recipients are using, and therefore the capabilities of their software. If you send email in the wrong format, your recipients may only see a mass of jumbled characters usually as an email attachment. Therefore, unless you know otherwise, the safest course of action is to use simple plain text.

In Outlook Express, you can change the default format using the Tools > Options command pair and choose the Send format you want. In Netscape Messenger, open the Edit menu and choose Preferences and click on Mail & Newsgroups.

3. Keeping order: using left alignment

For those who communicate in languages that use a left-to-right and down-the-page sequence like English, to prevent any possible text misalignment at your recipient's end, if possible use only the default left justified text alignment. That is, the text you enter is aligned vertically at the left edge of the screen. Try to avoid using indents, tabs, justified alignments and colours. Readers in countries that use other standard writing patterns can adapt this approach to their own language: the key point here is to make your message easy to read.

4. Using narrower columns for easier reading

Studies have shown that reading on a computer screen is generally acknowledged to be more tiring to the eye than, say, reading from paper. To make the job of understanding screen-based text easier and reduce eyestrain, consider narrowing

Word wrap ensures the text cursor is automatically moved to the following line when the end of the line is reached. Some email software defaults to 70 or even 80 characters – much too long, especially if you're reading from a larger screen.

the column width your readers have to read. An easy way to do this is to examine the program options in your email software and set or change the word wrap setting to about 60 characters or less.

5. Why short paragraphs make more sense

How about meeting a continuous 50-line paragraph just after breakfast! If you've got a lot to say, why not break your message into shorter paragraphs of up to about 5 or 8 lines maximum – and make someone's day! Most people hate to see long paragraphs of nothing but text – especially on a computer screen! If you're in business on the Net, your prospects and customers need to see and read your message if they're to respond to your call to action. Although readers are often more tolerant with longer paper-based paragraphs, on a business-oriented Web page or email especially, long paragraphs probably offer one of the quickest ways to lose money fast: few people feel like responding to your offer or reading about your latest incredible deal. Long spans of text often simply get scanned, skipped or not even read!

6. Keep it brief and get popular

Try to be concise and to the point in your emails. People who receive hundreds of emails each day welcome consideration given for their valuable time and carefully considered emails are, arguably, more likely to achieve their objective. Again, brevity is especially important for business-oriented emails where most people simply do not have the time to spend reading anything that is not relevant to the current theme or discussion topic.

7. Grammar reborn, ouch!

Technology drives us relentlessly towards a supposedly paperless society. Yet the widespread use of text-based email forces us to be more aware of and think about the words and sentences we use in our communications. Just when we thought that watching our grammar was a school-time activity that perhaps is not really relevant today, someone invents email!

Certainly when communicating about work and business, our sentences need to make sense; we still need to dot our I's and cross our T's – you never know who is going to be reading your email message. In personal emails however, we can loosen up, break the rules and have a lot more fun – and yes break the rules just because you can, if that's your bag!

8. Watch the file size

Why should the size of an email message make a difference? Some email software may reject or bounce messages that are larger than a specific file size. For most emails, file size is not really an important issue; for longer emails – newsletters (ezines) for example – file size does need to be considered. Early AOL email readers may not even deliver messages that are over 32Kb in file size. One way around this problem is to either split the message into several parts as needed, or consider using an email attachment approach. But again, check the limits on attachments.

Also, most users can set their email software to reject file attachments above a specific level, for example 100Kb, to help limit the amount of time online and save money. Therefore, if you plan to send a larger email message, consider sending a brief announcement email first to let your recipient know. This gives them time to change their settings (temporarily perhaps) or to contact you saving time and resources and avoiding confusion for all involved.

9. Focusing on your readers: email etiquette

Email is essentially just another form of communication; it reflects real life. People usually interact and work together better when a certain amount of politeness and consideration is involved. Email etiquette is simply just that: having consideration for other users.

Essential email address books

To send an email, you need to know your recipient's correct email address. However, although email addresses can sometimes seem confusing and difficult to remember, when you use an email address book, the task is much easier. When you send an email to a new contact the first time, you'll probably need to type the email address into the "To" box. However, to avoid having to

Gradually keep adding entries to your email address book. The extra time needed in the early stages pays off later when you want to seek an address quickly.

repeatedly type the same email address on subsequent occasions, you can copy or store email addresses in an address book using a nickname or the person's real name. Email address books usually come with email software or you can buy separate add-on utilities. To see the Address book in Outlook Express for example, simply choose the Address Book command from the Tools menu. In Netscape Messenger, you can find the Address Book command in the Communicator menu.

To help reduce the number of incorrect email addresses in your Address book or to avoid sending multiple identical messages to the same destination, regularly check for duplicate email addresses and delete those not needed.

Microsoft Outlook 2000 includes a superb Personal Information Manager (PIM) address book. Whenever you want to enter a recipient's email address, you only need start entering the desired nickname or real name into the box, and leave the software to remember the entire precise and sometimes-tricky email address sequence.

The Address Book in Outlook Express by default attempts to use what you type into the recipient field. However, sometimes you may need to manually edit a record to create an entry. To open the Address Book in Outlook Express while creating an email, click any of the little book icons placed next to the "To:", "Cc:" and "Bcc:" labels. Select the email address you want and use the buttons provided to copy it into the relevant recipient field.

In the Address Book dialog box, you can also enter a "New Contact" and easily edit the contents of an existing contact using the Properties button. In Netscape Messenger, just click the New Card button in the Address Book dialog box and enter details about a new contact. You can quickly add an email

Although Outlook Express provides a "Check Names" or "Check Addresses" command if an email address is invalid, your Internet Service Provider usually returns or "bounces" the faulty email back to you with an error message identifying where the problem may lie.

address to your Address Book in Outlook Express: right-click the email address you want and choose the Add to Address Book command. In Netscape Messenger, you can use the Add Sender to Address Book command from the Message menu.

Finding an email address

You can guarantee it will happen just when you're really busy and you haven't got the time to spend searching: you can't find that email address you need. But if it's unavoidable, and you're prepared to spend 15 minutes trying, how do you rectify this? Before looking for complex answers, try the obvious: friends, colleagues and acquaintances. Failing that, here are several other ideas to consider:

- Check any previous paper communications like letterheads, business cards, etc.
- Has this person had any contact with a Web site? If so, log on and go to that Web site. If you can't find the address you want, consider sending an email to an appropriate contact at the Web site.
- Try several Internet search services like: Big Foot at http://www.bigfoot.com/ and WhoWhere at http://www.whowhere.com/ and so on.
- Try to develop a habit of adding contact details to your email or other software address book to avoid the same problem later.

Creating a new email message

To create a new email message or reply to an existing message, remember you don't need to be online. You can create each email then transfer it to the Outbox in Outlook Express, or the Unsent Messages folder in Netscape Messenger, ready for sending later when you go online.

To reduce the possibility of making a typing mistake for an email address, use the correct pre-defined entries in your email address book whenever possible. Then you need only look for the recipient's name or nickname.

Usually, the command for starting a new message can be found on the File menu. In Outlook Express 5.x, simply choose the File > New Mail Message commands or click the New Mail button on the main toolbar. On other versions of email software, look for the equivalent commands and buttons like, "Compose Message" or "New Mail Message", and so on. A blank new mail window should then display with the mouse cursor placed in the "To" box.

In the "To" box, enter the email address of your recipient. Outlook Express then underlines the email address if the syntax appears to follow the correct rules for writing email addresses – in other words, if the address you enter seems correct to your email program.

Check an email address carefully. Even a single typing mistake can result in producing a "valid" email address, but which nevertheless may be the wrong recipient.

In Netscape Messenger, you can start a new email with the New Msg button, enter your recipient details and your message. If you're not online, you can queue email messages for sending later: click the Send Later command from the File menu of the message window for each message.

Doubling up with Carbon Copy (Cc) and Blind Carbon Copy (Bcc)

If you want to send an email to more than one person at the same time, you can enter additional email addresses into the "Cc:" (Carbon Copy) box. For more than one Cc recipient, place a comma, or sometimes a semicolon (;) between

each additional email address: check your email program documentation for the exact separator to use. If you use Carbon Copy, each recipient on the list can see the email address of every other recipient on the list. Sometimes, Cc: is not the most appropriate way to send a message. Some recipients, especially if they're sensitive about receiving a lot of spam email, may not appreciate their email address being openly displayed in this way. However, a remedy is available: use Blind Carbon Copy (Bcc) instead. With this option, the email addresses of all other members of this mailing list are not displayed openly – hence the name "Blind Carbon Copy." Often by default, the Blind Carbon Copy box may not be visible at first: you may have to switch on the command in your email program Option's dialog box or equivalent. In Outlook Express v5.x, you can make the Bcc: field visible by choosing All Headers in the View menu of the New Message window.

The email Subject box

The final component in the email header is the Subject box. Enter a short description in the Subject box, ideally using fewer than about 7 words outlining what your email message is about. The Subject is what your recipients usually see displayed in heavy lettering style until they read the message – a few seconds after which the "normal" lettering style usually applies to show that the message has been read.

Did you really mean to shout?

A continuous sequence of capital letters in an email message is considered to be the equivalent of shouting and is also generally harder to read. Capital letters force the reader to slow their rate of reading. Therefore, use capitals with care rather than simply to emphasise a point: your recipient may think you mean something very different to what you're trying to say.

Misunderstandings can easily arise possibly leading to problems that really have no basis – a definite no-no if you're trying to sell. Upper and lower case letters – like this paragraph – provide the easiest and fastest way to read an email message. However, capitals are ideal for headings and short sequences of text that have a clear meaning to which you want to give special attention.

Adding emotion with a Smiley

In a plain text email message, the options for putting over emotion or feeling are limited. However, you can use combinations of special characters to create Smileys – sometimes called emoticons. You can imagine how Smileys get their name: look at the list of popular Smileys below by tilting your head sideways to see the rough outline of eyes, nose and mouth.

Smiley:	Emotion:
:'-(	Crying
:-(	Frowning
:-I	Indifferent
:-D	Laughing
:-)	Smiling
:-0	Surprised
;-)	Winking

Saving time with abbreviations

Email abbreviations are a great way to type less, provided of course they make sense to all involved. Here are a few to get you started:

Abbreviation:	Meaning:
B4	Before
BTW	By the way
CUL	See you later
FAQ	Frequently asked questions
FOAF	Friend of a friend
FOC	Free of charge
FWIW	For what it's worth
FYA	For your amusement

Abbreviation:	Meaning:
FYI	For your information
FYIO	For your eyes only
HTH	Hope this helps
IME	In my experience
IMHO	In my humble opinion
IMO	In my opinion
IOW	In other words
KISS	Keep it simple stupid
L8R	Later
LOL	Laughing out loud

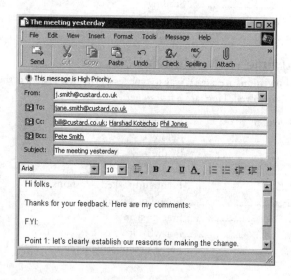

Abbreviation:	Meaning:
MOTAS	Member of the appropriate sex
MOTOS	Member of the opposite sex
MOTSS	Member of the same sex
NRN	No reply necessary
OBTW	Oh, by the way
OTT	Over the top
ROTFL	Rolling on the floor laughing
RSN	Real soon now
RUOK	Are you OK?
SO	Significant other
TIA	Thanks in advance
TTFN	Cheerio
TVM	Thank you very much
WRT	With respect to

The above are just a few of the hundreds of abbreviations used in email and Internet Chat communications, so if typing is not your bag, there's one answer.

Sending an email message

To create and send an email, here's what you'll need to do in sequence:

1. Enter the recipient's email address.
2. In the Subject box, enter a word or phrase describing what the email is about.
3. Type your email message (or for multimedia-based software: speak your message).
4. Check entered details: have automatic spell-checking turned on.
5. Click the Send button.

Once you click the Send button, depending on how your email program is set up, two possible results can occur:

- Your email software may immediately dial your Internet Service Provider and send the message, or…
- Your message is moved to the Outbox in Outlook Express or Unsent Messages in Netscape Messenger – both provide a temporary holding area ready for sending later when you dial up your Internet Service Provider to send and receive your email.

Usually by default, most current email software is set up to ensure you can Send and Receive email during the same session. Outlook 2000 for example, provides the "Send and Receive" button on the main toolbar allowing quick and easy email processing although you can fine-tune your choices. Usually, once an email is sent from the Outbox or Unsent Messages folder, the software either places a copy of the sent email in the Sent folder or marks an email in a special way to identify sent email messages from other emails.

For your first email, why not send yourself a brief message? This checks that your computer and email system are set up to correctly send and receive email. Before going online, set up your email not to automatically disconnect after sending and receiving email. Then after sending your email message, stay online and keep checking every few seconds until you have received your own message. You should receive your message ideally within seconds, but at least within a few minutes at most. After which you can disconnect and re-enter your preferred connect/disconnect settings.

Marking an email message as urgent

If you need the recipient of your email to respond quickly, you can mark the email as urgent. Microsoft Outlook and Outlook Express provide a command/button that allows you to indicate that an email is of "High importance". Then when your recipient receives a high priority email, an attention-getting marker – for example, an exclamation mark (!) – is included with the email Subject.

Replying to an email

To reply to an email, select the message you want, then click the Reply button or choose the Reply command from the Message menu. Then usually your email software copies your original message – including its original header information – into a new message window and places the prefix "Re:" – short for Reply – in the Subject line box.

You're now ready to enter your reply information and optionally edit or delete unnecessary information in the original email. People who use email regularly can receive many messages every day so when replying, your recipient will probably thank you for including only the relevant part of the original message. We refer to this as Quoting. Also by deleting the parts that are not relevant when replying, your message is shortened and so gets sent faster and helps keep the Internet less cluttered for everyone to benefit – resulting in faster, better connections.

You might ask, how can we ensure that the part we are quoting does not get mixed with our reply? Simple. Fortunately most good email programs provide an easy way to identify an original message when you hit the Reply button: often the "Greater Than" (>) character may be automatically placed at the start of every line of the original message.

Other email software may use text indents or even colour coding in the same way so that you and your recipients can identify all the parts of the original message from the new message. Often you can change the default character or indicator that email software uses through the Tools > Options command and look for the Send or Reply options in Outlook Express, or Edit > Preferences command in Netscape Messenger. Now all you need do is reply to the parts you want and delete the irrelevant parts of the original message – usually, simply highlight all the text you don't want and press the Delete key.

Forwarding an email

Sometimes, you may want to send a copy of an email message that you receive, to friends or colleagues for comment or feedback, or you may want to add your own comments first before sending. Most email software refers to this as Forwarding. Essentially, Forwarding is the online equivalent of sending a memo. Forwarding an email is simple; here's what you do. While viewing the email you want to forward, choose the Forward command or click the Forward (email) button. Then usually, your email software places the prefix "Fw:" or something similar in the Subject Line box. Next, in the "To:" box, enter the email address of the person to whom you want to forward the email.

Also, you can choose to forward an email message as an attachment to another message. Here's how: select the message and choose the Forward as

You can easily identify a forwarded email message: look for 'Fw:' or 'Fwd:' at the start of the Subject box.

Attachment command usually found on the Message menu – or you can right-click the message and choose the command from the floating menu.

If you want to send a copy of the email to others at the same time, include their addresses in the Carbon Copy (Cc) or Blind Carbon Copy (Bcc) boxes as covered earlier in this chapter. Optionally make any changes, add comments and delete parts of the message you don't want to forward and finish by choosing the Send command or button. Finally follow your usual procedure for actually sending emails.

Sending an email to several recipients

Earlier in this chapter, we mentioned that you can send the same email message to several people or many people. If you send an email newsletter, essentially that's all you're doing. However, in recent years, Internet Service Providers – in reflecting the views of many subscribers – have become sensitive to the issue of Spam – or bulk emailing. However, let's assume that you're a nice and sensible person who doesn't spam others. You simply want to send your newsletter to 600 people who have asked to receive it.

The obvious option would be to first open a copy of the message you want to send and enter one email address from your list into the "To:" box. Then Copy and Paste, the remaining several hundred others into the Blind Carbon Copy (Bcc) field. To do this, you would first have to make sure all the email addresses were valid and correct, then separate each one with a comma or semicolon (;) or whatever separator your email documentation instructs. When ready, simply choose the Send command. But wait!

Most Internet Service Providers put a limit on the number of email addresses you can put into the Blind Carbon Copy (Bcc) field – usually 50 or thereabouts. Any more, and they may assume that you're bulk emailing. Often, the simplest answer is to use a purpose-designed email list service. Providing you're not spamming anyone, you should have few problems with a genuine list. Your Internet Service Provider may even provide a list service – often called a listserver – free with your email or Web hosting account, so check with them before seeking an outside list solution. Some good quality free independent

Perhaps the best way to create a lengthy email list is to copy and past the list into a plain word processor window – say Windows Notepad or equivalent – then simply enter or arrange each email address with the separator character between them. Finally, save the file as a plain text file (.txt). Your email list is then ready for copying and pasting whenever required.

listservers are now available and if you want tight control, you can opt for a paid listserver service, but shop around, check out and compare what's on offer.

Re-sending an email message

If you sent your email message but, for some mysterious reason, your recipient hasn't received it, you'll want to re-send the message. If you're using Microsoft Outlook, in the left pane, simply click the Sent messages folder, select the message you want to resend in the right pane, and just choose the Resend command. If a direct Resend command is not available, you can copy the message contents window in the Sent items folder and paste into a new message window. But remember, you'll probably have to delete the header details in the original message and any other unnecessary characters, re-enter the recipient's email address and Subject box details and click Send to finish.

Attaching a file to an email message

Sometimes, you may want to send more than just a plain text file or a HTML-based document. Attachments are the answer. An email attachment is simply any document or computer file that is "attached" to an email message. For example, you might want to send a Microsoft Word document perhaps containing additional charts and pictures. Or even a computer program. However, sometimes the simplest solution is to copy and paste a document as plain text into an email window avoiding the need to attach the document.

If both you and your recipient are using a modern email program, then the business of sending and receiving attachments will probably go smoothly. For an attachment to be sent successfully, both parties must be using the same encoding standard. When you install your email program, the software chooses a common default standard, so the chances are you'll never need to change this. However, options include: MIME, Uuencode and Binhex. So although rare nowadays, if you come across problems, check that you're both using the same encoding format or consider both switching to using an easier

Here's probably one of the quickest ways to have your email (and optionally Web site) account closed without warning. Send an email to a large number of recipients without getting written evidence of their permission to receive emails from you.

automatic up-to-date email program like Outlook Express, Netscape Messenger, Eudora, Pegasus or Microsoft Outlook.

To attach a file to an email message, with your email message window open choose the Attach File or Send Attachments command, button, or its equivalent option in your email program. For example, Microsoft Outlook Express provides the Attach File button on the main toolbar in the message window. Your email software then usually displays a dialog box to allow you to choose the file you want to attach.

Microsoft Outlook identifies an attached file using a paperclip symbol. If you want to attach more than one file, usually all you need do is repeat the procedure. If you pay for every minute while online and if the file you want to attach is large in file size, to reduce the time spent online, consider compressing the file as examined in the following paragraphs. Also, do remember that the larger the file size, the longer the overall email transfer time and the more likely the possibility of transfer problems.

Before sending an email that contains a large attachment, consider sending a brief message to the recipient stating that you're about to send a large email and check if that is acceptable. For users who have to pay for every minute while online, downloading a large 'unannounced' email can be annoying and costly for the recipient – especially if they did not want or ask for the information or attachment in the first place.

Compressing an attachment

A file compressor program is designed to squash a file to a smaller file size where possible. Some file types already exist naturally in a compressed form and so may not compress much further, like Adobe Acrobat files for example, so usually these are probably best left in their native state.

So why bother compressing files? Well, here are several reasons. Transferring large files at their normal file size over the Internet is still not 100% reliable and may take a long time. If you pay for every second while online and can reduce the time needed to send a file by say 75% simply by compressing the file, you're going to save time and money.

Also, when sending or receiving larger, uncompressed files, hang-ups, dropped phone lines, and so forth may occur during the transfer, so the task of sending the entire message with the attachment will have to be repeated. After several hours of doing this when you really don't have the time, you can almost feel your hair falling out! So reducing the file size using a file compressor helps minimise these kinds of problems.

Thirdly, to prevent email boxes becoming jammed with spammed messages and unauthorised attachments, some users change the settings in their email software to limit the size of any file attachments that are automatically accepted when checking their email. A popular setting is 100 – 200 kilobytes. If you try to send a 250Kb file to someone who has set the upper limit to 200Kb, the email message will be rejected and you'll probably receive an appropriate but sometimes vague error message. Now if that same attachment were compressed to say 50Kb, it should transfer without problem – and do so more quickly.

One of the most popular file compressors today is WinZip, which I use regularly and consider this little program absolutely essential when working with the Internet. WinZip is shareware – that is, you get to try it first and if you decide to keep it, register and pay the small fee for your copy. For more information, go to: http://www.winzip.com/ Also remember, to decompress a compressed file, usually you must have the same type of software used to compress the file. Likewise, if you send a compressed file, your recipient must have the same type of software to decompress the attachment at their end.

To quickly and easily add an email attachment to a message, you can probably use drag and drop to simply drag a document/ attachment icon into the current message window. You can check your computer documentation to find out if your computer supports drag and drop.

About you: using email signatures

An email signature is a few lines of text describing who your are, what you do and perhaps a brief phrase promoting a Web site (yours or someone else's), special offer or product or service. Here's an example business-oriented signature:

/////////////////
Brian Austin MISTC
brian@mycompany.com
Author, publisher, webmaster,
http://www.mycompany.com
Fantastic NEW August promotion!
FREE Offers. Only while stocks last!
/////////////////

When creating email signatures for personal and not business use, you can have a lot more fun, creating patterns, faces and all sorts of Smiley-type symbols. To create an email signature in Outlook Express, choose the Tools > Options commands, then click the Signatures tab. In Netscape Messenger, choose Edit > Preferences and click the Identity tab under the Mail & Newsgroups category.

Consider including mailing address, phone and fax numbers in an email signature if this information is especially important for you.

Sometimes, having several different email signature files to serve different purposes, can be useful, save time and avoid unnecessary repetitive typing. For example, you could define one for private/personal use, two or three for business – one for Sales, one for Support, etc. – and additional ones perhaps for other members of your family or work colleagues.

Make an impact with a vCard

A vCard is a sort of online business card – a collection of details about you that you provide and make available, so that recipients can, if they choose, easily copy your details into their email address book.

To create a vCard in Outlook Express v5.0x, first choose the Tools > Options command pair. Then in the Options dialog box click the Compose tab. You can then create your vCard under the Business Cards category. Enter as many details as you wish to be made available. vCards made in Outlook Express have a .vcf filename extension. To create a vCard in Netscape Messenger, start by choosing Edit > Preferences. Then in the dialog box, click the Mail & Newsgroups Category, followed by Identity. Click the Edit Card button to start creating your vCard.

Dealing with email bouncers

If you send an email to an address that is incorrect or which does not exist, the sent message is usually returned to you as a "bounced" message. Check the email address again – remember, an email address has a certain structure. For example, all current email addresses must include an "@" character. For more information, see: What's an email address? on page 216.

Only a single-character typing mistake is enough to cause a message to bounce. If the email address you chose is "old", remember the person to whom you're sending the message may have cancelled that address or perhaps has a new address, so perhaps re-check your records.

Sending and receiving HTML email messages

Although most of this chapter focuses on sending email messages in plain text format simply because that is a universal worldwide standard, remember that you can also send emails in HTML or Web page format.

The advantage is you can add colours, text formatting, pictures, animations and so on to an email, in fact most of what goes into a Web page can be included. Like Web pages though, the more you put in, the longer a message takes to download, so just keep to the essentials unless your recipients know what to expect. To create and send email in HTML format, first make sure that HTML is turned on in your email software. In Outlook Express v5.x, choose Tools > Options then click the Send tab and edit the settings to make HTML format live. In Netscape Communicator/Messenger v4.6x, choose Edit > Preferences then click Formatting under the Mail & Newsgroups category and choose HTML formatting.

Setting up secure email

Although most current generation email programs like Outlook Express and Netscape Messenger are reasonably secure, when working with sensitive or valuable information, you might prefer better security. So let's examine the options.

Keep them guessing with PGP encryption

The best systems use encryption so that only the genuinely intended recipient who has the correct software key built into their email program can read the information. PGP – short for "Pretty Good Privacy" – is, despite the rather amusing name, one such system that uses what are called public and private encryption keys that work together to create a more secure email system.

Here's how it works. You freely send the public key to your contacts. When your contact wants to send information to you securely, they encrypt the information using the public key. As you are the only party with the private key, only you can open the encrypted message. For more information, see: http://www.pgpi.org/ and http://www.research.umbc.edu/pgp/pgpmain.html

Using a digital ID

A digital ID is another option that helps verify an email identity – however, remember this system is not as secure as PGP. Here's how it works. First you need a certificate from a secure and trusted third party like Verisign (http://www.verisign.com); more information is available at their Web site. When your personal certificate is installed, you'll need to turn it on in your email program. In Outlook Express, choose the Options command from the Tools menu, then click the Security tab and enter your settings. In Netscape Messenger, choose the Security command from the Help menu and follow onscreen prompts or see the Online Help. You then have two options:

- Include your digital ID with every email you send – but all recipients must also install your digital certificate.
- Or you can use normal mail for most operations and turn on digital ID-based email for specific recipients – and again those recipients receiving your ID-based email must install your digital certificate in order to read email from you.

When you send email with a secure digital ID, compatible email software from those recipients who have also installed your digital ID recognises that these secure emails can come only from you.

Converting a fax to email

Lots of Internet Service Providers and other companies on the Net now provide various additional services, like for example: fax-to-email and voicemail-to-email. Therefore, you may no longer need a separate fax machine and so make savings in electronic hardware and maintenance costs, electricity and fax paper. Web-based fax and voicemail services may also be particularly valuable to anyone who wants to stay in touch while travelling.

eFax at http://www.efax.com/ is just one of the many companies that provides a free service to convert faxes and voicemail to email messages. Some ISPs may include these additional fax and voicemail services free of charge with your email account – so if you think this might be for you, check what's on offer from your own Internet Service Provider before looking further afield.

Printing your email messages

It's got to be straightforward, hasn't it? To print an email, surely we just, well...
print it! Yep, that's true – usually. Often, however, you can set up various print
options. For example in the
superb Microsoft Outlook
2000, you can use:

- Print Preview –
  where you can see a
  representation of
  what your printed
  page will look like
  when printed suc-
  cessfully.
- Choose Table Style
  or Memo Style.
- Print each new item
  on a separate page.
- Print attachments along with your email message.
- Change your default printer.
- And so on.

Other email programs usually offer various printing options. Although
limiting the amount of printing is a noble aim, for businesses who have to keep
hard copy records of email invoices, receipts, etc., printing paper copies is, of
course, essential.

Managing your email messages

Many people nowadays use email daily to communicate with friends and work colleagues. The more you use email, the larger your email "collection" may become – unless you consider ways to manage your email messages. Plus, most email users eventually start receiving irrelevant email messages or "Spam." So let's look at ways to filter, organize and manage email.

Dealing with the garbage

Most of us get it! When you hear the mail hit the floor, you race to beat the dog before he does what some consider all good dogs should do: chew up the latest offering of junk mail. On the Internet, arguably, the practice of sending uninvited email usually in an attempt to sell a product or service is even more of a problem than conventional junk mail – and it's a problem that is probably getting worse for most Internet users.

Uninvited junk email, otherwise known as "Spam"; Unsolicited Commercial Email (UCE) or various other unmentionable terms dreamed up by real dedicated Spam haters. Few other topics on the Internet bring out such strong opinions both from those who send it and from those who receive it! Of course, there are always two sides to every argument and different people we've spoken to have different views on this sometimes emotive topic.

Some say that we tolerate it coming through our letterbox, so why not tolerate it online as well? Others vehemently hate Spam and would shrink in horror and plot your downfall if you should even mention the previous sentence as an option! Whatever your views on receiving junk email, if you don't want it, you can get pro-active and do something about it. If you're a real spam hater, here are some basic guidelines to help kill the beast:

- The most important first rule is to have more than one email address and keep your most important email address as private as possible – use with only trusted parties who know your views on spam.
- Use your second, less important email address for more public online activities, like mailing lists and newsgroups. You could even use a Web mail account, rather than have email sent through your email program. Many Web email providers have strict rules in an attempt to protect their users from email spam. When you examine your Web mail, you can easily delete any spam that gets through the net. At least then, you're in control.
- When you visit Web sites, check out their privacy statement and particularly their commitment to protect your email address and avoid interacting with Web sites that you think don't come up to the mark.
- Most good email software allows you to filter junk email, add any emails that come from selected sources to your "junk email list." Then, the next time an email arrives from that address you won't even need to see it – the little critter is sent straight to your computer's equivalent of the Internet garbage dump.

One option to consider is to quickly scan emails as you receive them and optionally add any junk emails to your junk list, or simply delete unwanted emails immediately – this is the approach I take and it is an acceptable compromise.

However remember, even with email filtering turned on, you still have to receive the email in the first place for the software to evaluate whether it should be filtered. The bottom line is most people can't effectively stop receiving all junk email – yet: the variables are just too complex for current generation software to handle.

If junk email becomes a particularly annoying problem to you, nevertheless, consider automatic filtering options carefully before activating them – especially if you're in business. A new customer or client may simply be testing you or your company's response timing. Not acknowledging a communication from a new prospective client is not an ideal way to foster new business. Answering a routine simple email enquiry may be the first step in gaining an order equivalent to your entire year's normal work: you just never know!

 With email filtering turned on, it's possible that you may receive email from a source of which you approve, but because of the way you may have set up your filter or the way the filter works, wanted emails may get deleted before you ever see them! The key point here is, you need to understand the junk email and filtering options available in your email software and decide what level of filtering you want to use or even whether filtering is really necessary.

How to keep spammers guessing!

If you particularly dislike receiving Spam emails, consider carefully whether you should vent your frustration on every Spam email that arrives. Even if "Unsubscribe instructions" to "prevent further emails being sent to you" are provided, unless you know this is a trusted and honourable source, my advice is to simply ignore the message and just delete the email manually, rather than replying. So why not just reply?

The problem is, if you do reply with an unsubscribe instruction, these people may decide to simply ignore your request anyway and if they do not have any genuine respect for your choices, they then know for sure that your email address is (1) valid and (2) that it's a "live" address – that is, someone is responding regularly.

Unscrupulous parties can then add your email address to the tens of thousands of others who may also have chosen to unsubscribe in disgust. These email "harvesters" can then sell this "live" emailing list to other parties, for another round of email spam! You then receive another batch of unwanted email. And so the cycle repeats. The best and safest advice we can provide here therefore is to simply delete any unwanted emails that you did not originally ask to receive.

Here's another way to limit or at least control junk email. However, this method does include the rather drastic step of first cancelling your current email address. Next, get two more addresses. Keep one of your new email addresses for serious communications and therefore only provide this to trusted parties. Then use your other email address for contributing to public forums like newsgroups, mailing lists, etc. – and if the amount of spam all gets too much a few months or a year later, simply cancel this address and start the cycle again with a new address. Drastic, I know, but it works!

Organising your email messages

As the number of email messages increases, if you don't delete or back up the ones you don't need, the efficiency of your email program may start to suffer. However, many people want or need to keep some or all copies of emails they receive.

The absolutely simplest way to handle email is to keep everything in a single folder. For most people, however, this approach is simply not practical: for example, you might want to separate emails you receive from your boss from those sent by Aunt Sally – just in case you accidentally send the wrong reply to the wrong person: not a great way to make a good impression on either party. Therefore consider the following guidelines to help create a more logical and easier email set up:

1. Creating new folders

Simply create folders with different names and organise them into a logical structure that makes sense to you. All good email software allows you to create different folder structures in this way. Other key organisation options include the ability to archive and compress older email messages and simply delete those no longer required.

2. Grouping and sorting messages

In Outlook Express, with the 3-panes visible in the main window (left: folders; top: files; bottom: contents of the selected file), you can also easily change the way Outlook Express sorts your items. Here's how. Notice in the top pane each column has a heading; simply click the column heading you want to sort the list of items by that column. So for example, if you wanted to group all emails received from Jane Jones, simply click the "From" column heading, then scroll down the list to the Js to find all Jane Jones' emails. To sort in reverse order, click the column you chose once again – in our example, the "From" column.

After replying to an email message, you can arrange for any messages older than a specific time to be archived, or you can simply delete the message to help control the overall quantity of emails. A large number of emails can make some email software unstable and slow down operation of the software.

3. Changing column widths

Place your mouse pointer on a dividing line between two adjacent column headings. When the pointer changes to an opposite-pointing double arrow, press and hold down the mouse button and drag the mouse left or right to increase or decrease the column width you want to change. This option allows you to quickly see more or less of the information detail in that column.

HOT TIP

If you have just "answered" your email box, you can easily identify new unread emails from those you have already examined, simply by clicking on the "Date" or "Received" option or by grouping your emails in the current folder using the Date or Received column. Sorting by date order is usually the best standard option for most people.

Rerouting messages automatically

Most email programs can be set up to automatically go online at regular intervals to send and receive email messages and then disconnect from the Internet. You can combine and enhance this approach with creating folders for specific email messages and rules that automatically route messages to the correct folders as soon as they're received: a great timesaving feature.

Automatic rerouting works by examining specific parts of an email message and comparing those parts with some reference text you provide. For example, the program might look at the sender's email address, the subject box, characters in the body text, and so on, and if any matches the reference text the program sends the email message to the folder set up for that particular rule.

For example, you can create a rule that ensures any email messages received from: john@custard.com are rerouted to the "Custard" folder. Or all messages containing the word sequence: "Internet Tips Today ezine" can be sent to a folder called Internet Tips Today ezine. Outlook Express handles automatic

rerouting of email using the "Create Rule From Message" command on the Message menu in combination with the Tools > Message Rules command pair. Netscape Messenger uses the Message Filters command on the Edit menu to automatically redirect email in a similar way.

If you receive a lot of email every day, this feature is definitely worth spending a little time to learn how to set up. It's the quickest way I know of cutting 30 minutes organising time to 30 seconds.

Flames, flame wars and email bombs

Slang terms and jargon have always been associated with computers and the Internet and, as we've already seen, email too has a few unusual terms that you might come across. An email flame is a single email message sent to one person designed to insult or annoy the recipient. When the recipient replies in the same manner, a flame "war" can start, with abusive emails travelling back and forth. Often, these events can also occur in public forums like newsgroups.

Sometimes, you may find that you're getting drawn into a heated Internet discussion, so what do you do? Obviously say your piece but if things start getting out of control, my advice is to simply never respond to an email flame – ever! As a reader of this book, you're an intelligent person. Just do the Internet equivalent of walking away; simply delete a flame and forget about it.

If you really don't want to hear from that person, most good email programs include commands that allow you to automatically send emails from a specific source straight to the email junk bin every time you check your email, so you won't even need to see another email from that source again – unless they use another email address. For instructions on how to make this option active, check your email program's Help documentation.

Listen to your email virtually anywhere

Here's an Internet gem! Using services like BT's SpeechMail or equivalent, you can listen to your emails over the phone line any time anywhere across the globe! Also, Genie and many other similar Internet Service Providers and other companies are now providing services that allow a PC user to send basic text messages direct to a mobile phone and surf the Internet with a new

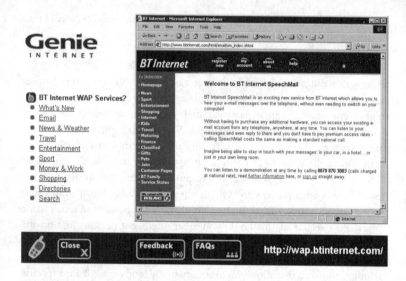

generation WAP mobile phone that contains a kind of mini Web browser. To discover more:

- Check out http://www.btinternet.com/
- Visit your own Internet Service Provider's Web site.
- Use the search engine boxes in your Web browser.

In this way, you can find other companies who provide these exciting new services and discover more about what's on offer now and what's just around the corner.

Mailing lists

The amazing development, growth and changing role of the Internet, from what was originally a military tool to that of a worldwide network, has spawned a rich variety of new ways to communicate. In this chapter, we'll examine how mailing lists and email work together to create an incredibly powerful yet simple communications method.

What is a mailing list?

A mailing list or discussion forum is a group of people who use email and the Internet to communicate, pass on news or discuss specific related themes. Mailing lists covering thousands of different topics exist, from cooking to climbing, and offer a great way to make new friends from around the world.

However, expect a lot of email after you subscribe. Unlike newsgroup information, mailing list messages are not stored on the Internet but distributed by email usually from a central coordinating email address. Popular automatic mailing lists include egroups, topica, listserv, majordomo and listproc.

Typically, the list name is included in the email addresses that you use to communicate with the list.

Although most mailing lists are open to anyone to join, some offer restricted access – for example, a mailing list about veterinary practice may quite reasonably be only open to vets: not many others may want to discuss the finer points of bladder infections in cattle. Specialist mailing lists offer an ideal way for experts to interact with their peers and keep up with current issues in their field. To get started, you can discover more information on mailing lists at:

- http://www.liszt.com/ (Liszt enables you to search for mailing lists that cover specific topics).
- http://www.reference.com/
- http://www.topica.com/

Or search for more mailing lists on the Internet; type: "mailing lists" or "mailing +lists" (without the quotes) into your Web browser search box.

How mailing lists work

Usually, when someone sends a message to a mailing list, everyone on the list receives a copy of that message. However, some mailing lists only allow messages to be received, not sent or uploaded to all the list members.

Although some email lists are run manually, most are automatically software administered, which means the email list owners have a life, but you need to be careful which message you send to which email address. Send a message to the wrong email address and your online credibility will probably take a battering – you'll almost be able to detect the fits of laughter coming from other more experienced but less forgiving list members. So here's the important information: a mailing list has at least two key email addresses that you need to know about in order to participate and contribute:

- The address of the mailing list. This is the main email address you'll use. Any messages you send to this email address get sent to everyone on the mailing list.
- An email address from which to subscribe and unsubscribe yourself from the list.

A mailing list may also make available other administrative email addresses for help, technical support, and so on. Remember: on lists that are run

Send subscribe/unsubscribe emails only to the special subscribe/ unsubscribe email addresses provided for these purposes as described in the following paragraphs and overleaf. Otherwise everyone on the mailing list will see your subscribe/unsubscribe email suddenly appear mixed in with the main discussion topics, when they're expecting information on the topic being discussed.

automatically, you'll need to use the correct email addresses provided. Therefore, there's little point in creating an email message as if it were to be read by a live operator.

Moderated and unmoderated mailing lists

A moderated list has volunteers (usually) who monitor email messages sent to the list and decide if a message is relevant, acceptable and has not broken the rules of the list. If a message is about a topic already covered, the moderator may refer the sender to the list archives where information about their chosen topic may already have been covered. If the message is accepted, however, the moderator sends it to all members on the list for possible comment and discussion.

In an unmoderated list, usually, all messages sent to the list are delivered to all members on the mailing list immediately with no checking or censorship being done. So with this type of list, what you see is what you get. Although unmoderated lists might seem a better option, sometimes the discussion topic can vary wildly with specific personalities trying to dominate. In a free environment like the Internet mailing list, personal insults can soon lower the value of a list.

Subscribing to a mailing list

In order to "join" a mailing list, you need to subscribe. Often, to subscribe, you need only visit a specific Web page and enter your contact details in the Web form provided. You might then receive an email message acknowledgement and have to reply to this message in a certain way to become fully subscribed. This approach is necessary to make sure that the person doing the subscribing is actually the person being subscribed rather than someone else playing a joke.

The simple steps to follow are usually found at the specific list you want or in advertisements about the list which you might receive by email. Most larger mailing lists are managed by a special computer, also known as a listserver (or listserv). To give you an idea of what's involved, the rules to perform a typical subscription could include putting the following words into the Subject box and sending the email to the subscribe email address:

subscribe your name

So if I were to subscribe to this imaginary list, I would enter the phrase: "subscribe Brian Austin" (without the quotes) into the Subject box and include a single space between the words "subscribe" and "Brian"; I would then send the email without any further text being added. Mailing list software can determine the email address of the sender as that information is automatically part of every email message and so, if I have followed the correct rules, my email address and name would be added to the subscription list. Another popular subscribe format might ask you to mention the precise list that you want, for example: subscribe star-trekies.

Follow the subscribe instructions exactly. Whether to use upper or lower case lettering may be important. For example, often the Subscribe wording has to be exact: "subscribe", "Subscribe", "SUBSCRIBE" could all be treated differently so only one of those three examples might be recognised as a genuine subscribe request, the rest simply rejected.

The Welcome message

Once a subscription is successful, the subscriber may then receive an automatic confirmation and welcome email message containing more details about the list and the rules for taking part and other key information. The more security conscious email lists might send another message first asking the sender to reply to a message – sometimes, someone may subscribe another person without their permission: asking for the email addressee to reply confirms that the email message must have come from the true subscriber, after which the sender would probably receive the usual "subscription confirmed and welcome" message.

Usually within the Welcome message are instructions on how to get help if you're unsure of how to proceed with a particular topic. For example, to get help you may only need to enter the word "help" (without the quotes) in the Subject box or body of an email which you then send to the administrative email address. This action may then cause a Help file to be automatically sent back to you, sometimes within seconds.

Receiving list messages

Joining a mailing list can mean that you may suddenly start receiving a lot of email messages within a short space of time, so ensure you check your email box regularly to avoid having to download a large backlog later in addition to your "regular" email. If the amount of email you receive from a list becomes so large as to be impractical, you might be able to change your deliver status from "regular" to "digest." A digest service groups the separate emails into one

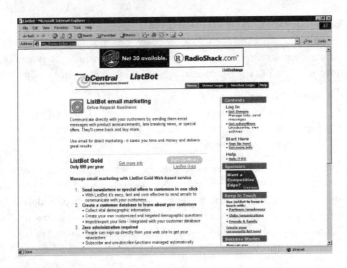

email message so this option, if available, may be preferable to receiving lots of individual messages.

Unsubscribing from a mailing list

Unsubscribing – or leaving the list – removes your email address from the mailing list and is essentially the same procedure as subscribing, except this time you might enter: unsubscribe your name … or something similar. Again, the appearance of the unsubscribe command must be correct to succeed: note the information in the Don't Forget tip on page 281 also applies when choosing an unsubscribe option.

Creating your own mailing list

If you can't find what you're looking for in any existing list, have a lot of time to spare and enjoy the thrill of creating something new, you can start your own mailing list. Here's a range of popular organisations offering free mailing lists:

- http://www.topica.com/
- http://www.onelist.com/
- http://www.listbot.com/
- http://www.coollist.com/

The trade-off is that these free lists gain income from including usually one or two discrete advertisements with every email they send out. If you want more control to create a list that contains only the content you provide, you can opt for a paid listserver. Ask your Internet Service Provider or Web host about providing a well-established and proven list management product like:

- Listserv: http://www.lsoft.com/
- Majordomo: http://www.greatcircle.com/majordomo/
- Llstproc.

Avoiding a holiday comeback mountain

During holiday periods, you probably don't even want to think about email! So if you belong to a lot of email lists or receive a lot of email, before taking a holiday find out how to avoid a large email build-up on your return.

Usually, you can contact the mailing list and either set your subscription to "holiday" mode – setting up a temporary email block for a set number of days to avoid an email mountain later – or temporarily unsubscribe and resubscribe on your return. Otherwise, you may return from holiday to find thousands of messages in your email box or, worse still, have an overflowing email box in which other more important emails may have become lost.

Part III
Interactive Internet

Playing online games

Playing games on the Internet is a compelling experience – especially if you're playing against live opponents and not just another computer program. Your opponents could be located anywhere across the globe and some take on their tasks with almost religious devotion and fervour. Online gaming can also be a great way to meet new friends on the Web – perhaps most of whom you might never meet otherwise. So if Internet games are for you, let's take a closer look at what's available and how to take part.

What you need to play online games

Computer muscle: most current games are designed for 3D. These often make high demands from computer hardware; the electronic video chips on 3D cards must be fast and powerful if they're to cope with the often high tension and speed of Internet games. To play 3D games, you'll need to have a 3D video card or capability built into your computer. Also, most games have a minimum specification for the main electronic chip – the Central Processing Unit (CPU) – and the amount of memory (RAM) installed. The faster the CPU and the more memory your computer has installed, usually the faster and more stable a game will run. Therefore, first make sure that you have the necessary computer hardware before getting on board.

Up to 2 players: for two players to participate in a computer game, both computers need to be connected together. If you're not connected to the Internet, you can use a special connector called a null modem cable and install each end into the serial port connectors of each machine. On the Internet, you can do the equivalent except you don't use null modem cables, rather modems or ISDN terminal adaptors can make the connection for you.

Three or more players: options here include using a Local Area Network (LAN) in which several computers are connected together in the same building. Each computer will need the relevant network cards or electronic networking chips installed, the cabling (although wireless networks are now available) to physically join the computers and the network software that allows each computer to "talk" to the other members on the network.

However, if you want more bodies to come to the party, why not go on the Internet – the ultimate computer network? Now things can really start getting interesting, challenging and yes, sometimes frustrating. I mention frustration because, as all regular Internet users know, delays and information "dropouts" can sometimes occur, so sometimes a command may need to be repeated – just hope that this doesn't occur at a crucial moment.

Downloading game software: some popular current games are quite large in file size, so rather than download them over the Internet, you're often better checking out the demo versions that often accompany computer and Internet magazines from your newsagent. And remember, you can check out online sources to discover what others are saying about specific games. See also: http://www.netgamer.net/

If you're physically located close to the server on which the game is hosted, you'll probably enjoy faster game response times and therefore enjoy a built-in gaming advantage. Also, if you play only with other participants from the same Internet Service Provider, overall game "quality" may be much better with shorter delays and fewer dropouts, compared to playing on the "open" Internet.

Getting started

With some online games, you can jump straight in as soon as you connect, while for others you'll need to hold back in a waiting area until a space comes up or the game you want becomes available. Some of the more recent games even allow you to talk to your opponents while playing – some interesting and colourful conversations can take place.

To discover the closest games to you – and therefore those that are probably the most stable – and set your system up for automated connections, you can install some purpose-designed software. For more information, see: http://www.gamespy.com and http://www.kali.net

Playing in teams

By combing the computing power and ingenuity of multiple participants – who may be located anywhere on the Internet – an online game can take on an entirely new look and feel. Power, emotion, intensity are three words that can help describe these experiences. Most new computer games designed for two or more participants can also be played on the Internet. Three of the most popular team games include Quake Team Fortress, Ultima Online and Unreal Tournament. See also: http://www.owo.com/

Finding online games

Current popular online games include: Commanche3, Age of Empires, Quake, TombRaider and Chessmaster to name but a few. To get started and discover what's currently available, consider visiting the following Web sites:

- WirePlay:
  http://www.wireplay.com/
  (UK & Australia)
- FreeLoader:
  http://www.freeloader.com/
- MSN: http://www.zone.com/
- Gamespot: http://www.gamespot.com
- GamesDomain: http://www.gamesdomain.com
- Happy Puppy: http://www.happypuppy.com

Good luck, have fun and try not to become addicted!

Internet
newsgroups

Newsgroups and mailing lists have much in common: both are great for meeting new friends, creating profitable business relations and generally interacting with lots of different people from around the world. However, mailing lists and newsgroups do have striking differences. Let's examine those differences by taking a close look at newsgroups.

A cautionary note: computer virus warnings

Message files downloaded from newsgroups are one of the most common ways to spread computer viruses. Therefore, before participating in a newsgroup, make sure you have an up-to-date antivirus program working in the background.

Don't ever trust anyone from a newsgroup who says a file or message is virus-free: if you decide to download it, always check it yourself using your antivirus program.

Even when a virus is present in a file, remember that antivirus software may still not detect the virus if it is a new strain or your antivirus records have not been updated to cover that particular virus. Therefore, do keep your antivirus software tables up-to-date: as a heavy Internet user, I update mine once every 2 weeks – sometimes more often. The safest option is to make a rule not to download any attachments from newsgroups, period. Plus make regular backups of your computer data.

Sorry to spoil your fun but I needed to say that! From my own experiences, I've had a lot of fun in newsgroups and several times my antivirus software has detected infected downloaded attachments and zapped them promptly.

Introducing newsgroups

Also known as discussion groups, newsgroups are a branch of the Internet where you can meet Internet users with interests similar to your own. You can discuss issues, solve problems and upload and download files but unlike Internet Chat (page 315), newsgroups are not "live."

Thousands of newsgroups are available on the Internet covering thousands of different topics including: cooking, travel, employment, humour, current events, music, films, sports, religion, the environment, and television to name but a few. Currently, over 60,000 newsgroups exist with more being added daily! For a snapshot, see "The Newsgroup Directory", page 415.

A newsgroup can have many thousands of messages stored, however when you first connect usually only a few hundred may be displayed by default. If more messages are available, you can simply click a button to have your newsreader download another batch. By default, Microsoft Outlook, for example, downloads 300 messages each time, but you can change that amount if you wish in the "Options" dialog box.

Usually, an Internet Service Provider provides a newsgroup server to handle all newsgroups they provide. The term newsgroup server is a collective name for all their computers that handle only newsgroup information.

Top level newsgroup categories

All individual newsgroups are grouped under several "top level" categories. In fact, in a newsgroup name, the characters before the first full stop show to which "top-level" category a newsgroup belongs.

For example, the newsgroup: comp.sys.laptops shows that this newsgroup is about computers – portable computers to be exact as the ending characters suggest. The table below shows some of the most popular top-level categories:

Category:	Covers:
alt	Alternative topics to the other main groups.
biz	Business-related newsgroups.
comp	Computers.
news	News and newsgroup discussion.
rec	Recreation-related topics.
sci	Science.
soc	Social topics.
uk	UK-specific newsgroups.

Newsgroup names

A newsgroup name is made up of two or more words separated by full stops. The first word describes the theme – as shown above. The words that follow gradually focus on more specific parts of the theme of that particular newsgroup.

For example: "uk.jobs.wanted" discusses employment wanted in the UK. Or "alt.chinese.fengshui" discusses the ancient Chinese art of designing living and working spaces and what implications – if any – that has for you. For more examples, see the directory of newsgroups on page 415.

Newsreader software overview

To send and read information on newsgroups, you'll need newsreader software. Microsoft Outlook Express is an email program and newsreader that comes with the Microsoft Internet Explorer Web browser – which is available free of charge from http://www.microsoft.com/ or often from the free CD-ROMs that accompany many computer magazines.

Netscape Messenger, that comes with Netscape Navigator Web browser as part of the free of charge Netscape Communicator suite, also includes a fine newsreader. Other popular newsreaders include Free Agent and Agent from Forte and MicroPlanet Gravity.

Configuring your newsreader

The guidelines provided in this section relate mainly to Outlook Express and Netscape Messenger – both of these free programs include excellent newsreaders. If you choose another newsreader, you can relate the steps here to help configure your copy.

To recap, most Internet Service Providers have what is known as a news server – computers on which newsgroups are stored and which are made available to customers. Now, when you first install Outlook Express, you'll need to enter the address of your Internet Service Provider's news server. For example, BT Internet customers use: news.btinternet.com

If you ever want to add an additional news server, or just perform this step directly, in Outlook Express first choose the Accounts command from the Tools menu. Next click the Add News button and follow the instructions from the wizard to complete the news server installation.

In Netscape Messenger, open the Edit menu and choose the Preferences command. Then under the Mail & Newsgroups category, choose Newsgroup Servers and click the Add button to include the news server name that your Internet Service Provider has given you (example: news.btinternet.com). During your newsreader set-up, the first time you connect to your news server, usually you'll be asked if you want to download a list of available newsgroups. This operation can take some time and essentially depends on the size of the newsgroup file being downloaded, the speed of your Internet connection and the power of your computer. Also some Internet Service providers censor the type of material available to remove what they consider may contain "objectionable content", others do not. If you pay for every minute while online, consider completing this task during cheap-rate hours – evenings or weekends. After you have configured your newsreader and downloaded a list of available newsgroups, you can choose to subscribe to any individual newsgroups you want from the list displayed.

Protecting your email address in newsgroups

Just like mailing lists, contributing to newsgroups can cause you to start receiving a lot of irrelevant email messages – usually from people and organisations trying to sell something to you. You can reduce this effect by not using your most important email address – instead, use another spare and preferably Web-based email address that you keep especially for newsgroups, mailing lists and other more public Internet communications.

Alternatively, you can change your email address slightly to help block or confuse automatic email harvesters – these are software tools often used by spammers that regularly scan newsgroups trying to collect email addresses. Here's one way to help beat email harvesters. Imagine if my real email address is brian@mysite.com, I can change this to brian@NOSPAMmysite.com

As NOSPAMmysite.com is a domain that really does not exist, any uninvited email messages sent to that domain name would usually get bounced back to the sender – with an error message. Using this technique, you would probably have to include a line of text with your changed email address that says something like: "please remove the NOSPAM part when replying", so that genuine people know what to do in order to contact you.

Moderated and unmoderated newsgroups

Like mailing lists, individual newsgroups can be moderated or unmoderated. A moderated newsgroup may have the word added at the end of a newsgroup name, for example: rec.arts.sf.tv.babylon5.moderated.

A moderated newsgroup has volunteers (usually) who monitor email messages sent to the newsgroup and decide if the message is relevant, acceptable and has not broken the rules of the newsgroup. If a message is about a topic already covered, the moderator may refer the sender to the newsgroup archives where information about their chosen topic is covered. If the message is accepted however, the moderator makes the message available to all members on the newsgroup. In an unmoderated newsgroup, all messages sent to the newsgroup are made freely available to all participants of the newsgroup as they come in. In some unmoderated newsgroups, strong opinions and personal clashes can result in the language becoming "colourful" to say the least.

Discovering what's available in newsgroups

Usenet – shortened from Users Network – is a description covering all the powerful computers on the Internet that enable all the newsgroups to operate.

Although Usenet currently has over 60,000 newsgroups, your ISP usually determines the exact type and nature of available newsgroups. So if a newsgroup you want is not available on their list, simply ask if they can provide it. They naturally try to meet the needs of customers so may make your desired newsgroup available to you, but this may not always be possible.

Some newsgroups are deliberately omitted from an Internet Service Provider's list on moral or censorship grounds – no Internet Service Provider wants to be branded pornography-friendly or linked to any extreme political views – at least openly. Essentially, for business reasons, most Internet Service Providers prefer to reflect what it considers is the general public's view on sensitive issues. However, some providers prefer to let their customers dictate what they make available – within reason, so some negotiation may be possible.

However, if your Internet Service Provider does not include what you're looking for, check other providers or consider using publicly accessible news servers. To gain access to the content of a publicly accessible news server, you don't usually need an account. Take a look at:

- http://www.remarq.com/
- http://www.freenews.net/ and www.freenews.com/
- http://www.newsvillle.com/

New newsgroups are being created every day and some newsgroups simply close down through disuse. Therefore, to start with, try subscribing to the following newsgroup to see the current range of newsgroups available:

news.lists

Or examine and post to newsgroups without using a dedicated newsreader. Instead, you can use the Web's largest and most popular newsgroup directory Deja.com at http://www.deja.com/ On Deja.com's Home/Index page, click the link for "Usenet", and you can gain access to the list of newsgroups as shown in the screenshot below:

Subscribing and unsubscribing to a newsgroup

To participate in a newsgroup – even just to discover what is being said without contributing directly – you'll need to join or subscribe to the newsgroup you want – using a real email address, not a NOSPAM version as listed previously. Use your NOSPAM version when actually posting or replying to individual newsgroup messages.

Joining a newsgroup is free of charge and you can subscribe or unsubscribe whenever you want. Although each newsreader has its own unique procedure for subscribing to newsgroups, subscription methods of different newsreaders are similar. To subscribe to a newsgroup in Outlook Express, first click on the news server name in the left pane, then click the Newsgroups button on the main toolbar at the top of the Outlook Express window.

You can also find the Newsgroups command in the Tools menu, or by right-clicking the desired news server name and choosing the command from the floating menu. In the dialog box that appears, click the newsgroup you want

300 | Internet newsgroups

from the list and click the Subscribe button. Outlook Express then inserts a small marker next to each newsgroup to which you subscribe.

To download messages, select the subscribed newsgroup name you want and click the GoTo button. If you're not already online, Outlook Express prompts you to connect to the Internet and the first batch of message headers starts to download once your software connects to the news server.

For newcomers to newsgroups, an ideal way to try out posting a message is to subscribe to the alt.test newsgroup and practice sending test messages. Sending test messages to other newsgroups is often frowned upon by other members who may ask you to stop.

When you subscribe to an individual newsgroup, usually the first 300 – 500 message headers are automatically downloaded to your newsreader. Then

Newsgroups are open to anyone who wants to subscribe, so when you join a newsgroup and participate, other Internet users know and a permanent record is available at your Internet Service Provider.

If you see a message that you find offensive and just have to tell this person what you think, consider sending an email direct to the sender rather than voicing your anger to the entire newsgroup. Sending personal attacks to a newsgroup or list is called flaming, and is generally frowned upon. Flaming may not help you get answers to your questions, solve your problem or endear you to the list.

once the batch has finished downloading, to read a specific message you'll need to select the message header, the content of that particular message is then displayed usually in the lower larger pane. You can read, reply and sort messages as described in the following sections.

In Outlook Express, to unsubscribe first right-click to select the newsgroup you want in the left-side pane, then choose the Unsubscribe command from the floating menu. In Netscape Messenger, you can subscribe using the Subscribe command in the File menu. In the dialog box, navigate to find the newsgroup name you want, select it, then choose the Subscribe button and click OK to finish. Then click the newsgroup name in the left pane to start downloading messages. You can also unsubscribe from a newsgroup using the Subscribe dialog box: select the name you want and click the Unsubscribe button followed by OK.

Don't say anything on a newsgroup, mailing list, Internet Chat or WebCam-based system that you're not prepared to repeat in a court of law. The key point is: be careful what you say. Avoid making slanderous or libellous statements.

If you subscribe to several newsgroups, make sure you post the right message to the correct newsgroup to avoid embarrassing comments.

A newsgroup's money-saving strategy

Once you have subscribed to any newsgroup, if you have to pay for every second while online, you can save money by first reading only those messages that interest you. Then disconnect – those messages will still be present in your newsreader. Comment or reply to any message you want, then reconnect to the

Internet and send your messages before disconnecting again. Later – say perhaps every couple of days – you can re-connect to the Internet and view any comments or replies to your messages and those of others. Repeat the sequence as necessary.

In this way, you make use of off-peak telephone rates and avoid having to spend a lengthy period online. Of course, if you have free or low-cost access to the Internet, then staying online while participating in newsgroups offers the easiest method to use as you can react while information is fresh in your mind.

The Frequently Asked Questions file

Many newsgroups have a Frequently Asked Questions (FAQ) file, which is useful for new members to read before posting and may indeed answer your question. If you don't see the FAQ on display, email the newsgroup moderator or, as a last resort, email to the newsgroup.

If you're new to newsgroups, before immediately posting a message, consider viewing and reading some of the current postings to get a better idea of what is acceptable. Taking a little time to familiarise yourself with newsgroup ways is worthwhile to avoid asking the kind of questions that regular participants hear repeatedly – and some are less tolerant to newcomers.

To get the best from newsgroups and avoid potential intolerance or unpleasantness, taking a little time to learn newsgroup netiquette can help you solve your problem quicker and is much appreciated by other members.

Reading newsgroup messages and contributing

A newsgroup message is simply an email a contributor provides to the group – also known as posting to the group. People can contribute opinions, ideas, software, images, sound and video clips. Although a short message is usually preferable – it takes less time to read – a message can often be much longer.

You can simply browse through the newsgroup message "headers" – a line of text describing what the message is about – and read only those messages that interest you. Message headers can include the subject, email address of the contributor, date sent and an indicator of any file attachments, and sometimes the message file size.

If you see a header line that interests you, click the message header and the main message text appears in another usually larger pane. Just like any other computer file, you can also save or print interesting newsgroup messages. If you're replying or commenting on an existing topic, your message is added to

If you participate in any particularly popular or busy newsgroups and want to follow closely what is happening, check back at least every couple of days. Why? Busy newsgroups fill up the space available more quickly; the providers may then delete older messages every 3 days or thereabouts to make room for new threads (a single discussion theme) and new topics.

the other messages on that same topic and becomes a "thread" in that series, so keep to the topic in the thread, or start a new thread yourself and post it for discussion. Most good newsreaders – the software that allows you to send and read newsgroup messages – let you sort and arrange messages by thread to make tracking the progress of a specific discussion topic easier.

Posting to a newsgroup

Remember, people from around the world post to newsgroups and so in different cultures similar words may have very different meanings. Therefore, try to make sure your message is simple, clear and concise with no chance of being misinterpreted and spell-check it before posting. Before posting to a newsgroup, spend a little time watching how others post – also known as "lurking." Read some posts and observe how others reply; which parts of the original message they include, etc.

To post a message in Outlook Express or Netscape Messenger, first click to select the newsgroup name you want in the left pane, then click the New Post or New Message button on the main toolbar. Or you can use the New Message command in the Message menu.

The newsgroup to which you're sending the post is shown in the upper box. If you want to post the same message to several different newsgroups, after the first entered newsgroup name type a comma and a space, then enter the

Keep messages short and to the point and be sure you understand the kind of newsgroup to which you're contributing. For example, sending the entire script of Shakespeare's Hamlet to a newsgroup and then asking: "Is this dude great or what?" could result in some colourful replies!

remaining newsgroup names likewise. In the Subject box, enter a brief description of what your message is about. Try to provide a specific rather than general brief description so that users have a clear idea of what the topic is about. Click the Send button to finish.

After posting a message or reply to a newsgroup, your message soon appears with all the others in the newsgroup. However, if later you decide that you want to scrap the message you sent, you can use the Message Cancel command if available in your newsreader – but remember this option does not guarantee that every instance of your message will be removed and may take some time to implement. In Outlook Express first select the message header then choose the Cancel Message command in the Message menu. In Netscape Messenger, the equivalent message cancel command is available on the floating menu when you right-click the message header you want to cancel.

Newsgroup spamming

Don't post the same message to several (or more) unrelated newsgroups or you may be accused of newsgroup spamming. Often, newsgroup users can become very annoyed at blatant commercial self-promotion of a product or service in a post – especially if that post does not in any way contribute to the current theme or topic. Some newsgroups, however, will tolerate commercialised postings. Check the rules in the FAQ for the newsgroup you want before posting commercial emails. Many Internet Service Providers now take spamming very seriously and in some situations may close your email, newsgroup and Web access account, sometimes immediately and without notice. In extreme cases in which an ISP has had to handle hundreds or even thousands of email complaints, they may even send you an invoice for the time spent in getting their system back to normal! So consider carefully.

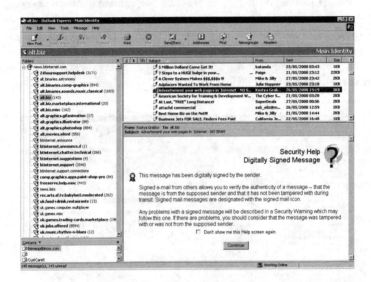

Replying to newsgroup messages

Once a message has fully downloaded, the Reply button is made available for you to use. To reply first click the message header you want, then choose the desired Reply command or button. Usually, you can reply directly to the sender, the entire newsgroup, or to all in a single action. Whichever Reply command you choose, a new window opens addressed to whoever you chose and containing the original message usually below the flashing text cursor prompting you to enter your reply, after which you click the Send button.

When replying to a post, you can save time for everyone concerned by only including (quoting) the part of the post that is relevant to what you're saying. Quoting only the relevant parts makes the task of possibly reading many posts so much easier, as all irrelevant parts are deleted before being posted. Reply to a post when you have something worthwhile to contribute. If you want to thank a member for their help, consider emailing this person directly rather than posting a heartfelt "thank you" to the entire newsgroup.

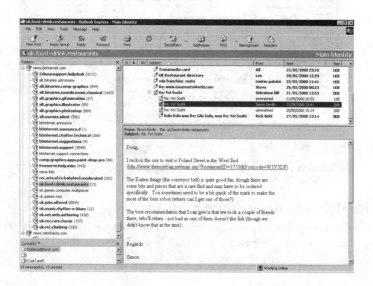

Downloading and uploading images, programs and audio/video clips

Sometimes, newsgroup messages may include attached images, programs, sound clips, video clips, and so on. However, do remember copyright laws may apply. If unsure, ask and if still unsure, simply don't download an attachment. Newsgroup names that include attachments are usually easily identified: look for the word "binaries" in the newsgroup name. For example: alt.binaries.pictures.cartoons. Good newsreaders like those found in Outlook

Express and Agent or Free Agent contain the necessary components to encode and decode information that is sent or received as an attachment. Larger images, sound and video clips can be huge in file size, so are often broken down

into smaller chunks. To view one of these images or to play a full sound or video clip, you'll first need to download all the individual chunks that make up the file. Usually, each chunk is given a number reference along with the name, for example if someone makes available a large photographic image of Niagara Falls from their last holiday, it might be split into 6 parts: niagara_falls1of6.jpg, niagara_falls2of6.jpg, and so on.

In Outlook Express, after you have downloaded all the chunks, you can select every chunk that makes up the entire sequence and choose the Combine and Decode command from the Message menu. Then if necessary, use the Move Up and Move Down buttons in the dialog box to arrange the sequence in numerical order and click OK. Finish by choosing the Save Attachments command and finding a location on your computer to save the file. Then move to the relevant location in your computer and double-click the file, then if it's:

- an image, your default graphics program for viewing those kinds of images (.jpg in our example above) starts up with the picture displayed.
- a video or sound clip, the full sequence should start playing – providing you have the correct player installed. The Windows Media Player can interpret several common video formats. Or you may need special video player software.

Automatically blocking unwanted newsgroup emails.

Sometimes, you may not want to read messages from a specific contributor or want to ignore a specific message thread. Newsreaders like those in Outlook Express and Netscape Messenger provide commands that allow you to block or ignore a specific message or thread. First select the message you want to stop, then look for the Block Sender command on the Message menu in Internet Explorer or the Ignore thread command in Netscape Messenger.

Dealing with flames

The Internet is made up of contributors from many different cultures, sexes and viewpoints – some mild and some extreme. Sometimes, someone can say something – often without meaning to suggest what someone else might think they mean – while contributing to a message thread and so "push someone else's buttons". Before the originator can draw breath, explain what they really meant or apologise, they're receiving a barrage of personal abuse.

This sometimes-animated event is known as a flame. Other members may then join in on the rapidly degrading debate, on one side or the other, some trying to control tempers while others just add more abusive insults to the chaos. Soon, the original discussion topic is all but forgotten in a sea of high emotions and vitriolic hate – resulting in a flame war.

Most reasonable Internet users won't want to get involved in these events. So what do you do if you're drawn into a flame war when you would rather be spending your time on more useful activities? Consider the following guidelines:

- Before contributing, get some foreknowledge: lurk a while and try to see how others use the group.
- When contributing to a newsgroup, don't use all CAPITAL LETTERS – unless you mean to shout. The tone of capital letters may be misinterpreted.
- Watch the jargon: keep it simple and make sure people can understand what you're saying so misunderstandings don't develop in the first place. Many flames start from ignorance or misinterpretation.
- Some newsgroup members enjoy starting an argument or handing out abuse. You'll get to recognize these characters. Avoid starting or getting involved in any kind of abuse or insult in the first place and remember, everything that you say in a newsgroup is on public record and you never quite know how long it'll stay that way.

- If you insult someone without meaning to, don't let them "push your buttons": stay calm, just apologise and leave the topic. If they still persist with abuse, don't respond. Use the commands in your email and newsreader to block their postings so you don't even have to read their sometimes colourful little messages.

- Make sure you're posting to the right newsgroup – some regular members become irritated with inappropriate postings especially if they're contributing week after week and are intensely interested in the theme and nothing else.

- If you're new to a newsgroup, check the Frequently Asked Questions (FAQ) file that is often made available so you know what's acceptable and what's not, before contributing.

- Business contributors often use newsgroups to market their products and services usually through their email signature file that they attach to every response. Try to keep this subtle and brief without being too obvious that you care more about your promotion than you do about genuinely contributing. Consider creating a completely separate signature file just for use in newsgroups. Or even create several for use in different newsgroups or for various purposes.

- If you openly try to promote a business product in a non-commercial newsgroup, expect big trouble. Therefore, keep open commercial postings to commercial newsgroups like biz.comp.services, biz.misc and biz.general.

Talking and viewing on the Internet

At the heart of the Internet is the strong need for humans to communicate. Although email, newsgroups and (to a certain extent) the Web each have their individual benefits, often you cannot get an instant response. But other tools like Internet telephony, video conferencing, Webcams, and online Chat have emerged to provide live Internet communications.

Internet phones

You can currently make telephone calls using the Internet in two main ways:

1. With this first option, users at both ends need a computer, modem, microphone headset, sound capability and access to the Internet plus special Internet phone software installed and set up. If your sound card/sound chips allow both sending and receiving at the same time (duplex transmission), then you can hold a normal telephone-like conversation. Otherwise, you'll each have to speak in turn: could be boring – unless you're a CB radio fan or already have had a taste of "walkie-talkie-speak", in which case you'll probably find the entire show a lot of fun.

   Here's an overview of how the above system works. First, your recipient needs to have the same software installed.

Then, once you know the Internet address of the person you want, you simply enter this email address into your Internet phone software, dial the address and wait to see if your recipient is available to respond.

2. The second option is to dial their number using a normal phone device that has been modified to route calls through Internet Service Providers rather than the normal phone network.

Internet phone headsets containing a microphone and at least one speaker can be bought from good local computer stores. With either approach, you can usually make international calls for the cost either at local phone call rate per minute, or if you have low-cost or free Internet access, the cost is minimal.

Once your Internet connection is set up, you only have your Internet Service Provider costs to pay – the same costs as you pay for say browsing the Web or using email! So with this system, whether your call is to Kidderminster, Khartoum or Kathmandu, the cost is the same. So what's the catch? Currently, the person you want to call must have an Internet address and using this system is often not as easy or reliable as an established phone network – yet! See also:

- The superb FireTalk service: talk to anyone around the world without having to call long distance rates: http://www.firetalk.com/
- MediaRing (software currently free) http://www.mediaring.com/
- And Microsoft NetMeeting as described below.

Conferencing with Microsoft NetMeeting

NetMeeting is a superb Internet telephony, video-conferencing and collaboration tool. NetMeeting also comes free with Internet Explorer Web browser suite. With NetMeeting you can talk with another person live on the Internet using Multimedia Chat, exchange files and even work together on the same publication. See: http://www.microsoft.com/netmeeting/

Internet Chat overview

Internet Chat offers a way to instantly communicate with people from around the world. As the cost of Internet access continues to fall and more people gain access to the Net, Internet Chat too has become popular. However, in contrast to newsgroups or email, remember, Internet Chat is always "live." Chat is available in two main forms:

- Text-based using a keyboard.
- Multimedia Chat is possible when both communicators have video and sound components installed and set up in their PCs or other Internet connection devices.

With Chat, usually you won't have to pay any long distance phone charges – check with your Internet Service Provider. For most people, the only cost is a local phone call or the standard connection charges through an Internet Service Provider. You can use Internet Chat to discuss ideas live and ask questions of family, friends and work colleagues or with anyone around the globe that also has Internet Chat installed and set up. Microsoft Chat is one popular Chat program that comes free as part of the Internet Explorer Web browser suite. Other popular Chat areas or "Conference Rooms" are present in MSN (UK section), CompuServe, AOL and Excite.

VICAM, Professional Quality Images Worth Looking At!
Compatible with Windows 3.1, 95, 98, 2000 & NT 4

Text-based Chat

To use text-based Chat, you'll need a Chat program installed and set up to communicate with a single person or – more usually – several. Internet Chat can involve interacting with lots of people that "enter the Chat room", also known as a "Channel" or Chat "forum." When your Chat program is "active", whatever you type immediately appears on the display monitor screens of all the people taking part in that particular Chat session.

Chat nicknames and maintaining your privacy

Many of those who take part in Chat sessions often prefer to use nicknames rather than reveal their true identity. A nickname must of course be unique so that no two members can use the same name or nickname. Also, don't reveal your real name, address or telephone number and consider using a common Web-based email provider, for example: http://www.hotmail.com/ rather than your "main" email address. This approach should limit the chance of anyone pestering or harassing you at other times.

If you do eventually decide to meet someone you originally met in a Chat room, meet in a public place and let trusted friends know what you're doing and the when and where of your meeting, until you're sure this new friend can be trusted. Kids, don't even consider it! Talk to your parents or guardian.

Internet Relay Chat (IRC)

Internet Rely Chat (IRC) provides Chat "rooms" or Chat Channels that focus on specific topics. Hundreds of subject areas are available; examples include: cooking, watercolour painting, tennis or beer.

IRC is also an ideal tool for distance learning: a tutor can interact with students wherever they may be located – although time differences around the world need to be considered. To use Internet Relay Chat, you'll need an IRC program. For more information, visit: http://www.mirc.co.uk

Chat commands

To take part in Internet Rely Chat, you'll need to learn some basic Chat commands. Although lots of different commands exist, most are logical and easy to learn. However, unless you're a real Chat enthusiast, you probably only need learn the basics. All Chat commands start with a slash (/) and are followed

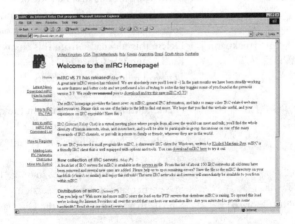

by the command itself. Text without a slash preceding it is interpreted simply as text. Here's an example of a Chat command: /JOIN. The /JOIN command shows that you would like to join the current Chat "room". When entering commands, you can type in capital letters or lower case letters. To discover the kinds of Chat topics available, with your Chat Program active enter the following command: /LIST. To help get you started, here are some of the most popular commands.

Command:		What the command means:
/AWAY		Tells others you've moved away from your PC and plan to return later, so replies may take some time.
/CLEAR		Clears the Chat window.
/HELP		Displays a list of all the commands available.
/JOIN		I want to join this Channel.
/IGNORE		Some contributors may be rude or worse. Lets you filter out or remove contributions from your Chat window that a specific person makes.
/KICK	[nickname]	Delete this nickname from this channel.
/LEAVE		I'm leaving this Channel.
/ME		Lets you tell other contributors that you are performing a task. For example: "/ME checking those figures" (without the quotes), would appear in each of the other members' Chat windows as: "Brian Austin is checking those figures."
/MSG		Allows you to send a private message to only one participant in the Chat session.
/SIGNOFF or /BYE		Signals that you're leaving the Chat session.

/TOPIC [new topic]	Change the current topic.
/WHO	Tells you who is participating in this Chat session.
/WHOIS	Provides some more information about a participant.

Using Web-based Chat

To take part in Web-based Chat, you don't need special Chat software, only a Web browser. To enter a Web Chat "room", you just click the relevant link on a Web page to open up another usually smaller window.

However, often the response time of Web Chat may not be as fast as Internet Relay Chat. Sometimes, you may need to wait a few seconds for the Chat window to appear and to refresh regularly. See also Chat options available at:

- http://www.wbs.net/
- http://www.100hot.com/
- http://www.aol.co.uk/ or http://www.aol.com/
- http://www.compuserve.co.uk/
- http://www.uk.msn.com/

Although communicating by typing live messages using a keyboard is the oldest and most well established Chat method, with the fast-paced development of the Web, multimedia-based Chat – using live Webcams and sound – is also growing in popularity and will probably dominate Internet Chat in a few years.

One-to-one communication with instant messaging

An instant messaging system enables you to communicate in private with another person live on the Internet.

Several messaging systems are now available. Some especially popular instant messaging programs include:

- America Online's Instant Messenger (AIM) with Netscape:
  http://www.netscape.com/chat
- ICQ available at: http://www.icq.com/
- Netscape instant messaging: http://www.netscape.com/

Internet Relay Chat and online games

Perhaps not surprisingly, many of the popular Internet Relay Chat Channels are dominated by computer and online games. You can play or compete with other Chat participants or the purpose-built automated programs or Chat bots. For more information, see:

- http://www.mpog.com/
- http://www.yahoo.com/Recreation/Games/Internet_Games/

For further information, see "Playing online games" on page 287.

Downloading and uploading information and software

The Internet is chock full of information files and software that are often available, free of charge, on a try-before-you-buy basis, or you can read the blurb and, if you like what you see, pay the fee online to gain access to the essential information you'll need to download the product.

So where are the goodies and how do you get them when you find them? The key to downloading information and software from the Internet is through the use of something called File Transfer Protocol (FTP). Don't be intimidated by the name – it simply refers to what's involved in sending and receiving files to and from other computers on the Internet. And to use FTP, you don't need to know the details of how FTP works, just what you need to do to grab or send files – and that is what we cover in this book.

Introducing File Transfer Protocol (FTP)

File Transfer Protocol lets you examine files that are stored on computers around the world and copy those files to your own computer if you wish. However remember, you can only view and copy those files that have been made available to you. Often, large files are also stored in compressed form and therefore must be decompressed after downloading before you can use them. Providers of some exceptionally busy FTP sites may generously make mirror FTP sites available. A mirror site provides the same information at different locations – possibly one near you. Therefore, if the "main" FTP site is busy and you're having trouble connecting, you could try other mirror sites if they're available. Using FTP, you can also upload your own files to any other computer that is set up for you to do this. For example, lots of people use an FTP program to help manage their Web sites. You can upload your Web files, make changes to the files already uploaded, and download or delete files that you no longer want stored on the computer containing your Web site. See also about publishing a Web site on page 357. First though, let's examine what an FTP site is and how to access it, and find and copy selected files.

What is an FTP site?

Files that you may get authorisation to view and copy are stored on computers at an FTP site. Individuals, companies, schools, colleges, universities and governments have established many thousands of FTP sites around the world. An easy way to picture an FTP Web site is to imagine it as a large office building containing hundreds or thousands of filing cabinets. In each filing cabinet,

Before connecting with any FTP sites – or the Internet – you should install suitable antivirus software and make regular backups of your computer's files. Computer viruses can be found anywhere on the Internet and may be hidden in files at FTP sites. For information about computer viruses and the action you can take to protect yourself online generally, see page 149.

there may be several drawers each containing many categories of files. Each category may itself contain many individual files.

Private and anonymous FTP

Some FTP sites provide private access but most offer public access. Private FTP sites usually ask you for a password to gain access. An example of a private FTP site could include an international company that provides access to essential company files for employees around the world and support materials for customers in different countries. Some private FTP sites may restrict access or charge for access to some files. Anonymous or public FTP sites allow anyone to access their files free of charge without having to enter a password – a user simply logs in as "anonymous". More later.

What's available from FTP sites

All kinds of files and documents can be stored at an FTP site. Often FTP sites provide key documents in the "top" level or "entry" folder or directory that shows what is stored at the site; look for files with names like "index" or "readme" to discover what's available at that location.

Also, files for different types of computers may be stored in different parts of an FTP site for good reason. For example, files for IBM-compatible PCs will probably not work on Apple Macintosh computers and so files for different "platforms" need to stored in separate locations on the same site. Key point: you need to make sure that the files you download are of the correct type for your computer. As various computer standards exist, often when you connect to an FTP site you may be asked to choose which standard you want. Usually, available options include:

- DOS.
- PC/Windows.
- Apple Mac.
- UNIX.

Therefore, if necessary, choose the correct standard before downloading any files or information.

An enormous range of file types is often available from FTP sites. A useful source containing links to thousands of FTP sites on the Internet is available from Filez at: http://www.filez.com/

You can download books, magazine articles, electronic magazines, images, computer games, shareware programs, word processors, spreadsheets and databases, speeches, music clips, simple sounds and movie and animation clips, to name but a few. Most files at an FTP site come under one of the following five categories. You can identify the types of files available by their filename

If you download and try to run program files for the wrong standard, you may damage the operating system of your computer.

extensions. The five main file categories including some of the most popular file formats are show below:

- Text. Filename extensions include: .txt, .doc, .htm, .html, .wpd, .msg and .asc
- Pictures. Filename extensions include: .bmp, .jpg, .gif, .tif, .eps, .pict and .pict
- Programs. Filename extensions include: .exe, .com and .bat
- Sound clips. Filename extensions include: .ra, .wav, .au, .mid and .snd. Remember, you'll need a sound card/motherboard sound chips and speakers to hear sound clips.
- Video clips: look for file endings like: .rm, .mpg, .avi, .mov and .qt. To see and hear video clips, you'll need the appropriate video player software – most now are available on free download – for the file you're viewing and a sound card/sound chips to hear any sound component.

Every file has a unique name and follows the standard computer naming system of a name followed by a full stop followed by an extension – which often determines the type of file. For example:

- report.txt is a text file.
- kathmandu23.gif – is an image file type that is usually quick to download and often used in Web pages.

Any computer system that contains hundreds, thousands, tens of thousands or even millions of files, needs to be highly organized if we are to gain relatively easy access to only the information we want and not get lost in a mass of irrelevant information. FTP files therefore, are usually stored in a highly organised manner. An FTP site also uses folders and sub-folders within which all the relevant files are (usually) stored in the most logical locations.

The procedure of uploading or downloading files using FTP software is often made much easier using simple drag-and-drop commands if they're available on your computer or other Internet access device.

Can I use these files free of charge?

Most files from FTP sites are available to use free of charge for non-commercial purposes. But do check the conditions of use available at the FTP site first. Often, a Frequently Asked Questions (FAQ) text document may be available so certainly examining this should be one of your first tasks.

Copyright usually stays with the author or owner of the file; check if necessary. Ignoring copyright – certainly in relation to the Web – can seriously damage your wealth if you're caught, so why take the risk? Always get written/emailed permission before use if unsure to avoid some nasty surprises later. Software programs are usually made available in five main ways:

- Public domain: suggests a program or file that is free for anyone to use and for which the originator has surrendered the copyright. Therefore usually you can modify, update, re-distribute or do whatever you want with public domain software.

- Freeware: usually means that the program can be used free of charge but the owner still maintains some or all of the copyright. Before editing or distributing freeware, check what restrictions are in force with the owner.
- Shareware: you can try the program for a limited period after which if you wish to continue using the software, you must pay the license fee for your copy. Usually, copyright stays with the owner and you cannot change the software but may be able to distribute copies. Read the documentation that comes with the software.
- Chargeable license: you pay for the software before buying it, and this includes a license to use your copy of the software. The owner keeps copyright and usually you can't change the software and need permission to distribute copies. Most commercially developed software is sold under chargeable license conditions.
- Beta software: as a company develops a software product, when the product development is almost complete, sometimes they may make a limited number of copies available – to try out – often for free, on condition that you report back to them about any problems you come across while using the software. Often, beta software is essentially fully working – at least to meet the needs of most people, so can provide a superb opportunity to use a product.

However, don't rely on beta software for doing important tasks: it may be unstable, could muddle your computer's file system or even damage some files. Usually, no guarantees are available for beta software and you'll probably have to agree not to hold the software provider responsible for any damage if you choose to use a beta copy. The risk is all yours. You'll probably come across strange quirks, bugs, unusual program crashes, but hey, if the software is free…

Working with compressed files

A large file or program, if left in its native format, can take a long time to download from an FTP site or anywhere else on the Internet and occupies a set amount of storage space. Large files therefore are usually compressed using special software to reduce their file size. A smaller file takes up less storage space and therefore can be downloaded quicker whatever the speed of your Internet connection.

However, compressed files need to be uncompressed once they reach their destination before use and some may uncompress automatically on first use, while others need to be manually uncompressed. Popular file compressors include WinZip (http://www.winzip.com/) for the PC, and Stuffit Expander (http://www.aladdinsys.com/) for Apple Macs. You can easily identify if a file is compressed: look at the filename extension. Popular compressed formats include: .zip, .arc, .tar, .z, .arj, .hqz, .gz and .sit.

Single compressed file archives

A single software program may contain many different individual files. To make the process of transferring software across the Internet easier and more reliable, many software providers compress all the relevant program files in a special way to create a single all-in-one file called an archive.

One great benefit from using an archive is that you only need to download the archive file and often simply click or double-click it to automatically start installing the file on your computer. Many popular IBM-compatible PC archive files use the .zip, .exe, or .lzh filename extensions.

So for example, imagine that you're downloading a freeware interactive Calendar program that sits on your Windows desktop. After downloading calendar.zip, you simply move to the relevant folder and double-click on calendar.zip – which then automatically de-compresses the various installation files to a temporary folder. You can then double-click the "setup.exe" file to complete the installation of your Calendar.

Configuring your FTP program

To set up your standalone FTP program, follow the installation instructions that come with your FTP software. Often, during the installation, an FTP program may automatically install and configure settings for some existing free access (anonymous) FTP sites for you. Take a little time to examine these settings, then you can gain a better understanding of the kind of information you'll need when visiting the FTP sites you want.

Usually however, to gain access to any new FTP site, three settings especially are important to ensure that your computer connects to the FTP computer:

- The FTP domain name: example formats include:
  ftp.companyname.com
  or for uploading Web pages to a Web host, some accept:
  www.companyname.com
  However, the FTP name may be longer, for example, look at this imaginary FTP address:
  ftp.mysite.com/files/pc/pdf/net-tips.zip
  From the above address, we know that the compressed file "net-tips.zip"can be found in a folder called "pdf" that is a sub-folder of a folders "files" and "pc" on the "mysite.com" FTP server.
- User name: if the FTP site has private access.
- Password: again if your FTP site has restricted access, keep this information secure.

How do I download something from an FTP site?

FTP programs that come built in as part of a successfully installed Web browser don't need any further configuration. You simply visit the Web page containing the file you want, click the link and the file download automatically starts. Follow the onscreen prompts and dialog boxes usually appear asking if you want to open or save the file. For now, choose the Save option – you can open it later – and decide where on your computer you want to store the file you're downloading. The download window then appears and shows the progress of the download.

The most popular way to download files from the Internet is to use a separate FTP program, which must be correctly installed and configured before use for the FTP site you want to connect to as covered in Configuring your FTP program on page 329. The main window of most standalone FTP programs is usually much like that of Windows Explorer and may be split into multiple panes.

One pane may show the location on your computer where you want to store or upload files. Another pane may show the folder or directory structure of the FTP computer to which you're connected. A third pane may be available to show the progress of files as they are uploading or downloading between your computer and the FTP computer. Usually, you can move from folder to folder in the destination and target panes.

You can download information in text or binary mode. When downloading a file, in most instances your FTP program should be set to binary mode or automatically know which mode to use. Usually, the binary option is set for you, but if a downloaded file appears faulty, certainly double-check this option.

If you're downloading a file to the location of a file with the same name, your FTP program erases the original file and replaces it with the new one – and you may not get a warning that the original file is being wiped. Use a different file name if unsure.

If you download many FTP files, first create a folder structure on your computer that makes sense to you. Then download the various programs and files to their most appropriate folders or directories, rather than store them in one folder. Otherwise, when you expand compressed files, you can never be sure which uncompressed file belong to which program or archive.

Once connected to an FTP site, if you stop using your FTP program, after a specific time delay most FTP servers will disconnect you (not from the Internet, just from their server). When ready, simply choose the command to reconnect.

While downloading files from FTP sites or the Internet, you can complete other tasks with your computer – like surfing the Web or working on a document. Usually when a file has completed downloading to your computer, your FTP software shows a message on the screen or it may sound a beep to let you know this task is complete.

Once a download has started, most good standalone FTP programs also provide a regularly updated estimate of how long the download is expected to take. So if some time is needed, at least you can work on other tasks and re-check the download progress occasionally.

Also install a program like Go!Zilla (currently free of charge from http://www.gozilla.com) – which can handle downloads for you. One of the most important benefits of Go!Zilla and similar FTP programs is that if you temporarily lose your Internet connection, after you reconnect again you can resume the broken download from the last point reached, providing the server you're downloading from allows resumed downloads. Superb – Go!Zilla can save your sanity if you're downloading a file that takes several hours or more. The following paragraphs also include information about a few popular programs.

Previously, we introduced the idea of compressed and archived files. Remember, to use one of these files you may have to manually uncompress or "unpack" a downloaded compressed archive file before you can use it. Therefore, if the file you want to download is compressed, you'll also need the correct decompression software installed and set up. Often, FTP sites also provide copies of popular decompression programs free of charge. Popular compression/decompression programs include: WinZip and PKZip for IBM-compatible PCs and StuffIt Expander for Apple Macintosh computers.

Busy FTP sites

Each FTP site allows only a specific number of users to connect at any one time. If you try to connect but keep receiving an error message, perhaps the user limit has already been reached; try again later. Some FTP sites are extra busy during business working hours, so again maybe try connecting in the evening or at weekends.

If you cannot connect to any FTP site, then double-check your FTP set-up – log-on Web addresses, user names and passwords particularly have to be correct for the FTP site you're using and we all know how easy it is to type an incorrect character in a password. However, usually you'll only need to enter your correct password the first time you connect to the particular FTP site. Each individual password along with other key information is usually stored in the relevant FTP profile you create on your computer.

Uploading files with FTP

Instead of accepting or downloading files, you can also send or upload files to another computer on the Internet. A popular example is if you publish your brand new "ritzy-glitzy" Web site. When you're ready, either directly through your Web design software or using a dedicated FTP program, you can transfer all the relevant Web files from your computer to the Web server on which your

Web site will be stored. The process is much the same as when downloading files. Here's what to do:

- You'll need a Web or ftp address using the format: ftp.domainname.com, for example: ftp.mysite.com or even the standard format www.mysite.com may be acceptable with some Web hosts. Check this information with your Web host or Internet Service Provider.
- Next you'll probably need a User name.
- A password.
- And a location where to upload the files.

If you're publishing a Web site, all this information is provided by your Web hosting company. If you're uploading some files to an FTP server, you'll probably need to know some or all of the information above. Again, check what you need to provide with whoever is receiving the files you're sending.

However, don't send important data, programs or sensitive information using conventional FTP and always keep backup copies of what you're sending, just in case your files get lost somewhere on the Internet. Once computer files go beyond your computer, you lose a certain amount of control and these free providers usually cannot accept responsibility for any loss.

To find a particular variety of compression/decompression software, check the "INDEX" or "README" files in the introductory areas of FTP sites. Or the compression/decompression software you want may be provided on some CD-ROMs that accompany popular computer magazines.

If you're getting low on hard drive space, some Web sites provide free space on their servers to which you can upload some files. For example, see: http://www.freedrive.com However, never upload any files containing private or sensitive information.

Popular FTP programs

Let's recap: to gain access to an FTP site, you'll need to install an FTP program. FTP programs are available either as standalone separate software or a basic version may come built-in to your Web browser. Internet Explorer and Netscape Navigator both include basic FTP components that will probably meet most needs.

Whenever you visit a Web site that offers something to download, after you click the relevant download link, an FTP-compatible Web browser automatically starts the download.

However, some tasks – like uploading a Web site for example – are best left to Web design software that includes a built-in FTP program, or use a separate dedicated FTP program.

Popular standalone free/shareware programs include:

- FTP Explorer: http://www.ftpx.com/
- WS-FTP: http://www.ipswitch.com/
- CutFTP: http://www.ftpx.com/
- Windows Commander: http://www.download.com/

All the above standalone FTP software programs allow you to:

- Identify the files you want to copy to another computer on the Internet (upload).

- Find and choose those files you want to copy to your computer (download).
- Manage and find your way around FTP sites.

When downloading large files, try to avoid using your Web browser. Instead use a standalone FTP program that supports resume downloads. Then, if your Internet connection is temporarily broken for any reason, you can reconnect at the earliest opportunity and continue the download from that last point reached. CuteFTP – the author's favourite – for example, can resume downloads, as does FTP Explorer.

Retrieving broken downloads

While downloading files from an FTP site, sometimes your connection may break and you'll need to reconnect to the Internet and to the FTP site again. If the file you're downloading is large and perhaps you've already been online for several hours, you don't want to have to restart the download again: your patience and sanity will probably be stretched to the limit! The best FTP programs now allow you to resume the download from the position you were last at just before becoming disconnected, so all previous effort is not wasted, providing the FTP site to which you connected before the break also supports resume downloading.

In order for resume downloads to work, the FTP program installed on your computer and the relevant FTP server must both support resume downloads. If either doesn't, then unfortunately, you'll have to try the download again. When downloading large files from FTP sites that do not support resume downloads, whenever possible try to consider other options if available – CD-ROMs, DVDs, Zip & Jaz disks and even floppy disks.

If your chosen FTP program does not automatically support resumed downloading, my advice is get one installed as soon as possible: you can have more than one FTP program installed on your computer. WS_FTP is free, so is Go!Zilla, a relatively new kid on the block.

How to find FTP sites

So many files are available using FTP and a common question people ask is: "But how do I find the kinds of files I'm interested in?" Answer: like most other search problems on the Internet, use special search tools. Two popular ways to find FTP sites around the world is to use a tool called Archie and other Web sites that include FTP search tools. Archie is examined in more depth below.

Popular FTP Web sites include: http://www.shareware.com. Using Shareware.com, you can browse through FTP sites around the world or you can use their search engine to find specific files. To see a list containing most of the FTP sites available, try: http://hoohoo.ncsa.uiuc.edu/ftp-interface.html Additional popular FTP sites include:

- ftp.lysator.liu.se (gardening)
- ftp.microsoft.com (wide range of software support products)
- ftp.dell.com (Dell computers: support software and files)
- ftp.mirrors.aol.com (AOL's music ftp site)
- ftp.mcp.com (an ebook site)
- ftp.apple.com (Apple Macintosh operating system support)
- ftp.zdnet.com (wide range of software products and games)

Using WSArchie to find files on the Internet

Archie is a great general-purpose tool to seek out files you know exist somewhere on the Internet but you don't know where. However, to find a specific file with Archie, you at least need to know part of the file name you want. You can find WSArchie and WSArchie services at:

- http://www.shareware.com/ (then enter WSArchie in the search box)
- http://www.lerc.nasa.gov/archieplex
- Rutgers University: archie.Rutgers.edu/archie.html
- http://archie.emnet.co.uk/services.html
- ftp://ftp.hkstar.com/.2/simtelnet/win95/inet/wsarch32.zip
- ftp://ftp.orst.edu/.1/simtelnet/win95/inet/wsarch32.zip

Part IV
Creating
Web Pages

Software for creating Web pages

The Web allows anyone with the right tools and a little know-how to create their own Web pages and publish these to the Web for other people around the world to share and enjoy. Individuals like to create Web pages about their favourite hobbies and interests or perhaps to share photos of special events, family gatherings, and so on. Business users can use the low cost but long reach of the Web to sell more goods and services and make new customers for a fraction of the normal offline cost.

In fact, businesses can benefit from the Internet in a variety of ways. For example, they can advertise and sell their products/services to a potentially much larger number of customers, again usually for a much lower cost; provide company forms and information for employees travelling around the country or aboard; and advertise employment vacancies, to name but a few applications. See also: On the road and using the Net on page 188.

Establishing what you need to create Web pages

Essentially, four main components can help create a great Web site:

- A sound plan of action plus an understanding of why you want to create your Web pages and who they're intended to benefit.
- Software to help you design and publish your Web pages.
- Ability to use your preferred Web design software and basic graphics editing software like Paint Shop Pro.
- Web space to hold and display your Web pages.

Armed with the previous information, let's look at the two basic steps you'll need to perform to create a working Web site. First you create your Web pages using Web design software. Then you'll need to send copies of your Web pages to a special location reserved for you on a computer that is connected to the Web called a Web server. You can gain access to a Web server in three main ways:

- Through an Internet Service Provider – many provide some free Web space with email accounts.
- You can buy Web space from a Web host – a company that rents Web space by hosting Web sites for other people.
- A third option is to set up your own Web server with a permanent connection to the Internet! However, have a big wad of money available. This option is often ideal for larger companies and organizations that have higher security needs and want total control. You'll probably need at least £15,000+ available annually and if you employ people to maintain and manage your Web site, multiply that rough figure many times. It's not hard to see why most people use free Web space or the services of a Web host, is it?

Planning and organising on paper

When you have some new Web design software, you can spend as much time as you need trying out the commands and generally getting familiar with how to use it.

However, before starting to design your Web pages or Web site, often you can save a lot of time later by roughly sketching on paper what you want to achieve and noting down any possible alternatives and various ideas – however wacky they might at first appear. Later, you might be able to include those "wacky" ideas to help create a better Web page or Web site.

Generally, the main rule to consider – unless you have a compelling reason not to – is to divide up and organise your information so that you keep each different topic to its own page. A "page" in Web design terms can be considered to be about 1 – 3 times the height of your display monitor screen. Using this approach, you can avoid putting what some might consider too much information on to any single page.

You can discover new ideas about the different ways you can create, build and publish Web pages from books like "Web Page Design in easy steps" and similar sources on the Internet. Make sure that what you intend to publish does not break any Internet Service Provider rules, decency and trade laws or regulations. Remember that even though the Web has a global reach, it is not 100% anonymous: with the right tools, almost every contributor can be traced.

A note about creating business Web sites

For businesses especially, as the Web is a strong graphical medium, your Web site must look professional and stand out. Often the services of a suitably experienced graphic designer can help produce a really stunning Web site that blends perfectly with your business. Usually, sophisticated and expensive software tools cannot substitute for a superb graphic designer. To learn more about using the Internet for business purposes, see page 371.

More on HTML

HyperText Markup Language (HTML) is a simple computer language used to create Web pages. The more recently updated version – Dynamic HTML (DHTML) – can provide interactive components and lots of control over how a Web page looks. Essentially, to create a Web page, either directly or through Web design software, you write the HTML in plain text, include special text to make formatting tags, include the text to display images and create the text codes that form hyperlinks or links to other Web pages.

You can create HyperText Markup Language (HTML) Web pages using:

- Most basic text editors like Windows Notepad or word-processing software like Microsoft Word.
- A HTML editor: more user-friendly but you still face raw HTML.
- Web site design software: here you can see how your Web pages look as you create your layout and designs and the better packages can often help with the management of your Web site. Clearly, the best option.

Although HTML/DHTML is probably not one of your most exciting discoveries, it is useful and can create some amazing effects. Creating HTML character by character using a basic text editor is useful for "tweaking" the design of a Web page or for those times when you want to create a precise look and feel. The next best option is to use a HTML Editor. However, for most of us nowadays, you can go one better and use any of the wide range of great WYSIWYG (What You See Is What You Get) Web design software tools. These can help you complete almost all Web design tasks using a Desktop publishing approach, so you can see a page as you're building it and you don't need to have an in-depth knowledge about HTML commands to get the job done.

Nevertheless, if you're serious about Web design, consider investing some time to learn about HTML and DHTML – you'll almost certainly need to know the details at some stage and sometimes even purpose-built Web design software may not be able to create the precise effect you want easily.

Web design software

A wide range of standalone Web design software is available in the shops and on the Internet. Alternatively, some word-processing, DTP and graphics software – for example: Microsoft Word, Adobe PageMaker, Corel WordPerfect and CorelDRAW! – let you save documents in Web (HTML) format, so depending on your needs, you may not even need a more powerful and flexible Web design package. Also, many HTML editors are available free of charge on the Internet and so can provide a great way to try out different programs to discover which approach you prefer. Popular favourites include:

Basic text editors:

- TextPad: http://www.textpad.com/
- Windows Notepad, Microsoft Word: http://www.microsoft.com/
- CuteHTML: http://www.cuteftp.com/

WYSIWYG Web design Products:

- Adobe GoLive: http://www.adobe.com/
- Adobe PageMill: http://www.adobe.com/
- Homesite from Allaire: http://www.allaire.com/

- HotDog Pro from Sausage Software: http://www.hotdog.com/
- HotMetal Pro: http://www.hotmetal.com/
- Macromedia Dreamweaver: http://www.macromedia.com/
- Microsoft FrontPage: http://www.microsoft.com/frontpage/
- NetObjects Fusion: http://www.netobjects.com/
- WebExpress: http://www.webexpress.com/

Included with the later versions of Microsoft Internet Explorer Web browser, FrontPage Express is another free Microsoft product and is great for learning about how to create basic Web pages and uploading (publishing) pages to the Web. A completely different approach involves using the services and tools of an online Web design and hosting provider. Often, space for several Web pages may be made available for free and the software tools you need are also provided. For example, take a look at: http://www.zy.com/

Creating simple
Web pages

A Web page is nothing more complex than a combination of various blocks of text, links to other pages and, optionally, images and possibly other graphical, multimedia or animated special effects. For businesses, however, a Web page can be considered as an electronic brochure, so getting the right look and feel is particularly important.

Copyright and legal issues again

Although the Web may be a public domain-type environment, unless a Web site states that their text, graphics, designs and other components are free for anyone to use, they're probably not. However, if you want to use some components from an existing Web site for your own site, email the Webmaster and ask first. Even graphics that you can buy for use in Web pages may have certain restrictions on how you can use them. Check the small print.

Often, you can see the raw HTML structure of Web pages while online. Use the "View Source" command – look in the View menu or choose the command from the floating menu that appears when you click the right mouse button by default.

Introducing HTML tags

Here's an example Web page showing the basic HTML structure:

```
<HTML>
<HEAD>
<TITLE>Welcome to my Home page!</TITLE>
</HEAD>
<BODY BGCOLOR="BEIGE" TEXT="NAVY" (more here...)
(most of the page content goes here)
</BODY>
</HTML>
```

The HTML tags are shown in capital letters enclosed between the (<) and (>) symbols. Often, these tags work together in pairs to form a command, with the ending tag having a forward slash (/) to signal the end of the tag command. You can learn about HTML in plain English from "HTML in easy steps" and "Web Page Design in easy steps" (http://www.ineasysteps.com/), or from other similar books or check out sources on the Internet.

Establishing page size

You need to consider page width and length. Page width is affected by the resolution visitors use to view a Web page and is measured in pixels (dots of light). For example, three popular browser resolutions include: 640 x 480, 800 x 600, 1200 x 740. Arguably, most computers now use 800 x 600 – which means 800 pixels wide by 600 high. Therefore, keep your page width to less than about 780 pixels to avoid forcing your visitors to have to scroll left to right – never popular. Or, if you're happy to lose some control, you can create your design using percentages instead of pixels so that your page content wraps to fit the current window size.

Page height: ideally, ensure your page content fits into a single browser window height or, if using lots of text, fewer than about 4 screen heights to avoid making a page too long. But this is not a hard and fast rule: use your own judgement here to create your best presentation.

Web page background

Your background can be a solid colour, variable or shaded colour, or even a watermark-type image. The most important consideration is that the overlying text can be clearly read and so has adequate contrast with the background, and that graphics and other overlying elements can also be viewed clearly. Also don't forget to consider using "white" (empty) space to frame your main page content and provide an uncluttered appearance. "Active" white space around an object actually helps the eye maintain focus on that object in a subtle way.

Working with colours on the Web

Colour has a powerful pull on the eye, can help suggest various moods, and contrasting colours add vibrancy to a Web page. Use colours that complement or work well together to create a superb finish. Most computers today can product 256 colours. However, 40 colours are reserved for use by the computer operating system and other functions. That leaves 216 "safe" colours. Most Web design software will provide more information about using safe Web colours. However, as many computers nowadays can display thousands (64 thousand) or millions (16 Million) of different colours and shades, you may decide to have more flexibility in the colours you choose.

Inserting text onto a page

You can enter text much the same way as you would using word-processor software, add formatting like bold, italic or underline and use lists – both bullet point and numbered – and so on, to place special emphasis on specific text.

Adding links to a page

Links – or hyperlinks – are one of the most important components in a Web page as links allow visitors to quickly move to the parts that interest them most. Specifically, a link allows visitors to quickly move to:

- Somewhere else on the same page.
- A different page in the current Web site.
- Another Web site or new location on the Internet.

Web design software provides simple ways to create hyperlinks:

- Insert a text-based link onto a Web page.
- Change the purpose of a normal image so that it becomes a graphical hyperlink – the object still looks the same except when a user moves the

mouse pointer onto the image, the mouse pointer symbol changes to show that the image is also a link.

Usually by default, a text link is shown in underlined blue; however, you can use the later versions of HTML or DHTML to create links that are of different colours and to keep or remove the underline, while being viewed with the latest Web browsers.

HOT TIP

You can install more than one Web browser. First install your preferred browser (I choose Microsoft Internet Explorer). Then while installing a second browser (like Netscape Navigator), the software may ask if you want to make this browser your new default browser. At this stage ideally, choose the "No" options. You can still view any Web page with either browser at any time after each has been correctly installed.

Things to consider when using images

Pictures and other graphical Web objects can add interest, provide contrast, form the main component of a Web page, or supplement the theme of the text, to create an interesting, compelling result – if done carefully and with consideration. Pure text displays quickly in a Web page; images usually take longer and the larger the physical size of an image the longer it takes to fully display in a browser. Therefore, consider the following guidelines when working with Web images:

- Choose your images carefully – avoid "tacky", poor quality images.
- Keep the size of an image as physically small as is acceptable to fulfil your goals for that image. The size of an image is given in pixels and each pixel is a dot of light. For example, a rectangular image of 100 pixels wide by 50 pixels high is simply described in HTML as HEIGHT=50 WIDTH=100.
- Images for use in a Web page should be converted to the correct format. This ensures that an image will download as quickly as possible to a visitor's browser, so minimising the time they need to wait. More on this important topic in the following paragraphs.
- Avoid having too many images on a Web page: the more images present, the longer a page takes to display in a visitor's Web browser.

Finding suitable images for your Web pages

You can find the images you need using a variety of methods:

- Create the images you want to use on your computer using an image-drawing program or take your own live pictures using a digital camera.
- With the right permission (see copyright and legal issues earlier in this chapter) modify an existing image using image-editing software.

- Copy (save) existing images from the Web or Internet. WARNING: get permission in writing from the copyright owners of the images you want to use before using them. Depending on how you want to use the images, copyright restrictions may apply, you may have to pay a fee, or permission may be refused.
- Using a scanner, you can copy existing images from printed pages. WARNING: the same legal implications apply as listed in the previous paragraph. Remember, even though information on the Internet may be considered by some to be "in the public domain" or available for anyone to use as they wish, how this is interpreted in law can vary from country to country. The essential point to understand is that all images are "owned" by someone.

Image owners appreciate being asked and I suspect many will give permission with some reasonable conditions, especially for non-commercial uses.

Search engines usually like "ugly" Web pages. Or, to be more precise, "simple" Web pages designed with the search engines in mind first and foremost, with look and feel second, usually fare better than those Web sites that are primarily designed to look visually attractive. Why? Simply designed Web sites do not usually have all the extra HTML/DHTML code and so make the job of indexing a site easy for a search engine and less prone to error.

Image formats and preparing images for the Web

Images for use on Web pages come in two main formats: GIF (pronounced "JIFF" or "GIFF") and JPEG (pronounced J-Peg). Other formats are available like Portable Network Graphics (PNG), but these have not yet gained widespread acceptance. GIF (.gif) is ideal for small images that contain only a few colours or shades like logos or simple geometric shapes. JPEG (.jpeg or .jpe) is ideal for any image that uses many different colours and shades, like photographs.

However, all images for the Web should be converted to use 256 or fewer colours – the fewer used, the smaller an image's file size, the faster it displays on a visitor's Web browser. In your graphics program, reduce the number of colours to as few as possible without degrading the image quality. However, if you use too few colours an image can look patchy. Usually, you'll choose 256 or 16 colours or, for simple black and white images, even 2 colours.

256 colours

16 colours

Placing an image on a page

Placing an image on a Web page is as simple as doing the same job in a word processed or desktop published document, except you'll use the HTML <IMG> tag. For example:

<IMG SRC="welcomelogo.gif">

If you're using Web design software, you won't need to be concerned about the exact HTML format, just place the image where you want it on the page. You can then choose from various image alignment options including: left, right, middle, text top and baseline.

Also, don't forget to use the ALT image tag to include a brief text description for each image. Example: ALT="holiday in Venice, 2000"

An ALT description is necessary just in case a visitor has turned off image display in their Web browser settings to reduce the download time of Web pages, and for helping the search engines index your page.

Creating a site navigation structure

When using Web sites that contain many pages, unless you design pages carefully, a visitor may soon become confused and lost – absolutely not on, especially if you want to create a successful business-oriented Web site. Therefore, create a clear page navigation structure using navigation bars and buttons where appropriate and always include a link on every page back to the Home/Index page and to the main categories of your Web site.

Saving a Web page

Usually, you save your Web pages using the .html or .htm filename extension (although more complex database-driven pages may use other filename extensions). While working on your pages, practice saving often – ideally every 15 minutes to protect your work and keep regular backup copies.

Previewing your Web pages

When ready, you can first see how your Web page might look on the Web by using the "Preview" command in your Web design software if available. Then when you're happy with the finish, open the Web page you want using your own installed Web browser. Often, all you need do to start up your Web browser with the desired Web page displayed in the Window, is to double-click the Web page filename you want in Windows Explorer or equivalent. But remember, not all browsers interpret the same Web page in the same way. Therefore, ideally have at least the latest versions of Internet Explorer and Netscape Navigator installed on your computer (choose one as the default). Then check your Web page using both Web browsers to confirm the end result is what you expect. If not, you can make your changes and re-check the results.

Spell-checking, proofreading, checking & testing

Before publishing your Web page or Web site, use a spell checker to catch those that you miss visually. Also ideally, print out each page and check layout again and make any necessary changes.

To get the best finish possible, you may have to repeat this checking and editing cycle several times, but hey, it's your baby right?

Publishing a "local" copy of your Web site

When you have finished your Web page design you can publish. However, to make sure your Web pages will appear as you expect, publish a "local" copy to your own computer first then open the Web page using your Web browser to view your page. If you have created a series of related Web pages or an entire Web site, you can open the main Index or Home page – usually called something like: index.html – and then check all the other related pages by navigating around your Web site just as your visitors will when you go live.

In this way, you can double-check all pages and make sure all the links that you can check offline are working as they should. Obviously, the links you include that point to other Web locations can only be properly checked once you publish your pages to the Web.

Finally, view your Web pages as described above using several different Web browsers if possible. Certainly, check your pages with the latest versions of Microsoft Internet Explorer and Netscape Navigator/Communicator. Ideally, also use some earlier versions of each browser in the same way. Once you're happy that the local published copy of your Web site works perfectly, you're ready to make your Web site live and publish to the Web.

Going live: publishing your Web site to the Web

To publish your Web site, you'll need an FTP program. Often, Web creation software may include this within the product. Alternatively, you can use a standalone product. See page 321 for more information about FTP software. You'll also need some Web space to which you have permission to publish. Several options may be available. If you use an Internet Service Provider (ISP) to gain access to the Internet and for email, they may make some free Web space available to you. If you're in business, you'll probably want a true business domain name. See page 376 for more information on this important topic.

Getting web space for individual and personal Web sites

Free Web space that may be available from an Internet Service Provider is ideal for individual, hobby, or non-business-oriented Web sites. However, do remember that, usually, the final Web address available from free Internet Service Providers may be longer than that of a true domain Web address like: http://www.ineasysteps.com.

To illustrate, here's an imaginary Web address dreamed up by my teenage daughter, that we might be able to use with the generous free Web space available from the well-established British Internet Service Provider BT Internet: http://www.btintenet.com/~amanda.hugandkiss/index.html

Not the shortest Web address you'll come across, and perhaps not the easiest to remember, but it may be perfectly acceptable for your needs. Just think twice before you consider trying to run a business using longer Web addresses like these.

Preferred business Web hosting options

Serious business Web sites are usually published to the Web using the facilities of a Web hosting organisation, or to a dedicated Web server that may be owned by the company publishing the Web site. Follow the instructions provided in your Web software for publishing to the Web. Your software may mention that you're publishing to a Web server – remember, this is just another name for a powerful computer that will hold your Web site and make it available for anyone with Internet access to view on the Web.

Creating fancy
Web pages

If you want to make an impression, create impact, provide more flexibility or make interactive Web pages, you'll need to go beyond the simple. Lots of options are available so let's look at some of the more popular choices.

Using cool mouseover effects

A popular current trend is to set up a link, or some text or a graphic that changes in some way when you move the mouse pointer over it, or which changes some other component on the page – perhaps to display some alternative text. As soon as you move the mouse pointer away from the object, the page design re-displays its original look. The currently popular mouseover – also known as rollover or hover – technique is often used to highlight Web site navigation buttons or other links and can provide an ideal way to display more information in the same physical space. The best Web creation software packages like NetObjects Fusion and Microsoft FrontPage provide some pre-designed mouseovers ready for you to use or you can create your own if you wish. See your Web software guide for more information.

Getting noticed with animation

If you want to draw attention to one particular component on a Web page, make that component move. For example, you can create animated buttons, scrolling text messages, advertisements and small self-running programs or presentations that when carefully designed can hold the viewer spellbound – at least for a few seconds, but that may be all you need. But do remember that too many competing moving components can have the opposite effect, cause confusion, slow down the loading of a page and can sometimes make too many demands on a browser and so cause it to crash.

Several different types of animation are currently popular that may use computer scripting and programming languages like JavaScript, Java, ActiveX and VisualBasic. ActiveX components, for example, are building block programs that can be inserted into a Web page, so that when the Web page is viewed using an ActiveX-compatible Web browser like Internet Explorer, the ActiveX Components can run automatically.

Dynamic HTML and more about special effects

Dynamic HyperText Markup Language (DHTML) techniques can include their own animated components. As complicated as the name might sound, in a nutshell, DHTML simply allows the content of a Web page to change even after the code that makes the page work has downloaded to the visitor's Web browser.

DHTML mostly uses JavaScript, one of the easier computer languages to learn, to help provide all sorts of clever effects and useful additions to a Web page. Many JavaScript components are available on the Internet that you can use or add to your Web page designs.

For example, to get started with JavaScript and learn more about the kind of effects you can create, see what's available at: http://www.javascripts.com/ JavaScript is actually a cut-down version of the more powerful "big brother" computer language, Java (originally developed by Sun Microsystems). They developed Java so that applets – self-contained chunks of code – could (when placed on a Web page) be interpreted by any computer no matter what operating system was used. You can find many sources about Java on the Internet through your browser search engines.

Inserting META tags for maximum exposure

A Web page can include more information about what you want to say than just what is included on the page. Extra information that is normally invisible can be added using HTML META tags, that can help the search engines index your Web site. For example, you can include a brief description about your Web page and include various keywords that you want your site to be associated with. Often, this information is used to help form what a visitor sees about your Web site displayed in the search listing of various search engines. See your Web creation software guide for details. See also page 401.

Creating your online forms

Online forms are simply the electronic equivalent of the often dreaded paper-based forms, except that, arguably, online forms can be easier to deal with. On a Web site, you can use an online form to create a guestbook that allows a visitor to simply say hello, provide feedback or even take part in a quiz or competition. For Web designers, online forms offer a great way to get to know your visitors better – for business Web sites, online forms are essential as accurate information is the lifeblood of any online business. Although the best Web creation software allows you to create online forms easily, there are two aspects to consider when working with Web forms:

1. The design of the form and the kind of questions you ask.
2. How the information gets back to you once a visitor has clicked the "Send " – or equivalent – button.

If forms are important to your Web site, you'll need a Web host provider that can handle forms – fortunately most do and usually provide something called a cgi-bin to handle and process information received from a Web form. Speak to your Web host for more details. Some free services are available that can make the entire job much easier and process all information received from your Web page forms; for example, consider: http://www.response-o-matic.com/ and http://www.formmailer.net/

Inserting a search box for your Web site

If your Web site contains lots of information, one quick way to build in added value and make using the site easier and quicker for your visitors is to include a site search box. Installing your own search engine is no longer the black art that it used to be.

Now, several non-specialist options are available. You can use pre-designed JavaScript components that you just drop on to the page. For example, Coolmaps.com at http://www.coolmaps.com/ provide a superb range of

"Components" for NetObjects Fusion users (http://www.netobjects.com/). Other software products like FrontPage provide similar pre-designed modules that you can use. Or you can download pre-designed JavaScript blocks of code from Web sites like: http://www.javascripts.com/

If your Web site has fewer than 500 pages, Atomz at http://www.atomz.com/ currently make the Atomz Search tool available free of charge.

Including Multimedia content

Multimedia refers to the combination of various types of media – text, still and moving pictures, animation, and sound. If you decide to include, say, video clips or large sound clips, remember that download times for your visitors will increase. Longer download times may be tolerated by your visitors providing they consider that the end result pay-off is worthwhile.

Sound/video clips come in 2 main forms:

- Discrete format: here the entire clip has to be fully downloaded before it can be viewed or heard – not ideal for anything that takes longer than a few minutes using a typical modem connection speed.
- Streaming media: content can start to play while it is downloading. Streaming media typically offers less delay so this option is usually much better for most purposes, but your visitor will need the correct player software installed. RealPlayer from RealNetworks (http://www.realplayer.com/) and Microsoft NetShow (http://www.microsoft.com/netshow/) are two streaming multimedia players that are currently available free of charge.

Currently free programs like Real Slideshow let you mix pictures with voice, music and other sound effects. Real Presenter – also free – converts Microsoft PowerPoint presentations into Internet video format. Several of the free Web hosting sites can now host your streaming media presentations at no charge: http://www.tripod.com, one of the pioneers in free Web sites, at the time of writing offers a program called ShowMotion. You can combine still photos with clips of video, scanned images, and backed with your narration. What's more, Tripod hosts it for free!

Adding sound to a Web page

Sound information from a microphone is made up of lots of changing high and low notes or waves; electronically, we call this analogue information. Computers however, use only two levels: 0 (zero) and 1 (one), or highs and lows to communicate and this effect is known as digital communication.

Background music can add that extra something to a Web page or it can irritate your visitors. As you can't predict how a visitor is going to react to your taste in music, consider this option carefully and always include a button or other mechanism that allows a visitor to turn off music. Also remember, as music and other sound components slow down the loading of a page, in an already graphically complex page, you might benefit by simply omitting music – unless you're in the music business.

To use sound on a Web page, the sound information has to be converted to digital format. Fortunately, lots of digital sound clips, music and tunes have already been converted ready to use (check copyright issues though). Several varieties of sound file for Web pages exist but all can be grouped as discrete or streaming audio. If you include sound files that end in extensions like .wav and .au, these discrete files have to be completely downloaded to the Web browser and have the correct player software installed before they can be heard.

Whereas with audio streaming, to play a file on a Web page a user does not have to wait for the entire file to download before the sound file can start to play. However, the correct audio player must be installed in the user's computer. Most of these players are available free of charge. Rich Music Format (RMF) is a new interactive audio format that looks set to be "the" format for the Web.

Also, free or cheap programs are available on the Net to let you record audio as a simple WAV file, a RealAudio file or in the newer MP3 format. One easy to use program is Internet Audio Mix from http://www.aoustica.com/ which works with your sound card to record up to 4 digital tracks.

Another approach is use free programs like those available from http://www.GiveMeTalk.com/ that allow you to record your own talk show and then host it on their site ready for your customers to hear your masterpiece. Or you could record your information in MP3 format and upload articles to http://www.Live365.com/ where your talks can be made available continuously 24 hours a day and rotated regularly – and it's currently free of charge!

Using frames

Frames offer a way to keep one or more components in the same position while other parts of a Web page can be scrolled through. This approach is sometimes ideal for business Web sites that want to keep a logo, advertising banner or navigation bar in the same position. Using the <FRAMESET> </FRAMESET> tag pair in HTML, you can create the frame structure you want and apply it to all pages in your Web site. As you then don't need to repeat the exercise on every page, you can save many hours' work – plus updating is much easier. However, poorly designed frame Web pages can cause more problems than they solve. Therefore, see your HTML guide or Web creation software Help files for more information about using framed page designs.

How about a WebCam on your Web site?

Also called NetCams, WebCams are digital cameras attached to a PC that can send live pictures/moving pictures at specific intervals on the Internet. A digital camera combined with WebCam software takes live, repeating, still photographs and transmits these at certain intervals. For example, pictures might be transmitted at a rate of one frame each second. Images from a WebCam are sent to a video capture board that is typically installed in a spare slot in the main circuit board of the computer with the WebCam attached.

The video capture board changes the analogue information it receives from the WebCam that makes up each frame into a digital format that the computer can work with – as the make-up of each image is probably complex, the JPEG digital graphics format is usually used. JPEG images are quick to load and are ideal for rendering images that contain a wide range of colours, tones and shades, like photographs. Each JPEG image is then associated with a specific Web address (URL), so that whenever a visitor clicks the appropriate link on a Web page, the most recent image from the WebCam is sent to the viewer. This cycle is repeated so that while a user is viewing, a continuous stream of photos provides the illusion of movement.

Although current generation WebCams are not pure continuous video quality, a WebCam can provide an ideal basic communication device today, and usage is probably set to increase as face-to-face video communication becomes more commonplace through the continuing development and ever closer ties of mobile phones, video phones, the Internet and television.

Part V
Doing Business on the Internet

Web business basics

Results of recent surveys and commercial forecasts cite 60,000 new subscribers coming on to the Internet every day with over 500 million expected to join by 2003 (IDC Research)! In 1997, Internet sales amounted to US $5 billion; in 2000 some predictions suggest US $94 billion – an amazing increase! The highly respected Forrester Research suggest that by 2002 Internet sales are likely to reach US $3.2 trillion!

These figures alone are enough to predict that in the next five years, probably more millionaires are going to emerge as a result of the Internet than at any other time in history! And you could be one of them! Why not? Let's examine how you can get started.

The one question almost everyone who has any interest in the Internet may ask at some stage is: "Can I make money on the Net?" Answer: Yes, individuals, entrepreneurs, companies and organisations around the world are already doing just that! However, if you were to ask: "What about losing money on the Net?", the answer would be "Yes absolutely!" In business terms, the Internet is no different from other areas of life.

For pure Internet businesses, the risk is always present, as are possible incredible gains and benefits – if you make the right moves and become successful. The Internet today can be compared a little to the Klondike of the 19th Century in which gold diggers also faced many hazards in the hope of quick riches. However, thankfully the Internet is a lot less risky!

If you want to establish a profitable Internet business, ask someone who's already doing just that what you need to do. But be careful: the Internet has its share of tricksters eager to spin you a false picture and run after you've handed over your money. Learn as much about the Internet and what you want to do as you can and get professional advice all along the way from the genuine, honourable businesses, who are quite happy to put their name on their work and openly provide their true business address on their Web sites. Organisations like the International Association for Professionalism Online (IAPO) can help

promote good practice online and identify the good guys. Nevertheless, always check out their claims. Get second opinions. Don't necessarily believe what they say: you want verifiable proof, not unrealistic or over-inflated dreamscapes!

Doing business on the Net, compared to that of a "conventional" offline business, can be easier in some ways and more complex in other aspects. Most importantly, Internet business requires a different way of thinking. Many kinds of existing businesses can save money, make more sales and find new customers through using the Internet. As mobile phone and television technology continue to merge with the Internet, other new methods will probably emerge to help even the most unlikely types of business.

Key point: however, just because the Internet has a global reach it doesn't mean you can't use it for creating and servicing local or regional customers! Until recently, many businesses were using the Internet in various ways to "support" their more traditional methods of doing business. For example, a business might create a basic Web site simply to outline what they do and install some advertisements.

As the great benefits and potential of the Internet are understood better, all kinds of businesses are now looking at ways in which they can really use the Net to forward their aims more pro-actively, or risk losing business or being beaten to the finishing line by their competitors. As the Internet and television merge, for small businesses especially the value of the Net is enormous. Before long, even small businesses will run television-like advertisements for a fraction of the cost of current television ads! This single fact has enormous implications for business of all sizes but especially larger organisations who may suddenly find they have many more competitors.

Drawing up an Internet battle plan

The great benefit of the Internet – its huge size and far reach – can also be a drawback for new Web sites: no one knows you're on the Net unless they know you exist. Therefore, once your business Web site is up and running, you'll need to create and implement a launch plan AND an on-going promotion plan. Consider the following guidelines to help you get started:

1. Get a "true" domain name, not one created from an Internet Service Provider. For example: "www.companyname.com" is better than

www.internetserviceprovider.com/~companyname.com or something similar. Alternatively, you could consider a domain name that relates to your industry sector. For example: www.InternetTIPS.com, www.toys.com, www.holidays.com, www.ineasysteps.com and so on – but be quick: many of the good domain names are going fast.

2. Create a compelling, carefully crafted press release about your new site and use it like crazy to promote your new site.

3. Let all your staff, customers, suppliers and all other contacts know about your new Web site. Invite them to visit.

4. Contact other key Web sites that are connected with your industry or which could benefit your business and ask these Web sites if they will provide a link to your site. Keep adding reciprocal links.

5. Offer special promotional deals to encourage early Web sales.

6. Provide interesting competitions and quizzes to stimulate interest. Provide compelling prizes.

7. Consider having an article written for your local or regional newspaper. Ideally, link it to a human interest angle: editors are always looking for good, interesting and compelling material.

8. Make sure each and every page has a proper title, META description and appropriate META tags (see page 401 for more information).

9. Ensure your Web pages are "tuned" to the search engines. Consider recruiting a skilled Internet marketing person or company to ensure your Web pages are search engine-friendly to maximise placement.

10. Register your Web site with 10 – 20 of the most popular search engines and directories (see "Promoting your Web site", page 405).

11. Make a special and careful effort to get listed in Yahoo.com or Yahoo.co.uk, etc. Key point: Yahoo especially may become an important source of new business for you.

12. Check out other possible directories and search engines on the Web that might be useful to you. Use the search engines to get started.
13. About every month, resubmit your Web details to the most important search engines and directories.
14. Keep looking for and considering new ways to promote your business – however wacky at first, at least regularly consider new ideas.

The benefits of using the Net for business

On the Net, you can reduce costs, save time and improve efficiency. If you're already in business currently without a Web site and wondering whether you could benefit from a Web site, the answer is probably yes. Most businesses have the potential to gain income with a Web site, but some may need to think beyond how they currently get business to really make gains. This may mean completely rethinking the way you currently operate.

With a little imagination, vision, determination and a willingness to think outside of the normal ways of doing things, the Internet can provide incredible, highly profitable opportunities for earning money. Play with ideas – however crazy they might seem at first, then seek ways to test these ideas out cheaply on the Internet. A little unconventional groundwork may set you on course to become another Internet millionaire.

Joint venturing for extra income: an example

Lots of possibilities exist for earning extra income from the Web. To illustrate, imagine a window cleaning business – at first glance, perhaps one of the most unlikely candidates for a Web site. But wait: a window cleaner visits a range of houses every day. The obvious area of interest is, well, windows – or is that all? What if our window cleaner were to form a joint-venture business relationship with, say, a local, regional or even a national:

- Double-glazing company.
- Curtain manufacturer or retailer.
- Builder and repairer.
- Burglar alarm company.

And so on.

Window cleaners often develop friendly first-name relationships with their customers – providing a perfect opportunity to help solve all sorts of problems besides dirty windows. Every day, houses are burgled, windows break – or need replacing. Our window cleaner suggests to their customer a carefully selected solution and provides a name, a Web link (from his Web site) and enters the customer's contact details.

The joint venture company now has a possible new customer with a problem for which they can provide a quick and easy solution – if they're clued-up and ready to act swiftly. If they're shrewd, their representative contacts the customer to provide a competitive price. If the sale is successful, our window cleaner earns, say, 10% - 40% commission for bringing the sale to the joint-venture company – who now have a new customer on their list and may have further opportunities to sell further goods and services in the future.

Or if the problem is not urgent, our clever window cleaner can offer to contact the company directly from his own Web site in his own time – remember the Web operates 24 hours/day, so he can complete these kinds of tasks in 10 minutes or thereabouts while relaxing at home. He simply logs on to his Web site using his computer or WebTV and clicks the appropriate link placed on his Web site, enters the customer's details and sends the information to one of his joint venture partners. Finished!

Forming these kinds of business relationships can provide a win-win solution for all involved:

- Our window cleaner's customer can get a fast, reliable solution to a problem or potential problem.
- During the period of a year, our window cleaner could perhaps create 25% or extra income for a small amount of effort and a tiny cost – if any (most Internet Service Providers now provide Web space free of charge). How much extra he earns depends on the results he creates and the agreements he has with those companies involved; so he could earn much more or less than the example percentage above – he may even discover new interests and develop highly profitable new skills that might lead to an entirely new and different full-time job as a result.
- Joint venture companies gain more business and new customers.

Some shrewd companies may be prepared to pay higher initial commissions and so perhaps make little profit on this first sale in the knowledge that a new customer has been identified and that future opportunities can recover their profit they need many times over.

Highly profitable joint venture ideas can be applied to almost any business with a little imagination. Any individual, self-employed or employed, can use joint venture methods combined with a Web site to provide extra income. However, do remember to discuss any employment status changes with your income tax office.

Why juggling is great for businesses too!

What's a circus juggler got to do with an Internet business? Answer: to be successful, every Internet business must also juggle several key tasks continuously:

- Communication: sounds obvious, doesn't it. Communication for most businesses on the Internet is not yet done face to face; therefore, it's important that any possible misunderstandings are kept to a minimum. Currently, text through email and Web pages is the main driving force of most Internet businesses, or at least provides a stepping-stone from which phone, fax and face-to-face communication can occur later. Key point: keep it simple, clear and be up-front.

- Marketing: the right kind of marketing for the Internet is absolutely crucial. The Net is huge and more new competitors are coming online and setting up their stall every day. An Internet business needs to inform and persuade customers to buy from them in preference to other similar organisations. Find your uniqueness and build on it.

- Sell goods and/or services: persuading a customer to buy is only one essential part of a transaction. Next, you need to ensure that the order is fulfilled and that you receive payment. Central to almost every sale on the Internet is a slick-running e-commerce Web site "machine."

Internet domain names for your business

To recap, remember an Internet domain name is essentially a name for a Web site, for example: InternetTIPS.com or names123.co.uk. Although you can often use free Web space that comes with many email accounts to establish a business, just think about this for a moment. Imagine including the following kind of Web address on all your business stationery and advertising:

http://www.internetserviceprovider/~baustin/index.html

The question is, are these types of domain names too long and unwieldy? Businesses need to be taken seriously if they're to thrive on the Web. Therefore, if you plan to do serious business on the Internet, the best option is to get your own "true" domain name. So just what is a "true" domain name? Well, let's return to the imaginary examples above, using my own name. Here's what I would need to do to create a true domain for a commercial business:

- Use http://www.baustin.com if I wanted to use my own name and do business internationally.
- Or use http://www.baustin.co.uk if I preferred to be identified as a UK-based company.

Remember also, often the best choice for business is not necessarily your own name, the name of your company or organisation. Imagine, if someone wants to buy some books and decide to see what's available on the Net. Of the following two domain names, which do you think is the most memorable:

- http://www.johndoe.co.uk
  (in our imaginary example: John Doe owns a bookshop)
- http://www.books.com

Also in relation to search engine listings, www.books.com contains the single most essential keyword that most users would enter into the search engines when looking for books. So www.books.com in this example, would probably get listed much higher up in the search listings, compared to www.johndoe.co.uk. However remember, the Internet is full of surprises.

Most current Web browsers default to .com domain names. So for example, if someone searching for a domain name, entered "ineasysteps" (without the quotes), the Web browser assumes that we mean "ineasysteps.com". What this means is that currently ".com" is probably the best choice for businesses that want to create a serious international presence on the Internet.

When writing domain names on business stationery, etc., if you prefer you can use capitals to help make a domain name easier to read or for emphasis. For example, http://www.InternetTIPS.com is arguably easier to read and has more 'punch' than http://www.internettips.com.

Consider www.amazon.com – a well-established brand name for books and now other products too. Hardly a name that you might naturally associate with books, yet the key point here is that Amazon spend many millions of dollars promoting their brand name, so that in time we the public immediately associate the name with books on the Internet. Result: successful branding.

Registering your domain name

Domain names, like business names, need to be registered through domain naming authorities. For example:

- Network Solutions (USA): http://www.networksolutions.com/
- Register.com (USA): http://www.register.com/ or
- Nominet (UK): http://www.nic.co.uk/

If, on the other hand, someone else has already registered "baustin.com" or "baustin.co.uk" then I might have to look for another alternative. For example,

I might try www.brianaustin.co.uk Alternatively, I could offer to buy the domain I really want from the current owner. See pages 413 - 414 for a list of established organisations around the world from which you can find, check and register domain names.

Individual countries may have their own domain naming authority so certainly check out what's available in your own country. Often the procedure for registering and transferring a domain name is simpler when dealing with an organisation based within your own country. However, check the relevant facts: you may still save money by buying direct from the USA.

If you buy a domain name, make sure you register yourself as the "Administrative and Billing Contact" — not any other organisation like your Internet Service Provider or Web host. Why? Because if you sell or transfer ownership of the domain name, there is little doubt over the "ownership" of the domain and the transfer to the new owner should be completed more quickly.

Business Web hosting with streaming content

For Internet businesses, a Web site is the online equivalent of an office building, a retail shop, a warehouse, a factory, and so on. Therefore, take extreme care in choosing an organisation to host your Web site. Usually, this means you get what your pay for. The biggest threat for any Web business is downtime: if at any time, your Web host's Web servers are not "live", your Web "shop" is not open for business and you're then essentially invisible to customers. Also, with the ever-growing merger between the computers, the

Internet and television, consider seeking a Web host that allows you to include streaming multimedia files (sound and video clips) on your Web site at no extra charge. One forward-thinking company, http://www.tripod.com/ provides ShowMotion, a program in which you can combine video clips, photos, scanned images, with voiceovers you provide to make superb TV-like Web presentations – and all for free!

If you want professional video quality, take a look at http://www.wbcimaging.com – an Internet company taking an unusual approach in employing television engineers to look at the best ways to make video available on the Internet. We could soon

see some amazing developments from this organisation. To get a real idea of what can be achieved with a superb approach to interactive multimedia Web design, visit: http://www.eye4u.com/ See page 411 for a list of well established Web hosting companies from around the world.

Creating a profitable e-commerce Web site

E-commerce is simply about buying and selling over the Internet. An e-commerce Web site allows a business to accept payment online 24 hours a day! And the best e-commerce Web sites enable goods and services to be paid for using a variety of payment choices including the option to accept payment by credit card using a secure system. So let's take a closer look at the business of e-commerce.

Taking key decisions

To establish an effective, profitable and smooth-running e-commerce Web site, essentially you need to make key decisions in five main areas:

- Create a detailed start-up plan and an ongoing plan. From the outset, before establishing your working methods, imagine what a transaction feels like from your customers' viewpoint, then build everything to match and exceed their expectations.
- Decide whether you're going to use an e-commerce-compatible Internet Service Provider or establish your own e-commerce Internet server (most expensive option: see later).
- Make decisions about computer hardware and which operating system to use. Choices here will affect the overall cost and the type of skills you'll need to gain access.

- Decide on the Web site design and creation software you want to use (see also page 341) and how to gain access to the necessary technical skills for the kind of Web design you want.
- Establish your e-commerce components necessary to display a products/services catalogue and to provide secure shopping cart software to automatically process online payments 24 hours/day.

A low-cost way to start making money on the Net

However, you may not even need to perform all of the steps above in detail to start making money on the Internet. Here's one low-cost strategy idea. First register a dot.com domain name through a company like: http://www.freeparking.co.uk who allow you to "park" a domain name that you register through them on their servers.

Next create a Web site on topics that interest you and which you know something about – it's my guess that almost everyone knows more about a topic, a hobby, or an interest, than perhaps at first they may realise. Take some time to write down what you know and build this up in stages. Publish this information in a Web site to the free Web space that is usually provided by most Internet Service Providers. Then set up the domain name you registered earlier so that it points to your Web site. Visitors then only see a more realistic domain name like http://www.TryUntil.com instead of something like: http://www.internetprovider.com/~home-pages/jdoe/index.htm/

Next, contact an existing free e-commerce store provider like http://www.vstore.com/ Set up your store and link it to your Web site – then, to the visitor, all components seem part of the same site. Your free store provider handles all the sales and ships the goods while you concentrate on attracting customers and accepting settlement cheques regularly – hard but someone has to do it! Once you're up and running, promote your Web site to the search engines – http://www.submit-it.com can help here – and keep promoting!

Sounds simple, doesn't it, but in practice you'll need to put in time and effort. Nevertheless, if you're game to get started, why not check out the Web sites listed and discover the details for yourself?

Building trust and accepting orders

For any business wanting to accept money online for goods and services, the most basic question in the mind of any new prospective customer is: "Can I trust these people with my money?" The most effective way to meet this need

Normal email is not encrypted so may not be suitable for sending and receiving credit card details. However, one simple way to improve security – providing your customer agrees – is to split credit card details between two separate normal email messages. Send the first half of a credit card number and the first half of the expiry date in one email. Then send the remaining information in another email. However, remember this is not a secure system, just one quick option that may be appropriate for you.

and overcome this natural barrier to sales is for the e-tailer to be seen to be doing everything in their power to demonstrate genuine trust and integrity.

One of the most basic yet essential steps to this end is to provide a secure way for your customers to leave their credit card details while online and paying for goods and services. Also, on the Internet, lots of people have strong opinions on how they might want to pay for things and the easier you make the payment process, the more business you're likely to do. Consider providing a range of different payment and delivery options. For example, in addition to payment online by credit card, consider payment by debit card, cheque and banker's draft and look at other options: email, phone, fax, postal mail – affectionately known as snail mail – and even FTP delivery may be suitable especially for some electronic products like ebooks and downloadable software.

If you accept payment by cheque or banker's draft, let customers know at the time of ordering that goods are not sent until payment has cleared. Tell your customer what is happening at every stage of the transaction. Respond to questions quickly. Misunderstandings often result simply from people jumping to the wrong conclusions when they don't hear from you.

Also, display a Terms of Business page so customers always have easy access to your transaction rules (page 403) and provide a Privacy page (page 403) to explain how you use information they provide. Make these pages clear and simple to understand without any hint of double meaning. Let's examine these various payment options in a little more detail:

Email: although email is available to every Internet user, often it's not the easiest method for all customers to use and is prone to error – affecting your profits. For you to receive an order, a customer has to enter several pieces of vital information plus send the order to the correct email address. A mistake made at any stage could lose the order. Therefore, if you accept email orders, make the email ordering process automatic where possible. Ideally, ensure that users only need enter the order details they want; make absolutely sure that they always get the right email address.

Web forms: probably the best way to currently accept online orders. A Web order form can be set up so that it contains all the information needed to fulfil an order and process the payment – which is available only on a

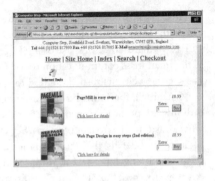

secure connection. Customers prefer this approach as their credit card details can be protected. Offering secure payment by credit card is, I believe, essential nowadays – an even slightly hesitant Internet buyer can be gone with a single mouse click, especially if they even pick up the slightest hint that you care more about getting the order than genuinely meeting their needs.

Usually, the best approach lists the items/prices a customer wants on a form; your customer can then click a box next to each item, to place a tick or a quantity in the box. The e-commerce software calculates the cost, adding any handling, postage and sales tax to the total value of the order. A customer can then examine the final amount required, choose their preferred payment method and click the Submit button, or equivalent, to order the goods.

Once an order is received, many e-tailers set up an autoresponder system whereby an email receipt acknowledgement and "thank you for your order" message is sent back to the purchaser's email address often within minutes. See page 404 for more information on using autoresponders. However always remember, not everyone can use Web forms or may wish to, so providing a range of ordering methods will almost certainly improve sales.

Phone: some customers will not order unless they can talk to a person. Often, the Internet can appear isolating whereas a real, live human is reassuring.

Fax: in many countries, use of the Internet and email is now replacing fax as the main mass communication tool. Nevertheless, fax is quick and is seen as a secure, well-established method to order products.

Postal mail: for online businesses, postal mail is the least preferred way of ordering: it's prone to error and can take the longest time to implement. Here's why: a customer has to identify what they want, print an order form, find a pen, fill in contact details, fill in payment details, find an envelope, place the order form in the envelope, seal it, find a stamp, leave their house and take the envelope to a post box. The previous list may seem trivial, but an interruption in any one of those stages can prevent your order from being sent.

Evaluating your e-commerce Web hosting options

To establish a Web site, first you need access to Web space and fast, reliable access to the Internet. Two main options are available:

- Use a leased line: this option provides a semi-permanent connection to the Internet so you have most control of your Web operation. Leased lines are currently the most expensive Internet access solution costing thousands of pounds each year, and so are more likely to be appropriate for mid- to large-sized companies and organisations who want absolute tight control of their Web presence. You'll need at least one powerful computer – preferably two running side-by-side, so if one fails the other takes over – on which to create, hold and manage all the Web information you install on it – this is your Web server. You'll also have to consider server maintenance costs and what is probably the largest single cost: highly skilled Web designers and programmers to run your Web empire. Solution: have a thick wad of currency at your disposal!

- Rent Web space from a Web host: lots of companies provide Web space for hire. You can rent as much Web space as you think you'll need and buy more, if you need it. Generally, the more space you rent, the cheaper the overall cost. Some Web hosts even provide basic pre-designed pages that you might want to use; others charge extra for these services. Check a range of different companies before deciding. Compare prices: the cheapest are not necessarily the worst and the most expensive may not necessarily guarantee you the best value for your money. Perhaps most importantly, if you've not had a Web host before, ask to see genuine testimonials before committing your hard earned cash!

At the time of writing this book, several established Internet Access Providers started offering low-cost and possibly free 24-hour/7-days a week Internet access. More competitors are expected to offer similar packages in the coming months. Therefore, soon lots more people will probably be getting hooked up to the Net and prices for creating and hosting business Web sites may also change. Key point: stay informed and shop around to save money.

Do check that low-cost and free Internet access packages do apply to businesses. A small business owner may be able to sign up as a private individual user if their business is operated from a home office and so save money. Check the subscription small print.

Accepting online credit card payments

A secure server is just another name for a powerful computer that protects a customer's credit card details while they make a purchase online. Customers can easily identify a payment page that uses a secure server: a closed padlock picture (small icon) is shown somewhere in the browser window – plus the Web address box contains "https://" rather than "http://" – the added "s" is included to show that the site is secure.

Without doubt, offering a secure server is essential for any serious Web business. It's probably the most secure way to properly protect your customers' private information while online. The Web pages that you use to accept and process credit card details and display other private information should always be secure Web pages. Why? These pages use functions built in to current browsers like Internet Explorer and Netscape Navigator to create an encrypted transaction that is extremely difficult to break.

So much research and development has gone into devising safe, secure online payment methods, that a properly set up secure online payment system can now be more secure than simply providing credit card details over the phone. Nevertheless, if considering establishing a Web business, you should always get professional advice especially on the security and liability aspects.

Even though a credit card payment may be "cleared OK" by your bank, the order could still be bogus. This may mean that after you have sent the goods, a few weeks later the credit card clearing bank may find that payment is not honoured and refuse to credit you as the Internet merchant with the value of that order. The Internet is creating conditions for a new breed of fraudster. Orders from certain names, addresses and even countries may be suspect. Examine this aspect carefully. Speak to your bank and find out how bogus orders affect you. Learn as much about the topic as you can to minimise your losses. Shrewd e-tailers now also share information on fraudsters.

A quick & simple 24-hour maximum security payment and ordering system

NetBanx at http://www.netbanx.com/ can help to provide a unique secure payment system. Here's how it works. All the product information and order details can be kept at your Web host. When the customer is ready to make payment, after clicking the "Buy" button or equivalent, the e-commerce software invisibly sends the customer to your special secure pages stored at the NetBanx secure computers where the payment is actually processed. On completion a few seconds later, the customer is returned to your Web site "Thank you for your order" page and links to the other pages.

The big benefit of this system is that at no time do you as the e-tailer hold any customer's credit card details: that information is held and processed at the highly secure NetBanx servers. So if hackers were ever to "break" into your Web host's computers, no credit card details would be available for them to steal. Therefore, at no time should you be held responsible for "not adequately protecting" your customer's credit card information. The chances of anyone hacking into highly secure computers like NetBanx are very slim. Although a superb maximum-security approach, NetBanx do charge a small fee on each transaction, so your card processing costs will be a little higher.

Choosing your shopping cart software

To display a range of products, shopping cart cataloguing software is available from a range of suppliers. You can set up your e-commerce Web site with a minimum of fuss and complexity. For example: Actinic Catalog is just one of a range of similar easy-to-use software products developed so businesses of all sizes won't need to hire expensive Web experts, designers or programmers for most or perhaps even all of their Web site development.

Actinic lets you set up a Web site catalog of products/services so that customers can easily browse, make their selections and pay online. Actinic handles orders, subscriptions and bookings logically and simply. Visit: http://www.actinic.co.uk/ or http://www.actinic.com/ (for international users).

Another popular alternative is Shop@ssistant Classic available from the Floyd Consultancy at http://www.floyd.co.uk which can integrate easily with a secure Payment Service Provider (PSP) like NetBanx introduced previously to process transactions. NetBanx (http://www.netbanx.com/) also provide a "bureau" option that is ideal for anyone who is just starting out in business or who does not already have a merchant account to accept credit card payments.

Other established Payment Service Providers include:

- Datacash: http://www.datacash.com/
- WorldPay: http://www.sitename.com/
- SecPay: http://www.secpay.com/

Alternatively, you could consider using built-in e-commerce components from a third-party provider like iCat at: http://www.icat.com/ As shopping cart software is so important, it's worth spending some time examining a range of options and how each links to the payment facility you want to identify as the best choice for you. Then make sure you allow enough training time to learn how to set up and get the best use from your shopping cart software.

Setting up an advance payment option system

Here's an order processing/payment method that, until the more widespread use of secure Web pages, was popular for customers who place regular orders, and which may still work for you. You direct your customer to a special Web form page that automatically allocates each new customer a unique reference number. Your customer then completes the form once only, providing essential contact details and so on. The customer then telephones and provides their credit card details or faxes the information. Now, every time your customer makes an order on the Web, they need only provide their no-risk unique reference number. As the seller, you can then ensure payment is made from the credit card details recorded previously before sending the goods.

On your Terms of Business page, if you provide a purchase ordering system, clearly state that purchase orders are not valid until adequate credit references have been provided and checked.

Handling purchase orders

If you plan to do online business with government departments, some larger companies and organisations, expect to be asked whether you provide a purchase order system. Most currently will not pay online. So decide whether you want to work with purchase orders and under what conditions.

Fulfilling orders

Once you've sweated blood and tears to establish a superb smooth running online payment system, people actually want the goods they've paid for – can you believe it? We consumers are not really interested in how much effort a

Web business has put into their online service, we just want the product – and preferably yesterday Key point: the sale isn't actually made until your customer has the goods AND is satisfied. This all feeds back to the earlier paragraphs on building trust and positive relationships with your customers.

Building your follow-up

Once a customer has bought something from you successfully first time on the Web and is pleased with how the operation went – that is, no problems – you have overcome a major hurdle when presenting future offers: they now trust you – at least for one more time. On the Internet, this is big medicine for businesses. Through personalised email communications, you can keep your best offers for those customers who have demonstrated loyalty and have bought from you in the past; why not? And with the right direct marketing approach, both parties can benefit from your online ingenuity.

However, don't ever forget that your customer can be gone forever with a single mouse click. This is the "flip-side": the amazing power of the Web that can bring so many benefits to Web business can also work against you like the plague. If you simply make a mistake on the Web, often the best approach is simply to own up and be seen to be doing all you can to correct the problem as soon as possible – then provide something extra to say sorry.

Here's a true story. A gift was ordered from a small Web store. However, a mistake occurred and the gift never arrived in time. After contacting the store, a genuine apology followed and the problem was soon put right. A couple of days later, a beautiful bunch of flowers arrived – and they already knew about any potential pollen allergies: an "actioned" apology. What a wonderful surprise and something that is not easily forgotten. Most people are reasonable and understand that mistakes occur sometimes. It's what happens afterwards that can often help determine the success of an Internet business.

Making money on the Internet

Like the Klondike and other gold fields of the 19th Century, the brave new frontier of the Internet has attracted its fair share of media hype, exaggerated claims and indeed true-life stories of amazing success! However, many who expected to make a lot of money fast on the Internet are coming away disappointed or worse still, heavily in debt. Some current statistics suggest that as many as 95% of Web business are not yet making a profit. In time, as the Internet and television merge, this will probably change. Nevertheless, there are ways to maximise your chances now.

The most important guideline

For anyone set on making a profitable living on the Internet, I suggest the first and most important point to make is that you can't make money on the Internet. Yes, you did read that correctly; it's not possible to make money from the Internet! Why? Because the Net is nothing more than a bunch of computers and other electronic devices connected together. However, the important point to realise is that you can make money from the people who use the Internet, if you provide what they want in the right way. I'm not just playing with words here, but the point I want to get across is that if you want to make money on the Net, remember that you're dealing with lots of different people who may live in many different countries, from different cultures, who have a variety of different opinions, feelings, likes and dislikes. Key point: treat your visitors and customers like gold (most don't)!

Harnessing the power of email

Try an experiment: take a few hours off and visit your local stores. Watch how people act when buying; what they like, what seems to work for them and what doesn't. Then you can "tune" your Web site into what people want.

Always remember, individual people buy products and services, not some faceless Internet. The Internet is just another convenient but powerful way to bring buyer and seller together. If you can build up a trusting relationship with customers, providing you don't betray their trust, ever, you can always contact them again through email in the future with your latest special deals.

Compare that to a conventional shop. Of course a high street store can record a customer's contact details, but sending out direct mail offers using the conventional mail system can be very expensive – and the results may not even cover the costs. The cost of email however is low or simply insignificant, so the same offers can be made for a fraction of the cost of conventional mail. If your offer doesn't bring as many sales as you hope, with email you've minimised your losses – and hopefully learned some valuable lessons.

Key point: Internet businesses and existing conventional high street businesses would do well to remember the power of email – a system that is already merging with mobile phones, WAP phones and television.

Your four paths to profit

So let's look at the four main ways in which you can directly make money on the Net. Whatever option you choose, always learn as much as you can about what you're getting involved in and don't just take someone else's word – me included. Do you own research. You can:

- Use intermediaries on the Internet to sell items or products. For example: online share dealing comes under this category, or selling an item through an online auction. Although this approach may seem like a stop-go approach to making money on the Net, some shrewd individuals are now earning their living full-time buying and selling stocks, shares, bonds and other products and services!

- Sell products and services on behalf of someone else in return for a commission payment: usually, you can earn anything from 10%-75% of the value of a sale. In this role, you're acting as an affiliate. Lots of affiliate programs are available on the Internet, for example, see: http://www.associateprograms.com/

There's little risk to you and this option can provide a low-cost way to get started making money on the Net. It's possible to earn a full-time living simply through low-cost email and Web marketing as an affiliate. However, you earn only by results – the more you sell, the more you earn. You may not earn a significant income until you have many sales or have built up an "active" email list: this all takes time – and you may need to create a free ezine to draw continual and growing interest.

- Join a Multi-level Marketing (MLM) scheme: to recruit other members who in turn also recruit other members. All members may also sell products or services of some kind and you can earn money for each member than signs up "under you", and perhaps a share of the profits from sales of other products or services too. This option can offer a low-cost way to get started. Once you've built up an active group, more money can flow in at a faster rate. However, this route probably demands a lot hard work and lots of email marketing effort, patience and incredible persistence to build an "active" group. Do not expect quick results; consider planning for the long term. Also, check for possible scams and dodgy companies. For example, see: http://www.scambusters.com/

- Set up your own Internet business from scratch: here, you take all the risk, have to perform all the marketing and support work and can capture all the profits. Another option that many who choose this route eventually consider is to set up your own affiliate program so that you can recruit others who can help build your business. This option is probably the best choice for serious Internet entrepreneurs, but also needs careful planning just like any other business opportunity. Lots of free and low cost help is available, for example, take a look at the superb WebHead Central: http://www.webheadcentral.com/

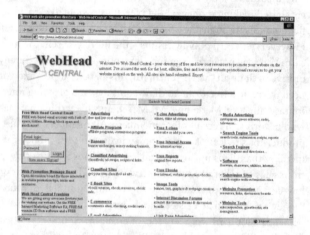

Creating your own profitable Internet business

If you decide to go the last mentioned route, the well known successful Internet entrepreneur, J Nicholas Schmidt from the Profitstream Corporation http://www.profitstream.com/ suggests there are 7 routes or "profitstreams" that if used properly can ensure your success on the Internet:

- Start your own free ezine with fresh content.
- Provide a discussion forum to encourage problem discussion/resolution.
- Install tools to create online events to create fresh interest.
- Create an effective online advertising strategy and implement it consistently.
- Ensure your Web site includes a trustworthy online shopping cart payment system and make the payment system reliable and easy to use.
- Set up your own affiliate system in which you pay others to sell your products and services.
- Set up joint ventures and co-ops with other parties.

Key point: the Internet allows you to test an idea for a relatively low cost. Therefore, when you try out a promotion, always measure and record the response. Also, check your Web statistics before and after running a promotion. Many Web hosts now provide these Web statistics and visitor information for free (or you can use free tools). In this way, you can make comparisons and modifications to arrive at the best ways to promote any product or service.

Using strategic Web forms

Key information about your customer is gold for Internet businesses. Any extra information that you can convince your customer to provide about them can help you put together offers that are finely tuned to their expectations and are therefore more likely to be successful! Easy to complete strategically designed Web forms can help you get the key information you need. So how do you create clever Web forms? Answer: ask the right questions – and provide the necessary incentives to get those answers. Prizes, competitions, draws, etc., can all help – but time spent thinking up entirely new ways usually pays off too. With free tools from generous sources like: http://www.response-o-matic.com/ you don't even need to know anything about the tricky technical aspects.

Some popular affiliate programs

Included in the following paragraphs are a few carefully selected affiliate programs, with their Web links, that I promote to help my friends, colleagues and customers to earn income from the Internet. You can discover more about each program simply by going online, copying the relevant Web link you want below into your browser Address box and clicking the ENTER key.

A combination of several key affiliate programs can in time, with regular and effective email promotion, provide a full-time income! Once you're up and running and creating new customers, every month (or payment period), you receive your commission cheque; some may pay in US dollars, others pay in the currency of your country: check these details with each affiliate program. Also, the best affiliate programs allow you to check your earnings at any time online using a password protected Web page:

1. Corey Rudl's Internet Marketing Center: Corey Rudl is a well-known and respected Internet marketer who earns millions of dollars annually. With this opportunity, he provides a comprehensive Internet marketing course that clearly explains how to market a business on the Internet successfully: http://www.marketingtips.com/t.cgi/12939/

2. Jim Daniels Internet marketing resources: just a few years ago, US-based entrepreneur Daniels was a TV engineer in a job he didn't much care for. So he learnt how to set up a Web site, wrote a best-selling book, gradually started selling a carefully selected range of other related products and services – and made a fortune – and still gives a lot of information away free of charge: http://www.bizweb2000.com/d3665.htm

3. Nothing But Net: Michael Cambell, working out of his parents' basement, created US $750,000 in Internet revenues using almost no advertising costs and using key free sources on the Internet and lots of know-how. Now he's telling how he did it in an a superb ebook:
http://activemarketplace.com/w.cgi?net-6694

4. AllAdvantage program: here's a nice surprise – get paid for doing what you probably already do anyway: simply use the Web! You can click a link like the one below to download a viewbar that sits at the bottom of your computer screen. I use it regularly, so whenever I'm on the Web, I'm earning money. How? While your using the Web in the normal way, small advertisements pop up on to the viewbar. However, whether or not you choose to click on an advert and follow it up, you still get paid simply for viewing. Superb:
http://uk.alladvantage.com/home.asp?refid=EVV508

5. Corey Rudl's Internet Marketing Center Associates Program: this program simply enables you to sell the entire program number 1 listed above.
http://www.marketingtips.com/sr/t.x/12939/

Top 10 Internet business success tips

1. If you already have an existing business and doing business on your Web site is a new option, decide how you're going to combine order taking and payment options into your existing business structure.

2. Create an orders machine: a set of procedures for taking orders, receiving and clearing payment, sending a receipt, fulfilling orders and for dealing with delays, that works the same way every time automatically – and which ideally does not need you to be on hand constantly: you can run your business, instead of letting it run you.

3. Assign responsibility to someone for running the system in Step 2.

4. Get to know your visitors and customers as individuals.

5. Aim to build trust; see the long term picture and avoid a short-term gains mentality – customers can pick up on this easily and be gone for ever in a single mouse click.

6. Look for ways to give genuine value. Be honest and up front.

7. Help your visitors and customers achieve what they're seeking quickly and easily by visiting your Web site.

8. Thank visitors for visiting and customers for buying from you. As far as possible, use one-to-one email communications.

http://www.ideasiteforbusiness.com/ideamenu.htm

9. Always remember that the Internet is the first commercial system in he entire history of human race in which the customer is in full control – if they don't like what they see, they're gone! If they don't like the way they're treated, they're gone – and they'll tell their friends, colleagues and acquaintances all about any bad experiences. So instead of losing one customer, you may lose 50 or 100 and not even know about it – until it's too late.

10. For successful Internet businesses, the rewards can be enormous. But becoming successful on the Net may mean completely re-thinking how you do business. Some shrewd entrepreneurs are actually changing their entire businesses to match the Internet way of doing things. Perhaps they've discovered something interesting...

Internet marketing
secrets revealed

Slick advertising, successful selling and fulfilling orders created through the Internet are achieved through shrewd Internet marketing. The more you learn about doing business on the Net, try out your ideas and measure the results, the better you become at it, the more sales you'll achieve. It's that simple.

Developing an Internet marketing plan

For business users or anyone who wants to make money on the Internet, having a carefully considered marketing plan is crucial for your success. But just as important is the business of carrying out the action steps in your plan, measuring the results, and adapting your plan if necessary as your Web site develops. Most importantly: don't give up too soon. Persist, persevere and learn from your mistakes. Everybody else who is ever successful has made many mistakes; the difference is, they learn from them, adapt, and usually keep going a little further just beyond the point where most people give up.

Web page titles, descriptions and special keywords

Title: the title of a Web page is what appears in the browser window Title bar when you access a Web page. The Web page title is absolutely essential for helping to get a higher ranking in search engines and directories. Make sure every page in your Web site has a title that is short, snappy and relevant to the Page it represents. You can easily create titles in your Web design software or directly in HTML using the <TITLE></TITLE> tag pair. Consider this imaginary title: "Welcome to gardening.com". It contains 24 characters including spaces (excluding quotes, included here for clarity). This title is short, snappy but doesn't include a key benefit. Perhaps a better title could be: "Access free gardening tips and great value gardening supplies". This version is longer with 61 characters including spaces but it's more meaningful and includes two benefits. Make sure your title fulfils the following conditions: (1) it's meaningful, (2) it contains your number 1 keyword (see below) but which is not the first word in your title, (3) it describes your Unique Selling Proposition (USP) – shows why someone should choose or

buy from you above anyone else. (4) it's (ideally) about 50 - 70 characters long, including spaces if possible.

META tags: allow you to include special extra information about a Web page that is normally invisible to visitors but which can nevertheless be seen by browsers and search engines. Lots of different META tags are available, but here we'll examine the two most important ones: the Keyword tag and Description tag. META tags are similar to HTML tags, except you place all META tags between the <HEAD> and </HEAD> HTML tags in your Web pages. You can manually place META tags in each of your Web pages or use the easy commands often available in Web design software packages. To form a better picture of the Keyword META tag, here's the basic structure:

<META name="keywords" content="widgets, Widget user guide">

The META Description tag: In the "content" section of the description META tag, you simply enter a carefully constructed and brief description of the Web page/site; consider the guidelines below. Here's the basic structure of the Description META tag:

<META name="description" content="Yourname.com's guide to designing your own Widgets!"> You can learn more about the art of creating keywords in "Web Page Design in easy steps" (http://www.ineasysteps.com).

Displaying a Terms of Business Web page

For businesses, a Terms of Business page is essential to help avoid problems and disputes later and may be a legal requirement in some countries. Check out the relevant business regulations in your country. Even a simple list outlining your business terms may be adequate for most small businesses.

If your Internet business has various methods of payment for goods and services, make payment conditions absolutely clear. For example: most people need to make clear to buyers that ownership of goods and services only occurs after full payment has been cleared.

Creating a Privacy Web page

As many people on the Internet receive lots of email messages they don't ask for – commonly called spamming – privacy is currently a hot topic on the Internet. You can help gain the trust of visitors by stating clearly and honestly how information you collect online is used. You can create your own text for a "Privacy page" or you could simply use one of the several online wizards available. One superb and thorough template to consider is the TRUSTe Wizard currently available free of charge at http://www.truste.org/wizard/

Working with Web banner adverts

Web banner adverts are those rectangular boxes that occupy the top and bottom of some Web pages – plus you'll often see miniature versions in the form of clickable "buttons." If you have a sufficient number of regular visitors to your Web site, you can make extra money by including banner adverts on your pages – however, usually they're best placed at the bottom of a page if you want visitors to read the main page text first (don't shoot yourself in the foot).

Adding a discussion forum

Sometimes called a discussion/bulletin board, a discussion forum enables you to communicate directly with people who are interested in your Web site theme. People can ask questions, get free advice and solutions to problems that might otherwise take a longer time to solve. Many organisations on the Web provide discussion forum services but first discuss options with your own Internet Service Provider. Or you can consider some of the free options – for example: http://www.network54.com/

Traditional and smart autoresponders

On the Web, people are impatient and first impressions count. Businesses especially need to respond quickly and efficiently to enquiries. One answer: autoresponders, one of the most powerful Web tools available. An autoresponder (or infobot) is an automated email-type fax back system. When someone sends an email to a Web address you create, your autoresponder replies automatically and usually within seconds or minutes. Working 24 hours a day even when your PC is switched off, an autoresponder sends your marketing, product or service information to potentially tens of thousands of people around the world. Autoresponders can also be set up for lots of different purposes. "Smart" autoresponder systems are now also available. These can be set to follow up on existing autoresponders several times to help close a sale. For more information, check out: http://www.aweber.com/ http://www.emailtoday.com/ and http://www.silverquick.com/

Promoting your Web site

To make a Web site successful, creating a superb useful Web site is the easy part. Now you'll need to let people know that it's available and open for business. Certainly make sure you make full use of all the relevant META tags in HTML as described earlier in this chapter, and you can discover more key promotion techniques on the Internet and from books like "Web Page Design in easy steps". If you do not have the time to manually tweak your Web pages, one option is to consider using an automatic Web promotion service like Submit It! at http://www.submit-it.com/. When you want to start advertising your Web site, simply send them your Web site address (URL) and they register your URL with about 20 of the most popular search engines. Also, quality software like WebPostion Agent at http://www.webposition.com can help monitor and improve your search engine rankings.

If you're in business, always think of your Web site as an electronic business card and include your Web address and key email details on all business stationery, brochures and other advertising devices. Also, try to get your Web site listed in any relevant conventional offline business directories. On the Web, you can form joint-venture working partnerships with other companies that are involved in your field and so exchange Web address links. By joint-venturing in this way with several carefully selected organisations, you can let many more prospects know about what you're providing for a small cost. Web success means meeting four main conditions:

1. Lots of continuous "targeted" traffic – that is, people who know about what you're providing before they visit (input).
2. Prospects have to trust what you say (belief/credibility).
3. A clear, easy-to-use Web design (output).
4. Get personal; after a sale, stay in regular touch with your customers and follow up. Demonstrate genuine help (follow-up marketing).

Making money with an email newsletter

You can also start a free daily, weekly or monthly email newsletter – to provide some free information and in return promote your products or services. This non-threatening approach is often considered one of the best ways to grow your Web business. Email marketing can be amazingly successful and profitable with the right approach. MotherNature.com is rumoured to have spent $23 million on television advertising alone in 1999. Yet arguably, the key to their strategy was to capture "opt-in" email addresses – that is, those who voluntarily provide their email address to receive relevant information. The company sent a promotional email to 65,000 of their opt-in subscribers; as a result, 3,000 units of chewable vitamin C products were sold. The email campaign cost practically nothing – a few hours perhaps crafting a carefully considered email message. Outcome: a tiny direct cost campaign produced a high profit result.

Submitting a Web site to the search engines

You can also learn more about what search engines and Web directories look for in a Web site and aim to get high placements in their listings – just make sure that you don't break their rules. Aim to get listed in the top 20 search engines and directories and any other niche search engines that are relevant to your field for a particular keyword that is essential for what you're promoting.

Currently, getting listed in most search engines and directories costs nothing and can, if used successfully, create high levels of "Web traffic." Or you can contract most of your Web promotion to a specialist company – just check them out first or, better still, look for personal referrals from friends and colleagues, to avoid the many "cowboy operations" that have emerged recently.

Advertising a Web site

Once your Web site is up and running, the most important first task is to encourage, compel and urge people to visit. An ideal first measure is to create a compelling press release. Consider creating a special kind of press release, one that has an "angle" – a human interest story that an editor would love to use. Make it interesting and unique. Or pay someone to write it for you. Then seek out relevant sources on and off the Internet and submit your article. As editors are always looking for interesting stories, this approach may get many hundreds or thousands of new visitors quickly for a small cost.

Another option that can bring quick results and which almost always creates interest is to include running competitions and quizzes, also perhaps with questionnaires and polls – your visitors love being asked about their views on topics that are relevant to all involved. For each individual communication, try to make sure you voluntarily capture an email address to consistently build your mailing list. Consider contributing to topics in newsgroups that are relevant to what you're offering and in each email you send, include your Web site address, and perhaps other basic contact information, and provide a compelling reason why new visitors should visit your Web site now – perhaps include a time-limited special offer or bonus. Always look for new and interesting ways to stimulate people who are interested in your products and services to visit your site.

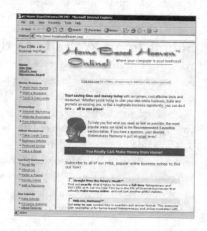

Evaluating new ways to advertise

TV and radio stations are making their material available live on the Internet. For businesses, advertisers can now reach tens of millions globally. Recently, a company called Arbitron carried out some significant research into Internet buying habits. They found that of those people who listened to their favourite radio station while online, 79% were likely to visit the Web site of an advertiser. Furthermore, 60% of those who visited made a purchase! Amazing revelations like these demonstrate that people are integrating the Internet into their day-to day lives. The key is to find a need, then supply what the customer wants in the simplest way – but not necessarily at the lowest price.

Part VI
The Internet
Guide

Internet Service Providers, domain name registers and Web hosts

This chapter includes popular Internet Service Providers but many other providers are available. When seeking an ideal ISP, do your own research and perhaps check out the latest reviews in popular computer and Internet magazines, in addition to the guidelines provided in "Getting online", page 70.

Internet Service Providers

UK: with "free" providers, you may only have to pay for telephone connection charges and technical support if needed. Some popular free providers include:

Name:	Phone from UK:	Web Address:
BT Click	0800 800001	http://www.btclick.com
BT ClickFree	0800 7317887	http://www.btclickfree.com
Cable & Wireless	0800 0923001	http://www.cwcom.net
Freeserve	0990 500049	http://www.freeserve.net
Free NetName	0800 3766910	http://www.freenetname.co.uk
FreeUK	0845 3555555	http://www.freeuk.com
ic24	020 7293 3726	http://www.ic24.com
LineOne	0800 111210	http://www.lineone.net
MSN	0345 002000	http://www.msn.co.uk
Netscape Online	0800 9230009	www.netscapeonline.co.uk
Screaming.net	0800 8450150	http://www.screaming.net
TESCOnet	0345 225533	http://www.tesco.net
Virgin Net	0500 558800	http://www.virgin.net
X-Stream	0800 3585678	http://www.x-stream.co.uk

UK: popular subscription-based providers include:

Name:	Phone from UK:	Web Address:
AOL	0800 3765432	http://www.aol.co.uk
BT Internet	0800 800001	http://www.btinternet.com
ClaraNET	020 7903 3000	http://www.clara.net
CIX	020 8255 5050	http://www.cix.co.uk
CompuServe (CIS)	0990 0002000	http://www.compuserve.co.uk
Demon	0845 2722999	http://www.demon.net
Direct Connection	0800 0720000	http://www.dircon.net
F9	0870 7058000	http://www.f9.co.uk
Global Internet	0870 9098000	http://www.global.net.uk
Netcom	0800 9809988	http://www.netcom.net.uk
NTL Internet	0800 607608	http://www.ntl.com
Which Online	0645 830240	http://www.whichonline.net
U-Net	0845 3308000	http://www.u-net.net
UUNet PIPEX Dial	0845 0884455	http://www.dial.pipex.com

Some interesting and relevant directories to help you find the ideal Internet Service Provider:

- http://www.thelist.com
- http://www.netalert.com
- http://www.internet-magazine.com
- http://www.limitless.co.uk/inetuk/

Some Internet Service Providers from around the world:

Africa: Africa Online. http://www.africaonline.com
South Africa. http://www.global.co.za

Argentina: Impsat. http://www.impsat.com.ar
Australia: Telstra Big Pond. http://www.bigpond.com.au
Brazil: Cybernet. http://www.cybernet.com.br
Canada: Concentric. http://www.concentric.net
Netcom Canada. http://www.netcom.ca
France: Easynet. http://www.easynet.fr Wanadoo. http://www.wanadoo.fr
Finland: Internet Finland. http://www.icon.fl
Germany: Deutsches Provider Network. http://www.dpn.de
Greece: Hellas Online. http://www.hol.gr
Ireland: Ireland Online. http://www.iol.ie
Italy: Itnet. http://www.it.net
India: VSNL. http://www.vsnl.net.in
Japan: Global Online. http://www.gol.com
New Zealand: Telecom XTRA. http://www.extra.co.nz
Pakistan: Brain Net. http://www.brain.net.pk
Spain: Madrid Online. http://www.mol.es
USA: AT&T WorldNet. http://www.att.net
Concentric. http://www.concentric.net
Prodigy. http://www.prodigy.com

Getting and registering an Internet domain name

Some "gold" advice: to see whether a domain name you want is available, check out the Better-Whois database at: http://www.betterwhois.com/

Why? Using the global shared domain registry, they provide an accurate way to check whether the name you want is available or if not, who currently owns it – so you can contact the current owner to discover if they will sell it and at what price. Do remember, most domain owners always list their best preferred price first, so if you're really determined to get the domain name you want, they'll probably reduce their asking price with some further negotiation. Also, some key domain name owners may consider leasing a name or allow its use in return for a profit share of some kind. Other tools and sources from which you can check out, determine and register domain names include:

- AfterNIC – one of the most popular places to buy and sell domain names: http://www.afternic.com/
- BestNames (finding domain names) – http://www.bestnames.net/
- E-gineer – http://www.e-gineer.com/dominator/index.phtml
- Kudosnet (search and registrations) – http://1-insternet-marketing.com/domains/
- GreatDomains, the Internet's number #1 place to purchase quality domain names – http://www.greatdomains.com/
- Nameboy (slick domain name generator) – http://www.nameboy.com/
- Network Solutions (registrations) – http://www.networksolutions.com/
- Nominet UK (registrations) – http://www.nic.co.uk/
- Unclaimed Domains (Superb tool that could make you rich. Allows you to register good previously registered domain names that people have allowed to lapse due to non-payment of the re-registration fee) – http://www.1-internet-marketing.com/ucd/
- WhataDomain (Premium domain names for sale, lease and partnerships) – http://www.whatadomain.com/
- Whois.Net (domain name lookup) – http://www.whois.net/
- WhoisPlus (domain name search) – http://www.whoisplus.com/

The Newsgroups Directory

With currently over 60,000 newsgroups available, almost every topic you can think of is probably covered in a newsgroup somewhere. You can find out more about working with newsgroups in "Internet newsgroups", page 291. To provide a "taster", we've included just a few here. However, when you set up your newsreader, usually you'll be prompted to download the full default list of all the newsgroups available from your Internet Service Provider.

If you want a newsgroup that your Internet Service Provider does not already include, check their acceptable user guidelines and if you think the subject of that newsgroup does not break their rules, simply ask if they will add the newsgroup you want to their list. We've omitted controversial adult-oriented newsgroups, like those from alt.binaries.pictures, alt.sex, .warez and so on as content from those groups may be illegal in your country. Even though you can gain access to extreme newsgroups, saving dodgy pictures and video clips or downloading pirated software usually passes the liability for any possible offence on to you automatically. Just because it's available doesn't mean it's legal, so beware!

Remember, you can usually work out what a newsgroup covers by its description. For example "alt.cardgames.magic" discusses magic tricks with card games and is found in the alt(ernative) category. Other popular categories include: aus(tralia), biz(business commercial), comp(uter), misc(ellaneous), rec(reation), sci(ence), soc(iety), talk (hot discussions) and uk (United Kingdom related). Finally, you can use alt.test to practice posting to newsgroups.

africa.news
alt.activism
alt.adoption
alt.alcohol
alt.aldus.pagemaker
alt.alien.research
alt.alien.visitors
alt.animals
alt.animals.whales
alt.aquaria
alt.archaeology
alt.architecture
alt.architecture.alternative
alt.aromatherapy
alt.artroom
alt.arts.ballet
alt.ascii-art
alt.astrology
alt.atheism
alt.backrubs
alt.beer
alt.binaries.multimedia
alt.books.pratchett
alt.books.reviews
alt.books.technical
alt.brain.teasers
alt.buddha
alt.business

alt.business.import-export
alt.business.misc
alt.business.offshore
alt.cad
alt.cardgame.magic
alt.cd-rom
alt.celebrities
alt.censorship
alt.child.support
alt.chinese.fengshui
alt.christnet
alt.collecting.autographs
alt.comedy.british
alt.comics.alternative
alt.comics.batman
alt.comics.superman
alt.comp.hardware.homebuilt
alt.comp.shareware
alt.comp.virus
alt.computer.consultants
alt.config
alt.conspiracy
alt.contraceptives
alt.co-ops
alt.crime
alt.cult-movies
alt.culture
alt.culture.www

alt.cybercafes
alt.cyberspace
alt.dads.rights
alt.dreams
alt.drugs
alt.education.alternative
alt.education.disabled
alt.education.distance
alt.elvis.sighting
alt.evil
alt.fan.monty-python
alt.fashion
alt.feminism
alt.fishing
alt.flame
alt.folklore
alt.folklore.herbs
alt.food
alt.food.fat-free
alt.food.wine
alt.forsale
alt.freemasonry
alt.games.doom
alt.games.duke3d
alt.games.mk
alt.games.sf2
alt.games.whitewolf
alt.gossip.royalty

alt.guitar
alt.hangover
alt.hindu
alt.home.repair
alt.homosexual
alt.horror
alt.html
alt.humour
alt.hygiene.male
alt.individualism
alt.infertility
alt.internet.access.wanted
alt.internet.services
alt.irc
alt.irc.questions
alt.journalism
alt.lefthanders
alt.life.sucks
alt.love
alt.magic.secrets
alt.medical.allergy
alt.meditation
alt.missing-kids
alt.music.bluenote
alt.music.dance
alt.music.hardcore
alt.music.jewish
alt.music.progressive

alt.mythology
alt.obituaries
alt.pagan
alt.paranet.paranormal
alt.paranormal
alt.parnet.ufo
alt.politics.british
alt.politics.greens
alt.politics.homosexuality
alt.prisons
alt.psychology.misc
alt.quotations
alt.radio.broadcasting
alt.rave
alt.religion.islam
alt.revenge
alt.rock-n-roll
alt.satellite.tv.europe
alt.security
alt.sewing
alt.sexual.abuse.recovery
alt.shenanigans
alt.showbiz.gossip
alt.skincare
alt.sports.darts
alt.starfleet.rpg
alt.startrek.creative
alt.stupidity

alt.support
alt.support.hemophilia
alt.surfing
alt.tasteless
alt.test (your test area)
alt.usage.English
alt.windows98
alt.writing
alt.yoga
alt.zen
aol.internet
aol.misc
aus.jobs
aus.jokes
aus.politics
aus.sport.ruby-league
aus.tv
biz.comp.hardware
biz.comp.software
biz.general
biz.misc
comp.databases
comp.fonts
comp.graphics
comp.graphics.animation
comp.infosystems.interpedia
comp.internet.net-happenings
comp.lang.java

comp.mail.eudora.ms-windows
comp.mail.misc
comp.newprod
comp.os.ms-windows.apps.misc
comp.publish.prepress
comp.sources.wanted
comp.sys.ibm.pc.games.adventure
comp.sys.ibm.pc.games.misc
comp.sys.laptops
comp.sys.mac.apps
comp.sys.mac.graphics
comp.sys.mac.hardware
comp.virus
compuserve.general
demon.adverts
microsoft.public.intexplorer.ie4
microsoft.public.office.misc
misc.consumers.house
misc.entrepreneurs
misc.fitness
misc.health.alternative
misc.immigration.canada
misc.immigration.usa
misc.invest
misc.invest.stocks
misc.jobs.offered
news.admin.misc
news.announce.groups

news.answers
news.groups.questions
news.lists (newsgroup lists)
news.lists.ps-maps
news.newsusers.questions
rec.antiques
rec.arts.anime
rec.arts.bonsai
rec.arts.books.marketplace
rec.arts.cinema
rec.arts.comics.marketplace
rec.arts.dance
rec.arts.fine
rec.arts.misc
rec.arts.movies
rec.arts.poems
rec.arts.sf.marketplace
rec.arts.sf.reviews
rec.arts.tv
rec.audio.marketplace
rec.autos.marketplace
rec.autos.misc
rec.boats
rec.climbing
rec.collecting
rec.crafts.brewing
rec.crafts.winemaking
rec.food.veg.cooking

rec.gardens
rec.gardens.roses
rec.humour
rec.martial-arts
rec.music.celtic
rec.music.classical
rec.music.info
rec.music.misc
rec.org.mensa
rec.pets
rec.pets.birds
rec.pets.cats
rec.pets.dogs
rec.photo.advanced
rec.sport.cricket.info
rec.sport.golf
rec.sports.soccer
rec.travel.air
rec.travel.asia
rec.travel.cruises
rec.travel.europe
rec.travel.usa-canada
rec.woodworking
sci.geo.geology
sci.math

sci.med
sci.space.policy
soc.history
talk.bizarre
talk.politics.drugs
uk.environment
uk.finance
uk.forsale
uk.gay-lesbian-bi
uk.jobs.offered
uk.jobs.wanted
uk.legal
uk.media
uk.misc
uk.music.alternative
uk.music.breakbeat
uk.net.news
uk.net.news.announce
uk.people.consumers
uk.people.deaf
uk.politics
uk.railway
uk.rec.gardening
uk.teachers
uk.telecom

The Web Directory

The directory includes a wide range of established Web sites and a number of more unusual developing sites arranged into basic categories. Some Web sites may handle similar topics in related categories. Enjoy!

Animals and pets

AcmePet.com: covers information on and products for dogs, cats, horses, fish, reptiles and exotic pets: http://www.acmepet.com/

Animail: extra treats and accessories for your pet: http://www.animail.co.uk/

The Cats Protection League: a charity-based Web site providing lots of useful information about the care of cats: http://www.cats.org.uk/

The Royal Society for Prevention of Cruelty to Animals (RSPCA): http://www.rspca.org.uk/

Arts, music and entertainment

101cd: includes music, videos, games and books: http://www.101cd.com/

Ain't It Cool News: film reviews: http://www.aint-it-cool-news.com/

<u>All-Music Guide</u>: information about a wide range of artists:
http://www.allmusic.com/

<u>Alphabetstreet</u>: for books, music, videos, games and news:
http://www.alphabetstreet.com/

<u>Audiostreet</u>: again, books, music, DVDs, games and news:
http://www.audiostreet.com/

<u>Boxman</u>: more music, videos, DVDs, games, gift certificates and features:
http://www.boxman.co.uk/

<u>CDNow</u>: for wide range of music, videos and gifts: http://www.cdnow.com/

<u>CDparadise</u>: CDs, books, videos and games from WH Smith Online:
http://www.cdparadise.com/

<u>Charlotte Church</u>: the renowned British classical music soloist:
http://www.charlottechurch.com/

<u>Classic Net</u>: superb amateur classical music site with lots of related information:
http://www.classical.net/

<u>Classical Insites</u>: lots of interesting information about classical music and
popular performers and composers: http://www.classicalinsites.com/

<u>ClassicFM</u>: the world-renowned ClassicFM radio station on the Web:
http://www.classicfm.co.uk/

<u>Coffeehaus</u>: an interesting visual journey into the history of coffee houses:
http://www.coffeehaus.co.uk/

<u>Comedy Central</u>: the title says it all: http://www.comedycentral.com/

<u>Comics.com</u>: Dilbert cartoons and a host of others to keep you sane:
http://www.unitedmedia.com/comics/ and http://www.dilbert.com/

<u>Cream</u>: Club music: http://www.cream.co.uk/

<u>CyberDance</u>: great information resource on ballet and modern dancing:
http://www.cyberdance.org/

<u>Dancing baby</u>: yes, it's that one: http://www.viewpoint.com/features/baby/

<u>DotcomedyTV</u>: web site to support the popular British TV programme of the same name, currently hosted by Gail Porter and Chris Addison:
http://www.dotcomedytv.com/

<u>Dotmusic</u>: music news, reviews and downloads: http://www.dotmusic.com/

<u>DVDplus</u>: buy everything DVD: http://www.dvdplus.co.uk/

<u>DVDStreet</u>: books, music, DVD, games etc.: http://www.dvdstreet.com/

<u>DVD World</u>: DVDs, CDs, video, Sony Playstation games and more:
http://www.dvdworld.co.uk/ or http://www.blockbuster.co.uk/ and
http://www.blockbuster.com/

<u>Entertainment Express</u>: CDs, videos and DVDs mainly:
http://www.entexpress.com/

<u>FreeServe</u>: a popular British Internet Service Provider that also provides information, news, sports and links to a wide range of other sites:
http://www.freeserve.net/

<u>Games Domain</u>: lots of gaming information and downloads:
http://www.gamesdomain.com/

<u>GamesSpot</u>: lots of reviews and information:
http://www.gamespot.co.uk/ and http://www.gamespot.com/

<u>GameSpy</u>: http://www.gamespy.com/

<u>Gramophone Magazine</u>: includes thousands of reviews and lots of classical and jazz information: http://www.gramophone.co.uk/

<u>HMV</u>: lots of music, video, DVD and games options available:
http://www.hmv.co.uk/

<u>Horror Online</u>: (adult content) for everything horror:
http://www.horroronline.com/

<u>Internet Underground Music Archive</u>: considered by many to be "the" place to visit if you want key information about all kinds of music:
http://www.iuma.com/

<u>Jazz Online</u>: a musical magnet for jazz fans: http://www.jazzonline.com/

<u>Klingon Language Institute</u>: make yourself clearly understood; learn to speak Klingon and help avoid a galactic war: http://www.kli.org/

<u>LifeRaft</u>: a graphically and musically rich highly animated journey about life: http://www.liferaft.com/

<u>Listen to hundreds of radio stations online from around the world</u>: http://windowsmedia.com/iradio/en_gb/radio.asp

<u>Macromedia ShockRave</u>: http://www.macromedia.com/

<u>MDC Classic Music</u>: cool site providing for an amazing range of classical music tastes: http://www.mdcmusic.co.uk/

<u>More Than Fifty Ways to Get Rid of Blind Dates</u>: http://www.cog.brown.edu/brochure/people/duchon/humor/blind.dates.html

<u>Motown</u>: all about music of the same name recording label: http://www.motown.com/

<u>MP3.com</u>: lots of MP3-related information: http://www.mp3.com/

<u>Mr. Showbiz</u>: information, news and reviews on the world of entertainment: http://www.mrshowbiz.com/

<u>MTV Online</u>: includes information, news and features about shows and music events: http://www.mtv.com/

<u>Multiple-Player Online Gaming</u>: discover all about playing games online: http://www.mpog.com/

<u>Music Boulevard</u>: a fine US-based online shop that serves a wide range of musical tastes: http://www.musicblvd.com/

<u>Net Casino</u>: yet another way to spend and help make someone richer: http://www.casino.com/

<u>New Musical Express</u>: the online version of the magazine of the same name: heavily news-oriented: http://www.nme.com/

<u>NetRadio</u>: like music? Then you can make your choice from 120 different channels covering rock to classics: http://www.netradio.com/

<u>Nintendo Direct</u>: lots of information about Nintendo games and features: http://www.nintendodirect.co.uk/

<u>Odeon</u>: discover what's on at your local Odeon cinema, book your tickets online and collect when you arrive at your cinema: http://www.odeon.co.uk/

<u>Playstation Direct</u>: gaming heaven for Sony Playstation lovers: http://www.playstationdirect.co.uk/

<u>SacredTreasures.com</u>: informative articles on antiques and collectables and items for sale: Egyptian, Celtic, Roman, India, Tibet and Africa. http://www.sacredtreasures.com/

<u>Second Spin</u>: buy and sell CDs, DVDs and Videos: http://www.secondspin.com/

<u>Shakespeare and the Globe</u>: a visually superb offering from Encyclopaedia Britannica: http://shakespeare.eb.com/

<u>The BBC Shop</u>: lots of videos, CDs, tapes, and CD/DVD-ROMs available here: http://www.bbcshop.com/

<u>The Bottom 100 Movies</u>: where better quality means lower marks: http://us.imdb.com/bottom_100_films

<u>The Daily Entertainment Network</u>: a male-oriented online magazine: htp://www.theden.com/

<u>The Hollywood Reporter</u>: gossip, TV, Music and film revues: http://www.hollywoodreporter.com/

<u>The Internet Movie Database</u>: an incredible amount of free information about movies: http://uk.imdb.com/

<u>The Official Star Wars Web site</u>: all about the famous galactic heroes and how they saved the universe: http://www.starwars.com/

<u>The Official X-Files Web site</u>: discover who's covering up what: http://www.thex-files.com/

<u>The Sealed Knot</u>: a charitable society dedicated to the re-enactment of the English Civil Wars: http://www.sealedknot.org/

<u>The Simpsons Archive</u>: where Homer, Madge, Bart, Lisa, Maggie and all their friends live on the Web: the amount of material makes you shiver: http://www.snpp.com/

<u>The Toaster Museum Foundation</u>: you'll be amazed at just what these people have to say about toasters: http://www.toaster.org/

<u>The Ultimate Band List</u>: news and information about thousands of bands: http://www.ubl.com/

<u>TheatreNet</u>: a superb guide to plays in London and other parts of the UK; includes related links: http://www.theatrenet.com/

<u>This is London</u>: the London Evening Standard newspaper online: http://www.thisislondon.co.uk/

<u>Ticket Master</u>: get your tickets online for a bewildering range of events; just superb: http://www.ticketmaster.co.uk/

<u>Time Warner Pathfinder Network</u>: entertainment, news and information: http://www.pathfinder.com/

<u>Warners Brothers Online</u>: discover what's on at the movies: http://www.wb.com/ and http://www.warnerbros.com/

<u>Warner Village</u>: see information on the latest films, what's on and where, plus you can book and pay for your tickets: http://www.warnervillage.co.uk/

<u>What's on Stage</u>: what's on at theatres across the UK: http://www.whatsonstage.com/

<u>What's on When</u>: a guide to world events: http://www.whatsonwhen.com/

<u>Windows Media site</u>: music, radio, video and the latest information on Microsoft Windows media: http://windowsmedia.com/

<u>World Wide Arts Resources</u>: an amazing guide to art and culture on the Web: http://www.wwar.com/

<u>Urban75</u>: anti and underground themes: http://www.urban75.com/
<u>VirginNet</u>: provides a range of information and interesting entertainment topics: http://www.virginnet.net/
<u>Wireplay</u>: all about BT Internet's unique non-Internet gaming system: http://www.wireplay.co.uk/

Television listings

<u>BBC</u>: http://www.bbc.co.uk/
<u>Carlton (UK TV)</u>: http://www.carlton.co.uk/
<u>Channel Four (UK TV)</u>: http://www.channel4.co.uk/
<u>ITV</u>: http://www.itv.co.uk/
<u>SceneOne (full TV & radio listings)</u>: http://www.sceneone.co.uk/

Auctions

<u>Amazon</u>: http://www.amazon.co.uk or http://www.amazon.com/
<u>Bid.com</u>: http://www.bid.com/
<u>Ebay</u>: http://www.ebay.co.uk / or http://www.ebay.com/
<u>FreeServe Auctions</u>: auction anything from £1 up. Popular for holidays, cars and electronic goods: http://www.fsauctions.co.uk/
<u>Loot</u>: http://www.loot.com/
<u>QXL.com (Quixell)</u>: http://www.qxl.com/
<u>Yahoo Auctions</u>: http://uk.auctions.yahoo.com/uk/

Books and literature

<u>Alphabetstreet</u>: for books, music, videos, games and news: http://www.alphabetstreet.com/
<u>Amazon</u>: arguably the Internet's premier online bookseller: http://www.amazon.co.uk or http://www.amazon.com
<u>Barns & Noble</u>: online bookshop: http://www.barnsandnoble.com/

<u>Bertelsmanss's Online Bookshop (Bol)</u>: http://www.bol.com/

<u>Bibliofind</u>: online book supplier: http://www.bibliofind.com/

<u>Blackwells</u>: online book shop: http://www.blackwells.co.uk/

<u>Britannica Internet Guide</u>: Encyclopedia Britannica doing what it does best: http://www.britannica.com/ and http://www.britannica.co.uk/

<u>Buy.com</u>: branded as the Internet superstore: http://www.buy.com/

<u>Computer Manuals</u>: an impressive range of computer books: http://www.compman.co.uk/

<u>Computer Step</u>: UK's largest independent computer book publisher: http://www.computerstep.com/ or http://www.ineasysteps.com/

<u>Cookerybooks.com</u>: http://www.cookerybooks.com/

<u>HarpWeek</u>: provides compelling visual access to the content of the newspaper that covered the American Civil War: http://www.harpweek.com/

<u>Internet Bookshop (WH Smith online)</u>: http://www.bookshop.co.uk/

<u>Jane Dorner</u>: superb resources for writers and researchers: http://dspace.dial.pipex.com/jane.dorner/

<u>Society of Authors (SoA)</u>: authors support: http://www.writers.org.uk/society/

<u>The London Review of Books</u>: http://www.lrb.co.uk/

<u>Waterstones</u>: http://www.waterstones.com or http://www.waterstones.co.uk/

Business

<u>AskAlex</u>: searchable directory of businesses from the UK: http://www.askalex.co.uk/

<u>Beenz</u>: an interesting online currency idea: http://www.beenz.com/

<u>Better Business Online (formally Home Run Online)</u>: business resources: http://www.better-business.co.uk/

British Chambers of Commerce: provides information on events, services and publications available from members: http://www.britishchambers.org.uk/

BT OpenWorld: options for fast Internet access through ADSL connections: http://www.btopenworld.com/

Business consultants: http://www.austinhall.co.uk/

Business Plan software (free): plus a great source of sound business advice: http://www.natwest.com/

Business planning with Peter Thomson: http://www.peterthomson.com/

CNNfn: the latest business news from around the world: http://www.cnnfn.com/

Companies House UK: registration of companies, and company information: http://www.companieshouse.co.uk/

Data Registration Protection Registrar (UK): http://www.dataprotection.gov.uk/

Department of Trade and Industry (UK): http://www.dti.gov.uk/

eFax.com: a superb service that converts faxes and voicemail to email messages for free – great if you're on the road: http://www.efax.com/

Enterprise Zone: lots of information relevant to small firms in the UK from this government-financed site: http://www.enterprisezone.org.uk/

Europemedia.com: free weekly news report covering the most important developments in online business markets: http://www.europemedia.com/

Forrester: superb site for Internet research data: http://www.forrester.com/

Fortune: business information and features from Fortune Magazine: http://www.fortune.com

Ideas For Business: great site for experimenting with new business ideas: http://www.ideasiteforbusiness.com/

Karen Blakeman's superb business information site: RBA Information Services:
http://www.rba.co.uk/sources/

Learning Matters: discover surprising skills you didn't think you had:
http://www.learning-matters.co.uk

Marketing: information and advice on marketing, plus various key publications
are available for sale: http://www.marketinguk.co.uk/

PlusNet: free fax2email included with this provider:
http://www.plus.net/

The Financial Services Authority (FSA): provide information to help determine
scams from genuine business opportunities: http://www.fsa.gov.uk/

UK Business Net: a business-to-business information source that covers key
topics like: planning, marketing, training and public relations management.
Includes over 2500 pages of free information:
http://www.ukbusinessnet.com/

WebHead Central: a superb resource with a huge range of help options to aid
anyone promoting a business on the Internet: http://www.webheadcentral.com/

Yell: the UK online Yellow Pages: http://www.yell.co.uk/

Make money on the Internet

All about working with affiliates on the Internet:
http://www.associateprograms.com/

Corey Rudl's Internet Marketing Center:
http://www.marketingtips.com/t.cgi/12939/

Corey Rudl's Internet Marketing Center Associates Program:
http://www.marketingtips.com/sr/t.x/12939/

Dale Publishing: a respected UK-based resource for online marketers:
http://www.dalepublishing.com/

Greg Schliesmann's Internet marketing resources: superb range of free downloads, business tips and advice for creating a successful Internet business: http://www.jvmarketer.com/

HomeBasedHeaven.com: Lady Harmony Major's excellent ebook: "Learning the Ropes" and resources to help anyone set up an Internet business from home: http://www.homebasedheaven.com/

Jim Daniels Internet marketing resources:
http://www.bizweb2000.com/d3665.htm

Nothing But Net: Michael Cambell created US $750,000 in Internet revenues using almost no advertising costs – instead he used free sources on the Internet and lots of know-how. Now he's telling how he did it in a superb ebook: http://activemarketplace.com/w.cgi?net-6694

Vstore: set up your own e-commerce store without the hassle. US-based but expected to come to Europe soon: http://www.vstore.com/

Business training

Abacus Virtual Training College: http://www.abacus-uk.com/

Computer Step: plain-English computer guides designed for quick, easy learning: http://www.incasysteps.com/

DfEE: the UK Department for Education and Employment:
http//www.dfee.gov.uk/

Learning Direct: http://www.lifelonglearning.co.uk/

Learning Tree International: http://www.learningtree.com/uk/cbt

Open University: http://www.open.ac.uk/

Resources to help you set up an e-commerce Web business

JShop: http://www.jshop.co.uk/pro/index.html

SetUpShop UK: http://www.setupshop.co.uk/

Virgin: http://www.virginbiz.net/

Cars, motorcycles, scooters and bicycles

Auto Trader: covers key topics you should know about when buying a car: http://www.autotrader.co.uk/

Autobytel.co.uk: an Internet-based new and used car service: http://www.autobytel.co.uk/

BikeNet: resources and product reviews for the biker community: http://www.bikenet.com/

British School of Motoring: learn all about learning to drive in the UK: http://www.bsm.co.uk/

Carbusters: Superb European car savings site originally set up by Which.net: http://www.carbusters.com/

Edinburgh Bicycle: lots of information on bikes plus you can buy bikes and accessories: http://www.edinburgh-bicycle.co.uk/

Hertz: going travelling? Reserve a car in almost any country: http://www.hertz.co.uk/

RAC: find out about the RAC car breakdown and recovery services and includes the latest UK traffic news: http://www.rac.co.uk/

The Automobile Association (AA): learn about the AA car breakdown and recovery service and join online if you wish: http://www.theaa.co.uk/

The Official Mini Site: for Mini car fans everywhere: http://www.mini.co.uk/

The Official Vespa Site: for Vespa scooter owners worldwide; who said art and Vespa can't mix?: http://www.vespa.com/

Top Gear: a car enthusiast's online magnet: http://www.topgear.com/

Children

Blue Peter: http://www.bbc.co.uk/bluepeter/

<u>Buffy the Vampire Slayer fan sites</u>: Sarah Michelle Gellar and friends pounding the guys from the dead zone:
http://www.cdmeetens.freeserve.co.uk/home.html
http://www.spidernet.ndirect.co.uk/

<u>Children's TV Workshop</u>: entertainment and stories from favourite television characters: http://www.ctw.org/

<u>CITV</u>: spin-off Web site for the popular British Children's ITV programme series: http://www.citv.co.uk/

<u>Crayola</u>: lots of ideas for kids to experiment and have fun with colour: http://www.crayola.com/

<u>Disney Online</u>: all the favourite Disney characters in one place; visually stunning: http://www.disney.co.uk/ or http://www.disney.com/

<u>KZuk.net</u>: have established a safe and fun place for kids with more than 20,000 interactive pages available: homework club, fun section, quizzes, games, pen pals, music, chat and a magazine: http://www.kzuk.net/

<u>Matthew Porretta fan site</u>: the New Adventures of Robin Hood series:
http://www.geocities.com/TelevisionCity/Station/1924/fanclub/matthew.html

<u>Warner Bros Kids</u>: lots of games and fun things to keep children amused:
http://www.kids.warnerbros.com/

<u>Whoosh (online TV episode guide)</u>: includes reviews of Xena Warrior Princess
and Hercules the Legendary Journeys:
http://www.whoosh.org/whooshfake00.html

<u>Xena Warrior Princess</u>: fan sites for Lucy Lawless, the New Zealand leather
queen: http://www.xenafan.com/ and http://xenite.virtualave.net/

<u>Yahoo for kids</u>: includes lots of links to great Web sites for kids everywhere:
http://www.yahooligans.com/

Computers, computer accessories and software

<u>Acer</u>: computers and accessories: http://www.aceruk.co.uk/

<u>Action Online</u>: computer and office retailer; wide range of products available:
http://www.action.com/

<u>Adobe products store</u>: all Adobe software products for European customers:
http://eurostore.adobe.com/

<u>Apple computers</u>: http://www.apple.com/

<u>Beyond.com</u>: sells wide range of big name computer software and hardware
and includes a popular download section: http://www.beyond.com/

<u>Buyonet</u>: http://www.buyonet.com/

<u>Dabs Direct Online</u>: http://www.dabs.com/

<u>Dan</u>: http://www.dan.co.uk/

<u>Dell</u>: a superb online resource and virtual computer store:
http://www.dell.co.uk/ or http://www.dell.com/

<u>Elonex</u>: computer hardware, add-ons and software:
http://www.elonex.co.uk/

Evesham: http://www.evesham.com/

Firewall software: you can protect your computer and network while online with ZoneAlarm from ZoneLabs: http://www.zonelabs.com/

Gateway: http://www.gw2k.co.uk/ or http://www.gateway.com/

Gibson Research Corporation: computer data recovery and Internet security: http://www.grc.com/

GregoryBraun.com: a range of great value Windows shareware products for the PC: http://www.gregorybraun.com

Hewlett Packard: http://www.hp.com/

Insight: online catalogue for computer hardware, software and add-ons: http://www.insight.com/

Jungle: lots of special offers and big brand names in computing: http://www.jungle.com/

Micro Warehouse/Technomatic (both Web addresses link to the same site content): http://www.microwarehouse.co.uk/ and http://www.technomatic.co.uk/

Microsoft: an absolutely massive site covering an enormous range of issues; use the search facilities as much as possible; start at: http://www.microsoft.com/

Netscape: for popular Web browser software and related tools: http://www.netscape.com/

Opera Web browser: a neat alternative Web browser from Norway: http://www.operasoftware.com/

PC World: online access to popular British high street computer store chain: http://www.pcw-software.co.uk/shop/

Quicken financial software: http://www.intuit.co.uk/ and http://www.intuit.com/ (international users)

Simply Computers: http://www.simply.co.uk/

Software Savings Limited: http://www.softwaresavings.com/

<u>Software Warehouse</u>: http://www.software-warehouse.co.uk/

<u>SpotShop</u>: http://www.spotshop.co.uk/

<u>TechWeb – the IT Network</u>: Ideal information source for those employed in the computer and Internet fields: http://www.techweb.com/

<u>The Association of Shareware Professionals</u>: promotes the shareware concept; excellent resource for anyone considering publishing software as shareware: http://www.asp-shareware.org/

<u>The Learning Store (educational software)</u>: http://www.learningstore.co.uk/

<u>Time Computers</u>: http://www.timecomputers.com/

<u>Tiny Computers</u>: http://www.tiny.com/

<u>Tom's Hardware Guide</u>: covers the basics of PCs and includes reviews of various peripherals: http://www.tomshardware.com/

<u>Viglen</u>: computers and accessories: http://www.viglen.co.uk

<u>Ziff-Davis</u>: superb range of information and downloads: http://www.zdnet.com/ or http://www.zdnet.co.uk/

Popular software download sites

<u>32bit.com</u>: includes software news and downloads: http://32bit.com/

<u>DaveCentral</u>: http://www.davecentral.com/

<u>Download.Com (CNET)</u>: http://www.download.com/

<u>Linux Online</u>: http://www.linux.org/

<u>Paint Shop Pro</u>: http://www.jasc.com/

<u>Rocket Download</u>: http://www.rocketdownload.com/

<u>Shareware.com (CNET)</u>: http://www.shareware.com/

<u>The Java Centre</u>: http://www.java.co.uk/

<u>TuCows</u>: http://www.tucows.com/

<u>WinFiles</u>: http://www.winfiles.com/

<u>ZD Downloads</u>: http://www.zdnet.co.uk/software/

Education

<u>AngliaCampus Home</u>: general children's education; used in schools and for educating children at home: http://www.angliacampus.com/

<u>BBC Education</u>: http://www.bbc.co.uk/education/

<u>Click2Learn</u>: IT/business and general courses: http://www.click2learn.com/

<u>Discovery Channel</u>: http://www.discovery.com/

<u>DIYnet</u>: learn about everything DIY: http://www.diynet.com/

<u>Floodlight</u>: all about training courses available in London: http://www.floodlight.co.uk/

<u>How Stuff Works</u>: discover how things work in today's world: http://www.howstuffworks.com/

<u>Learning Matters</u>: discover surprising skills you didn't think you had: http://www.learning-matters.co.uk

<u>Letsfindout.com</u>: a Pandora's box for the curious about anything: http://www.letsfindout.com/

<u>Oncourse</u>: discover what's available in further education courses in the UK: http://www.oncourse.co.uk/

<u>Pearson Publishing</u>: educational books, etc.: http://www.pearson.co.uk/

<u>QA Training</u>: further training options in the IT sector for commercial and public sector organisations: http://www.qatraining.co.uk/

<u>SmarterKids</u>: educational resources for children: http://www.smarterkids.com/

<u>SmartPlanet</u>: wide range of subjects: http://www.smartplanet.com/

<u>The Open University (OU)</u>: all about the OU's amazing range of training courses and degree courses: http://www.open.ac.uk/

<u>WebNovice Online</u>: ideal to help new Web users learn all about how to use the Web: http://www.webnovice.com/

Email and Web newsletters (ezines)

<u>Affiliate Today</u>: all about making money on the Internet with affiliate programs: To subscribe, send an email to: affiliate@affiliatebroadcast.Com?subject=SUBSCRIBE

<u>Amazing Golf</u>: enjoyable ezine includes lessons, articles, news, and links to other golf sites: http://www.winningoffers.com/signup.htm

<u>BestEzines.com</u>: how to find the quality ezine nuggets: http://BestEzines.com/ To subscribe, send a blank email to: join-bestezines@bestezines.com

<u>BizWeb2000</u>: http://www.bizweb2000.com/d3665.htm Ace Internet marketer and ebook author Jim Daniels, shares what he knows in this regular free ezine: To subscribe, send an email to: freegazette@bizweb2000.com

<u>Email TV</u>: http://www.ondigital.co.uk/

<u>Incredible People</u>: uplifting ezine about people who are living life's challenges every day: http://www.incrediblepeople.com/

<u>Innovative Professional TIPS Letter</u>: superb motivational ezine from respected author and Life Coach, Philip E Humbert PhD, that includes practical tools for managing and succeeding in business and in life:
http://www.philiphumbert.com/

<u>Internet Scambusters</u>: renowned and respected free resource on exposing scams and scam artists on the Internet: http://www.scambusters.org/
To subscribe, send an email to scambusters@scambusters.org and put the word SUBSCRIBE in the Subject box

<u>JNCZ Marketing Newsletter</u>: http://www.Information-Web.com/news/
a free newsletter biased towards home-based businesses in the UK. To subscribe, send an email to: lloyddaley@totalise.co.uk

<u>John Labowitz</u>: includes links to thousands of ezines
http://www.meer.net/~johnl/e-zine-list

<u>List-Universe</u>: network of various types of ezines covering a wide range of topics: http://List-Universe.com/

<u>Monday Memo</u>: the superb official weekly ezine from the International Association for Professionalism Online (IAPO):
http://www.MondayMemo.org/
To subscribe, send an email to: subscribe@MondayMemo.org

<u>Namaste (Deepak Chopra) Mailing list</u>: from the Chopra Center for Well being: Send an email to: listserve@chopra.com with a blank Subject box and "subscribe namaste" (without quotes) as the email message:
http://www.chopra.com/

<u>Neat Net Tricks</u>: a regular ezine that provides computer and Internet tips in a light-hearted and not-too-technical format. For information on subscribing, send an email to: info-neatnettricks@silver.lyris.net

<u>One Minute Diet Tip</u>: quick easy advice on eating right, losing weight and staying healthy: http://www.ValuHealth.com/

<u>Suck</u>: the cult zany Webzine that arguably started it all; chances are, you'll either love it or hate it: http://www.suck.com/

<u>The Onion</u>: caustic witty comments on newsy issues with just so many layers: http://www.theonion.com/

<u>TipWorld</u>: get free daily tips in your email box on hundreds of topics you choose: http://www.topica.com/tipworld

<u>Women's Wire</u>: explores key issues that matter to women everywhere: http://www.women.com/

Employment and the world of work

<u>Ageism</u>: Fighting ageism in the workplace: the Campaign Against Age Discrimination (CAADE): http://www.caade.net/

<u>Best</u>: contract and permanent jobs advertised plus career advice: http://www.bestpeople.co.uk/

<u>BigBluedog.com</u>: the job shop from London's Evening Standard newspaper: http://www.bigbluedog.com/

<u>FutureStep.co.uk</u>: Online executive recruitment and search company for management professionals: http://www.futurestep.co.uk/

<u>GisAJob.com</u>: a large, well-established online recruitment resource: http://www.gisajob.com/

<u>Hunterskil Howard</u>: popular recruitment source: http://www.hunterskil-howard.com/

<u>Job Pilot</u>: http://www.jobpilot.com/

<u>Job World</u>: http://www.jobworld.co.uk/

<u>Netjobs</u>: http://www.netjobs.co.uk/

<u>Reed Computing Personnel</u>: http://www.reedcomputing.co.uk/

<u>Taps</u>: http://www.taps.com/

<u>The British Army</u>: all about the UK security forces: http://www.army.mod.uk/

<u>The Monster Board</u>: get the job you want:
http://www.monster.com/ or http://www.monster.co.uk/
<u>WorkLessMakeMore</u>: offers information and strategies for balanced living:
http://www.worklessmakemore.com/

Encyclopedias, language and reference

<u>Britannica Online</u>: access to the full online version of this superb world renowned encyclopedia: http://www.britannica.com/

<u>Dictionary.com</u>: includes various links to language-related sites and online dictionaries of various types: http://www.dictionary.com/

<u>Encyclopedia.com</u>: offers free access to an encyclopedia containing information from more than 17,000 articles: http://www.encyclopedia.com/

<u>Encyclopedia of Psychology</u>: lots of links to psychological topics:
http://www.psychology.org/

<u>Free Online Dictionary of Computing (FODOC)</u>:
http://wombat.doc.ic.ac.uk/foldoc/index.html

<u>Information Please</u>: includes an encyclopedia and dictionary with search facilities: http://www.infoplease.com/

<u>Internet Press</u>: includes a huge range of language-related links:
http://gallery.uunet.be/internetpress/diction.htm

<u>Learn2</u>: where you can learn step-by-step how to do things. Includes a wide range of topics: http://www.learn2.com/

<u>Microsoft Encarta</u>: http://www.encarta.com/ or http://encarta.msn.com/

<u>OneLook Dictionaries</u>: want to know what that strange word means? OneLook checks hundreds of online dictionaries at the same time:
http://www.onelook.com/

<u>Oxford English Dictionary</u>: http://www.oed.com/

<u>Phrase Finder</u>: for getting literate: http://www.shu.ac.uk/web-admin/phrases/

Quoteland: endless quotations till you drop: http://www.quoteland.com/

Research-It: includes lots of software tools to help you find answers to many questions. Research categories include: language, library, geographical, financial, shipping and Internet: http://www.iTools.com/research-it/

Family

Baby World: coming into the world; all about babies:
http://www.babyworld.co.uk/

Boden: online clothes shopping for all the family: http://www.boden.co.uk/

Mothercare: http://www.mothercare.co.uk/

Super Family: offers a great way for members of families to keep in touch wherever they may be located; unique: http://www.superfamily.com/

UKMums: topics cover pregnancy and child care, plus a UKDads section:
http://www.ukmums.co.uk/

Urchin: billed as "funky stuff for baby, nursery and small kids":
http://www.urchin.co.uk/

Vitago: a range of health and beauty products: http://www.vitago.co.uk/

Fashion, clothes and style

Alloy: lots of teenagers will love it: http://www.alloy.com/

Bras Direct: lots of popular brand names; this site is aimed as much for men who are seeking to buy gifts for that special lady, as well as women who wish to shop direct: http://www.brasdirect.co.uk/

Diesel: http://www.diesel.co.uk/

Dolland and Aitchison: this popular UK optician also provides an impressive selection of designer sunglasses: http://www.danda.co.uk/sunglasses

Dorothy Perkins: an online shop plus links to other Internet clothes e-tailors:
http://www.dorothyperkins.co.uk/

DeBeers: jewellery: http://www.debeers.co.uk/

Fashionmall.com: ties for sale, plus an interesting online necktie guide – even includes a graphical guide that shows you how to tie a bowtie, four-in-hand, half-windsor and full-windsor: http://www.fashionmall.com/guide/tie/doc/

Freemans: the catalogue shop online: http://www.freemans.com/

Gap.com: http://www.gap.com/

Guess.com: http://www.guess.com/

H Samuel: jewellery: http://www.hsamuel.co.uk/

MischiefKids: children's designer clothes: http://www.mischiefkids.co.uk/

Next: Next Directory online: http://www.next.co.uk/

Principles: fashion for men: http://www.principlesmen.co.uk/

Raffaello: designer neckties top names: http://www.raffaelloties.com/

SmartBras.com: UK firm providing bras and lingerie in a range of styles and sizes: http://www.smartbras.com/

The Tie Rack: international quality-oriented tie firm also includes scarves and pashminas to buy online: http://www.tie-rack.com/

Top Man: http://www.topman.co.uk/

Top Shop: http://www.tops.co.uk and http://www.topshop.com/

Van Peterson: jewellery: http://www.vanpeterson.co.uk/

Zoom: covers a wide range of topics and products: including money, headline news, books, travel, fashion, gifts, and health: http://www.zoom.co.uk/

Finance

Bank of England: information, press releases and job vacancies: http://www.bankofengland.co.uk/

Bank of Scotland: http://www.bankofscotland.co.uk/

Barclaycard: http://www.barclaycard.co.uk/

Barclays: http://www.barclays.co.uk/ and online banking at: http://www.barclays.co.uk/online.html

<u>Charles Schwab</u>: for investing services and up-to-the minute information. http://www.schwab-worldwide.com/Europe/

<u>Citibank</u>: online banking: http://www.citibank.com/uk/

<u>Co-Operative bank</u>: British banking site: http://www.co-operativebank.co.uk/

<u>Currency converter (164 currencies)</u>: http://www.oanda.com/convert/classic

<u>Dow Jones</u>: investment big player news source: http://www.dowjones.com/

<u>Egg</u>: popular online bank: http://www.egg.com/

<u>Electronic Share Information</u>: allows you to buy and sell UK shares on the Net: http://www.esi.co.uk/

<u>E*trade</u>: investing on the Internet: http://www.etrade.co.uk/

<u>FinanceWise</u>: search engine for financial information: http://www.financewise.com/

<u>Financial information directory (UK)</u>: http://www.find.co.uk/

<u>First Direct (UK bank)</u>: http://www.firstdirect.com/ and http://www.firstdirect.co.uk

<u>FT Quicken</u>: lots of key financial information, tools and resources: http://www.quicken.co.uk/

<u>HSBC Midland</u>: banking site: http://www.hsbc.co.uk/ (see also First Direct)

<u>Inland Revenue</u>: tax help: http://www.inlandrevenue.gov.uk/sa/ (self-assessment section only)

http://www.inlandrevenue.gov.uk/home.htm (general info: wide range)

<u>Interactive Investor International</u>: financial advice, products and services on key issues that matter: http://www.iii.co.uk/

Lloyds TSB: http://www.lloydstsb.co.uk/

London Stock Exchange: background information:
http://www.londonstockex.co.uk/ or http://www.stockex.co.uk/

Management Web Resources Database: contains links to many useful British
and international resources on management:
http://www.keele.ac.uk/depts/mn/teach/mgtlinks.htm

MoneyeXtra: UK site providing financial guidance on a range of topics:
http://www.moneyextra.com/

Moneygator.com: loans, mortgages plus other personal finance products from
which you can compare prices: http://www.moneygator.com/

Moneywise: information and advice about personal finance:
http://www.moneywise.co.uk/

MoneyWorld: investment, personal finance and financial help guides:
http://www.moneyworld.co.uk/

Nasdaq: all about the Nasdaq: http://www.nasdaq.com/

National Westminster Bank: http://www.natwest.co.uk/

Nationwide: http://www.nationwide.co.uk/

Offshore profits: from OPC International: how to opt out and still make
money; become a Cyber gypsy and live off-shore, plus a free ebook:
http://offshoreprofit.com/

Reuters: http://www.reuters.com/

Royal Bank of Scotland: http://www.rbs.co.uk/dbpc

Smile the Internet bank: part of the Co-operative Bank plc:
http://www.smile.co.uk/

The Motley Fool: an entertaining way to money management advice:
http://www.fool.co.uk/

The New York Stock Exchange: http://www.nyse.com/

The Office of Fair Trading (UK): lots of useful information and great advice about secure Internet shopping:
http://www.oft.gov.uk/html/shopping/index.html
The Street.com: a superb investing resource: http://www.thestreet.com/
The Wall Street Journal: http://www.wsj.com/

Food and drink

Beers Direct: a range of popular and "specialist" beers available to buy online here: http://www.beersdirect.com/ and http://www.lastorders.com/
Berry Bros and Rudd: superb wine shop selection:
http://www.berry-bros.co.uk/
Buitoni: an Italian flavour: http://www.buitoni.co.uk/
Cambell Soup: if soup takes your fancy: http://www.campbellsoup.com/
Cheese & Co: if cheese means more to you than..., then here you can buy Yorkshire's best: http://www.tasteofyorkshire.co.uk/
Cheese Hamlet: a wide range of cheeses available:
http://www.webart.co.uk/clients/hamlet/cheese.htm
Edibilia: proves that food and humour can make a perfect match:
http://www.pcug.co.uk/~owls/edibilia.html
Food and Health: more information about food and nutrition:
http://www.readersdigest.co.uk/food.htm
Food Channel: wide range of different kinds of information about food:
http://foodchannel.com/
FoodWatch: all about healthy eating: http://www.foodwatch.com.au/
Fuller Smith and Turner: all about this London brewery:
http://www.fullers.co.uk/
Godiva Chocolatier: chocolate heaven for chocaholics everywhere:
http://www.godiva.com/

Harmonie Organic Dairy Foods: dairy foods that come from happy cows:
http://www.harmonie.co.uk/

Kellogg's: like cereals? Then discover more:
http://www.kelloggs.com/

Milk – the National Dairy Council: lots of information about milk, cheese and
nutrition: http://www.milk.co.uk/

Pillsbury Central: for all who want to know more about Häagen-Dazs ice
cream or Green Giant vegetables: http://www.pillsbury.com/

Recipes for all tastes: the title says it all:
http://www.geocities.com/NapaValley/1111/

Smirnoff: if you like a vodka tipple, here you can find 365 vodka cocktails:
http://www.smirnoff.com/

Taco-L: recipes and ideas "discussing the world's most perfected food: the
taco": http://www.ashlists.org/taco-l

The Good Pub Guide: discover who's offering quality food, drink and
accommodation in England, Wales and Scotland:
http://www.goodguides.com/pubs/search.asp

The Rare Wine Cellar: buy your favourite wine online:
http://www.rarewine.co.uk/

Thorntons: chocolate heaven: http://www.thorntons.co.uk/

TuDocs: provides a superb directory of links to great cooking sites on the Net:
http://www.tudocs.com/

Vegetarian Resource Group: for everything vegetarian:
http://www.vrg.org/

Veggies Unite: vegetarian heaven: http://www.vegweb.com/

Whisky Shop: if whisky is for you, you'll find a wide variety on display,
including some rare blends: http://www.whiskyshop.com/

<u>Wine on the Web</u>: ideal tipple for wine drinkers and wine makers everywhere: http://www.wineontheweb.co.uk/

<u>Winecellar</u>: a wide range of fine wines and spirits are available to order here: http://www.winecellar.com/

<u>Young & Co Brewery</u>: mainly about Young & Co's range of real ale treats: http://www.youngs.co.uk/

Government and politics

<u>Government Information Service (UK)</u>: lots of information about the activities of the UK government: http://www.open.gov.uk/

<u>HM Treasury (UK)</u>: what the Chancellor of the Exchequer and the Treasury has to say: http://www.hm-treasury.gov.uk/

<u>Number 10</u>: take a virtual tour around the symbolic home of the British Prime Minister: http://www.number-10.gov.uk/ or http://www.pm.gov.uk/

<u>The White House</u>: visit Bill Clinton and the First Lady's main residence: http://www.whitehouse.gov/

Health and fitness

<u>American Heart Association</u>: cut your risk of getting heart disease: http://www.justmove.org/

<u>Children's health</u>: http://www.childrenshealth.co.uk/ch/ (see the facing page)

<u>Condomania</u>: condoms galore in a variety of styles – plus accessories (don't even ask): http://www.condoms4u.com/

<u>E-sthetics</u>: about plastic surgery from Patrick Hudson: http://www.phudson.com/

<u>FitnessLink</u>: resources to help you get fitter: http://www.fitnesslink.com/

<u>Gay Men's Health</u>: a thoroughly practical and useful resource including lots of superb information: http://www.gmhp.demon.co.uk/

<u>HealthSCOUT</u>: includes a powerful "ask a question" search tool to check out a wide range of health-related topics, side-effects from certain medicines, and so on: http://www.healthscout.com/

<u>Life on Purpose Institute</u>: guidelines for re-evaluating your life: http://www.lifeonpurpose.com/

<u>Mediconsult.com</u>: support and information about a range of ailments: http://www.mediconsult.com/

<u>Medisport</u>: information about sporting injuries and products to help treat them: http://www.medisport.co.uk/

<u>Sivananda Yoga</u>: relax and learn all about Sivananda Yoga: http://www.sivananda.org/

<u>The Quit Smoking Company</u>: can help you do just what it says: http://www.quitsmoking.com/

<u>ThinkNatural.com</u>: a UK-based health site – naturally with lots of health tips, information and remedies, plus an online shop: http://www.thinknatural.com/

<u>World Health Organisation (WHO)</u>: all about the WHO and what it stands for: http://www.who.int/

Help and Advice

<u>Buy.co.uk</u>: includes: tools to help you shop for the lowest rates on electricity, gas and water suppliers: http://www.buy.co.uk/

<u>Citizens Advice Bureau</u>: http://www.poptel.net/cab/

<u>Drug abuse</u>: discusses why it's simply not worth it: http://www.freevibe.com/ and http://www.freevibe.com/headsup/marijuana.shtml

<u>Expert Central</u>: solve your problem; ask a guru: http://www.expertcentral.com/

<u>Free2Try.com</u>: a US-oriented site with lots of free things on the Web: http://free2try.com/

<u>National Center for Missing and Exploited Children</u>: US-based site helping to find missing kids and fight exploitation of children: http://www.missingkids.com/

<u>The Samaritans</u>: one-to-one help if you're feeling low: http://www.samaritans.org.uk/ and http://www.mhnet.org/samaritans/

<u>TipWorld</u>: a great source of computer tips, news and gossip: http://www.tipworld.com/

<u>Which Magazine Online (consumer & legal advice)</u>: http://www.which.net/

Hobbies and crafts

<u>Bushido Online</u>: if you're into martial arts, here there's lot of information, news and details about events: http://www.bushido.ch/

FunTriva.com: if you like trivia, the amazing range of content on this site should tie you down for a while: http://www.funtrivia.com/

Lladró: all about these renowned and beautiful superb Spanish porcelain figures: http://www.lladro.es/

Holidays and Travel

@UK: superb tourism and travel guide to the UK:
http://www.atuk.co.uk/index.html

1Ski.com: current prices relating to skiing holidays around the world and what's happening on the slopes: http://www.1ski.com/

A Virtual Tour of Ireland: no explanation necessary
http://ireland.iol.ie/tip/

Automobile Association: a superb travellers resource; includes car breakdown services and accommodation in the UK: http://www.theaa.co.uk/

Bargainholidays.Com: go on, you know you need a break. Discover what's on offer: http://www.bargainholidays.com/

Bed & Breakfast Channel: information on bed and breakfast accommodation worldwide: http://www.bedandbreakfast.com/

Britannia: ideal resource for travellers coming to Britain; includes lots of useful links: http://www.britannia.com/

British Airways: http://www.britishairways.co.uk/

British Midland: http://www.britishmidland.com/

British Tourist Authority: an absolutely essential resource for anyone looking into travel around England, Scotland, Wales and Northern Ireland.
http://www.visitbritain.com/

Cheap Flights: search for cheap flights and related links:
http://www.cheapflights.com/

EasyJet: for simple no-fuss holiday deals: http://www.easyjet.com/

<u>Excite Travel</u>: information and links covering many destinations across the globe: http://www.city.net/ and http://www.excite.com/travel/

<u>Expedia (Microsoft)</u>: travel-related offerings: http://www.expedia.co.uk/

<u>Farebase Electronic</u>: check out holiday deals and book scheduled, charter and last-minute flights, plus links to other relevant sites: http://www.farebase.net/

<u>Glastonbury, England</u>: find out more about this compelling area with a rich history: http://www.glastonbury.co.uk/welcome/welcome.html

<u>Go</u>: British Airways low-cost airline: http://www.go-fly.co.uk/

<u>HolidayDeals.co.uk</u>: another late-break holiday deals provider: http://www.holidaydeals.co.uk/

Hotel Discounts: information on hotels and tools to make reservations: http://www.hoteldiscounts.com/

Hotel World: search for and check out over 9000 hotels in over 200 countries: http://www.hotelworld.com/

Infotel: ideal to help you find accommodation in the UK: http://www.infotel.co.uk/

Internet Holiday Rentals: for holiday homes to rent worldwide: http://www.holidayrentals.co.uk/

KLM (airline): http://www.klmuk.com/

Last Stop: Feel like you need a lift? Check out some great holiday deals at: http://www.laststop.co.uk/

LastMinute.com: for last minute travel, hotels, holidays, shows and gifts: http://www.lastminute.com/

LateRooms.com: the hotel industry's late availability database; snap up a bargain; get informed: http://www.laterooms.com/

Lonely Planet: superb resource where you can find out about destinations around the world: http://www.lonelyplanet.co.uk/

Lufthansa: http://www.lufthansa.com/

Multi Media Mapping: provides an interactive atlas of the UK; useful for touring and finding your way around: http://uk.multimap.com/

National Express: provides information about travelling across the UK by long distance coach: http://www.nationalexpress.co.uk/

Online Air Guide: flight times and hotels information: http://www.oag.com/

P&O Cruises: all about P&O and includes sailing departure and arrival times: http://www.pocruises.com/

RAC: local travel information throughout the UK: http://www.rac.co.uk/

Railtrack: provides basic information about the UK rail network: http://www.railtrack.co.uk/ or http://www.railtrack.com/

Rough Guides Travel: lots of guide books and information on many travel destinations around the world: http://travel.roughguides.com/

Ryanair: http://www.ryanair.ie

Silicon Village: travel directory: http://www.silicon.village.co.uk/

The Bayfair Website: a close look at the quaint seaside village of Robin Hood's Bay on the coast of North Yorkshire, England: http://www.bayfair.co.uk/

The Hawaiian Chieftain: tour around the beautiful San Francisco Bay in this tall sailing ship: http://www.hawaiianchieftain.com

The Internationalist: ideal resource for the international business traveller: http://www.internationalist.com/

The Train Line: find the train you want and book online: http://www.thetrainline.co.uk/

Thomas Cook: travel and holiday deals: http://www.thomascook.co.uk/

Thomson Holidays: general information about the different types of holidays available through Thomson: http://www.thomson-holidays.com/

Tjapukai: superb genuine Aboriginal site http://www.tjapukai.com.au

Travelcity: http://www.travelcity.co.uk/

Travelog.net: follow the adventures of a geek with a digital camera and a laptop as he travels the world: http://www.travelog.net/

UK Online: includes a huge range of links: http://www.ukonline.co.uk/

Virgin Atlantic: http://www.fly-virgin.com/

Virgin Express: http://www.virgin-express.com/

Virtual Tours: take a virtual tour of hundreds of locations around the world: http://www.virtualfreesites.com/world.html

World Travel Guide: an amazing amount of information on travel to every country in the world including B&B accommodation: http://www.travelguides.com/ and http://www.wtg-online.com/

<u>Yosemite.com</u>: discover the great outdoors in what Theodore Roosevelt called "The most beautiful place on Earth": http://www.yosemitepark.com/

Main UK Airports and airport information

<u>a2bAirports.com</u>: listing UK and Ireland airports: http://www.a2bairports.com/

<u>Belfast</u>: http://www.bial.co.uk/

<u>Birmingham International</u>: http://www.bhx.co.uk/

<u>Bristol</u>: details at: http://www.a2bairports.com/bristol.shtml

<u>Cardiff</u>: http://www.cial.co.uk/

<u>East Midlands</u>: http://www.eastmidsairport.co.uk/ema.html

<u>Edinburgh</u>: http://www.baa.co.uk/edinburg/navigaed.html

<u>Gatwick</u>: http://www.gatwickairport.co.uk/BAAHome.htm

<u>Glasgow</u>: http://www.glasgow.pwk.com/

<u>Heathrow</u>: http://www.heathrow.co.uk/BAAHome.htm

<u>Leeds/Bradford</u>: http://www.lbia.co.uk/
<u>Luton</u>: http://www.london-luton.co.uk/
<u>Manchester Airport</u>: http://www.manairport.co.uk/
<u>Newcastle International</u>: http://www.newcastleairport.com/
<u>Stanstead</u>: http://www.baa.co.uk/BAAHome.htm

Home, home improvement and garden

<u>Argos</u>: the online equivalent of the popular British chain store:
http://www.argos.co.uk/

<u>B&Q</u>: popular home improvement, DIY and garden centres:
http://www.diy.co.uk/

<u>British Gardening Online</u>: lots of gardening products and information:
http://www.oxalis.co.uk/

<u>Burncoose Nurseries</u>: a virtual garden nursery from which the intractably
green-fingered can buy plants, shrubs and all things gardening:
http://www.eclipse.co.uk/burncoose

<u>Cookson's Tools</u>: if you're into DIY tools, start drooling:
http://www.cooksons.com/

<u>Crocus.co.uk</u>: includes lots of gardening information, ideas, tips and gift ideas:
http://www.crocus.co.uk/

<u>Exhibition Seeds</u>: suppliers of quality seed products: http://www.exhibition-
seeds.co.uk/m

<u>Gardening.com</u>: lots of useful gardening information and products:
http://www.sierra.com/sierrahome/gardening/

<u>Greenfingers.com</u>: a UK site with lots of interesting information, hints, tips,
and ideas, an online gardening club, gardening news and a well-stocked shop:
http://www.greenfingers.com/

<u>Home Hunter</u>: ideal resource if looking for a home to buy or sell in the UK: http://www.homehunter.co.uk/

<u>Homebase</u>: DIY, home improvement and garden centres: http://www.homebase.co.uk/

<u>Ikea</u>: original yet simple home furnishing; find details about the store nearest to you plus lots of information and stuff for kids in the global site: http://www.ikea.com/content/

<u>Paint & Paper Library</u>: a beautifully designed Web site that provides an online "library of paint and wallpaper designs chosen for their innate sense of style, spirit and attitude": http://www.paintlibrary.co.uk/welcome.htm

<u>Pots and Pans</u>: in addition to pots and pans, this site from Scotland also sells a range of kitchenware and tableware products: http://www.pots-and-pans.co.uk/

<u>Royal Horticultural Society</u>: gardening books and gifts plus some plants: http://www.gardeningstore.com/

<u>The Antique Collector's Internet Directory</u>: deals with a range of antiques organised by category: http://www.acid.co.uk/acid

<u>The Citrus Centre</u>: selling a range of citrus fruit plants; useful information on cultivating citrus plants: http://www.citruscentre.co.uk/

<u>The Sofa Company</u>: Want a slick new sofa on the Net?
http://www.thesofacompany.net/

<u>Today's Homeowner</u>: includes useful resources on DIY and home improvement: http://www.todayshomeowner.com/

Insurance quotations

<u>EasyCover.com</u>: (includes CarQuote.com and HomeQuote.com):
http://www.easycover.com/

<u>Screentrade</u>: includes motor, home and travel insurance quotations:
http://www.screentrade.co.uk/

Humour

<u>Ask Dr. Science</u>: it's officially official: scientists are funny and here's the proof:
http://www.drscience.com/

<u>Cartoon Express</u>: more funny little pictures to split your sides:
http://www.cartoonexpress.com/

<u>Centre for the Easily Amused</u>: links to lots of funny Web sites:
http://www.amused.com/

<u>Comics</u>: lots of comic cartoons here: http://www.ctoons.com/

<u>Fade to Black</u>: a wicked comedy magazine: http://www.fadetoblack.com

<u>Funny</u>: the comedy Web directory: http://www.funny.co.uk/

<u>Good Clean Fun</u>: jokes resource: http://www.slonet.org/~tellswor/

<u>Humour.com</u>: information on famous comedians, jokes resource and cartoon comic strips: http://www.humor.com

<u>Jokes.com</u>: cartoons and joke of the day: http://www.jokes.com/

<u>Rec.humor.funny Home Page</u>: ...so many jokes – just make sure you don't pull a muscle through laughing too hard: http://www.netfunny.com

Internet

Anonymizer: one cool way to keep your email communications private:
http://www.anonymizer.com/

eFax.com: a superb service that converts faxes and voicemail to email messages for free – great if you're on the road: http://www.efax.com/

F9: UK Internet Service Provider and portal; includes information on business, technology, sports and TV listings: http://portal.f9.net.uk/

Free Agent (and Agent): popular standalone newsreader software:
http://www.forteinc.com/

FreewareWeb: dedicated to finding the best free stuff on the Web:
http://www.freewareweb.com/newsindex.html

HushMail: tools for setting up totally private email communications:
http://www.hushmail.com/

International Association for Professionalism Online (IAPO): a body formed to help raise the level of professionalism on the Internet:
http://www.IAPOnline.org/

Internet.com: includes lots of Internet-related news and information:
http://www.internet.com/

Internet Relay Chat Help: over 1000 Help files on IRC topics:
http://www.irchelp.org/

NetCafes: lists details of over 3000 Internet cafes in 135 countries:
http://www.netcafes.com/

Newsville.com: a huge list of newsgroups available on the Internet:
http://www.newsville.com/news/groups/

ProxyMate: ProxyMate enables Internet users to protect their privacy while online: http://lpwa.com:8000/

Reflex Macro Interceptor: great for zapping macro viruses:
http://www.reflex-magnetics.co.uk/

Response-O-Matic: add forms to your Web site without any programming needed and have the information emailed to you:
http://www.response-o-matic.com/

The CGI Resource Index: for experienced Web designers and computer programmers, contains hundreds of ready-to-use program snippets and scripts and related information: http://www.cgi-resources.com/

The Internet Traffic Report: provides information about response times of key areas of the Internet: http://www.internettrafficreport.com/

The Pocket: zany guide to the "best" content on Internet:
http://www.thepocket.com/

The UK Online Telephone Directory: find any individual or business phone number in the UK: http://www.bt.com/phonenetuk/

The Web 100: provides a great guide on the top 100 Web sites on the Net. Ranking is achieved by Internet voters and updated regularly:
http://www.web100.com/

The World Wide Web Consortium (W3C): all about one of the bodies that help the Internet develop: http://www.w3c.org/

Tools for the Net: lots of free tools to help you use the Internet:
http://www.toolsforthe.net/

Worst of the Web: is a useful guide to how not to design Web sites:
http://www.worstoftheweb.com/

ZoneAlarm: stop hackers poking about inside your computer while online. Get your own superb free personal firewall software:
http://www.zonealarm.com/

Zoomerang: create forms for your Web site without knowing anything about Web programming: http://www.zoomerang.com

Selected free email providers

Excite Mail: http://www.mailexcite.com/

Geocities: http://www.geocities.com/
iName: http://www.iname.com/
Microsoft Hotmail: http://www.hotmail.com/
Yahoo Mail: http://mail.yahoo.com/

Museums and galleries

Louvre Museum: access to an amazing collection of art from around the world:
http://www.culture.fr/louvre
Museum of the History of Science: from the University of Oxford:
http://www.mhs.ox.ac.uk/
Smithsonian Institute: http://www.si.edu/
Tate Modern: a superb collection of modern art from around the world:
http://fm370.facility.pipex.com/modern/
The National Gallery: http://www.nationalgallery.org.uk/
The National Museum of Science and Industry:
http://www.nmsi.ac.uk/
The Natural History Museum: discover all about living things:
http://www.nhm.ac.uk/
The Tate Gallery: http://fm370.facility.pipex.com/home/default.htm
Web Museum: http://sunsite.doc.ic.ac.uk/wm/

Nature and environment

Daily Planet: weather and weather-related topics:
http://www.atmos.uiuc.edu
Friends of the Earth: all about important environmental topics:
http://www.foe.co.uk/
Greenpeace: lots of information about topics that threaten our environment:
http://www.greenpeace.org/

<u>National Geographic</u>: some information relating to the magazine of the same name: http://www.nationalgeographic.com/

<u>Royal Geographic Society</u>: for information and news about the Society: http://www.rgs.org/

<u>Save America's Forests</u>: taking action to prevent the total destruction of America's last ancient forests: http://www.saveamericasforests.org/

<u>Shell UK</u>: proves there's more to oil than you might think: http://www.shell.co.uk/

<u>TerraServer</u>: using resources from the SPIN-2 (Space Information - 2 metre resolution) satellite, you can choose a geographical region, then zoom in from space to make out objects as small as 2 metres: http://www.terraserver.com/

The BBC Weather Centre: get the latest forecast:
http://www.bbc.co.uk/weather/

The Living Almanac of Disasters: discover about natural disasters around the world: http://disasterium.com/

The Met Office: lots of information about UK weather forecasting, plus other places around the world: http://www.met-office.gov.uk/

The Nature Conservancy: learn more about what's being done in nature conservation: http://www.tnc.org/

The RainForest Site: One mouse is all it takes to help protect more of the Rain Forest for free: http://www.therainforestsite.com/

The United States Environmental Protection Agency: discover what the USA is doing to help the planet: http://www.epa.gov/

The Weather Channel: provides detailed US weather information plus weather forecasts from around the world: http://www.weather.com/

The WorldWide Fund for Nature: here you can learn more about nature conservancy and actively help by signing petitions: http://www.panda.org/

Volcanoes.com: lots of interesting information about volcanoes around the world: http://www.volcanoes.com/

News, newspapers and magazines

About.com Internet News: http://today.about.com/

AutoExpress: the car news weekly source: http://www.autoexpress.co.uk/

BBC Online: all about the British Broadcasting Corporation:
http://www.bbc.co.uk/home/today/

BBC World Service: the world-renowned radio service now on the Web:
http://www.bbc.co.uk/worldservice/

British Magazines Direct: reference source for UK magazines; find the one you want and you can easily order it online:
http://www.britishmagazines.com/

CNet: The Computer Network includes news, information and downloads relating to computers: http://www.cnet.com/

CNN: includes US and world news with special categories covered: http://www.cnn.com/

Computer Active: a superb plain English magazine online with lots of information and downloads: http://www.computeractive.vnunet.com/

Computer Buyer: http://www.computerbuyer.co.uk/

Computer Shopper: http://www.computershopper.co.uk/

Daltons Weekly: the online version of this popular UK magazine: http://www.daltons.co.uk/

Electronic Newstand: provides many magazines to view online and you can even sign up to receive your copy: http://www.enews.com/

Empire Magazine: all about movie news and reviews of the latest films: http://www.empireonline.co.uk/

Europemedia.com: free weekly news report covering the most important developments in online business markets: http://www.europemedia.com/

Exchange and Mart: buy and sell in the motor, home & leisure and business areas: http://www.exchangeandmart.co.uk/

Fortune: business information and features from Fortune Magazine: http://www.fortune.com

FutureNet: publishing conglomerate Future Publishing shows what's available from their amazing range of magazines: http://www.futurnet.com/

Internetnews.com: covers news about the Internet and the Web and organised into topic categories: http://www.internetnews.com/

LineOne: popular British Internet Service Provider that also includes UK and foreign news and weather information: http://www.lineone.net/

Loot: UK financial magazine: share dealing, etc.: http://www.loot.com/

MacUser: for everything Apple Mac: http://www.macuser.co.uk/

New Scientist/Planet Science: interesting and easy to understand online version of the printed magazine: http://www.newscientist.com/
NewsNow: news headlines and links to other general news sources: http://www.newsnow.co.uk/

NewsPage: up-to-date news on a wide range of industries: http://www.newspage.com/ or http://www.individual.com/
PC Pro Magazine: http://www.pcpro.co.uk/
Private Eye: the online equivalent of the magazine: http://www.private-eye.co.uk/
Reuters: the world-renowned news service online: http://www.reuters.com/
Slate: an entirely Internet-based news and literary magazine: http://www.slate.com/

<u>Sporting Life</u>: the online version of this popular sporting newspaper: http://www.sporting-life.com/

<u>The Daily Mail</u>: popular British newspaper that includes lots of interesting links: http://www.dailymail.co.uk/

<u>The Daily Telegraph</u>: the online version of this popular British newspaper: http://www.dailytelegraph.co.uk/

<u>The Economist</u>: online version of the renowned business and current affairs magazine: http://www.economist.co.uk/ or http://www.economist.com/

<u>The Financial Times</u>: http://news.ft.com/

<u>The Guardian</u>: Guardian Unlimited provides the online equivalent of The Guardian and The Observer: http://www.guardian.co.uk/

<u>The Independent</u>: http://www.independent.co.uk/

<u>The Mirror</u>: http://www.mirror.co.uk/

<u>The Sun</u>: http://www.the-sun.co.uk/

<u>The Times</u>: http://www.the-times.co.uk/

<u>The Wall Street Journal</u>: http://www.wsj.com/

<u>The Week (political magazine)</u>: http://www.theweek.co.uk/

<u>USA Today</u>: access the online version of this popular US newspaper: http://www.usatoday.com/

<u>Wired</u>: online version of the renowned cutting edge computer magazine, featuring news about computers and the Internet: http://www.wired.com/

Religion and philosophy

<u>About Wicca</u>: informative site about the religion of Wicca and other links: http://www.stolaf.edu/people/petersol/

<u>Chijmes</u>: a beautifully designed, interesting and spiritually uplifting Web site that is well worth a look for those also interested in history: http://www.chijmes.com.sg

Christian Naturists: living and worshipping like Adam and Eve – literally! Perhaps just a little bit draughty: http://home.vistapnt.com/markm/

God Allows U-Turns: includes a variety of short stories written by people from around the world, plus a free ezine: http://www.godallowsuturns.com/

Hare Krishna Home Page: information about the religion of Krishna Consciousness as founded by A. C. Bhaktivedanta Swami Prabhupada. http://www.webcom.com/~ara/

Hinduism Today: a popular online Hindu family newspaper: http://www.HinduismToday.kauai.hi.us/ashram/htoday.html or http://www.himalayanacademy.com/ht/

HinduNet: a popular focal point for the Hindu outlook and Hindu values: http://www.hindunet.org/

How Can I Make Money: an unusual title that relates to a religious personal view from the life and experiences of successful businessman George Parry: http://www.georgeparry.com.au/

How to Know God: an interactive experience of best-selling motivational author Deepak Chopra: http://www.howtoknowgod.com/

Jehovah's Witnesses: http://www.watchtower.org/

Jesus Saves: learn all about the Bible and get guidance for modern living: http://www.jesussaves.cc/site_map.html

Latif.com: includes interesting information on Muslim issues, news and events and Qur'an verse: http://www.latif.com/

Maven: devoted to Jewish and Israeli issues: http://www.maven.co.il

Online confession: from the Universal Life Church; just tell it all by filling in the online form: http://www.ulc.net/confession.html

Ontario Consultants on Religious Tolerance: lots of information and links on many different worldwide religions: http://www.religioustolerance.org/var_rel.htm

<u>Religious Society of Friends</u>: all about Quakers and links to Quaker organisations; mostly text: http://www.quaker.org/

<u>The Book of Witches</u>: how to become a white Witch and make a difference: http://www.maxpages.com/witchesbook2

<u>The Celestine Vision</u>: relates to James Redfield's best-selling book "The Celestine Prophesy" and questions whether coincidences are really just coincidences: http://www.celestinevision.com/

<u>The Damanhur Community</u>: the amazing Federation of Damanhur, an international centre for spiritual research and alternative community based in the alpine foothills of northern Italy: http://www.damanhur.org/

<u>The Holy See</u>: the official site about the Pope and the Vatican: http://www.vatican.va

<u>The University of Science & Philosophy</u>: lots of information provided within a graphically stunning presentation: http://www.philosophy.org/

<u>Tyburn Convent</u>: take an incredible virtual tour of this amazing London convent. A superbly designed Web site: http://www.tyburnconvent.org.uk/

<u>Universal Life Church</u>: become an official minister of the Universal Life Church in minutes while online and print out your official certificate to prove it: http://www.ulc.org/

<u>Witches League for Public Awareness</u>: from Salem, Massachusetts, a kind of witching portal for people with an interest in paganism and the occult: http://www.celticcrow.com/

Search engines and directories

<u>About.com</u>: http://about.com/

<u>AltaVista</u>: one of the Internet's primary search engines for Web pages and newsgroups: http://www.altavista.digital.com/

<u>BarclaySquare</u>: http://www.barclaysquare.co.uk/

<u>Big Yellow Pages</u>: mainly US-biased content: http://www.bigyellow.com/

<u>BigFoot</u>: US-biased email address locator: http://www.bigfoot.com/

<u>Deja News</u>: hailed as "the" resource for searching newsgroups:
http://www.dejanews.com/

<u>Excite</u>: a powerful popular search engine that you can limit to the UK and
Europe as well as globally: http://www.excite.co.uk/

<u>FinanceWise</u>: search engine for financial information:
http://www.financewise.com/

<u>Find thousands of publicly accessible mailing lists</u>:
http://paml.alastra.com/

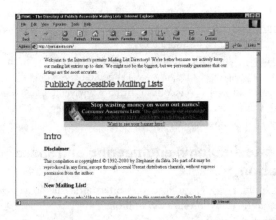

<u>Four11</u>: email address directory: over 6.5 million email addresses listed:
http://www.four11.com/

<u>Goto</u>: primary search engine that can give special emphasis to words using
values: http://www.goto.com/

<u>HotBot</u>: primary Internet search engine from Wired magazine:
http://www.hotbot.com/

<u>Infoseek</u>: primary Internet search engine for the Web, newsgroups and email addresses: http://www.infoseek.com/

<u>Liszt</u>: lists hundreds of mailing list sources: http://www.liszt.com/

<u>Lycos</u>: primary Internet search engine:
http://www.lycos.com/ and http://www.lycos.co.uk/

<u>Mama</u>: the Mother of all search engines: http://www.mamma.com/

<u>MindIt</u>: you can send an email message to track a Web page. When the page changes, MindIt emails you automatically: http://mindit.netmind.com/

<u>Search.com</u>: resource that lets you access many different types of Internet search tools: http://www.search.com/

<u>Shops On the Net</u>: http://www.shopsonthenet.co.uk/

<u>UK Shops</u>: http://www.ukshops.co.uk/

<u>Yahoo</u>: arguably the most popular search tool and directory on the Internet: http://www.yahoo.com/ or http://www.yahoo.co.uk/

<u>Yellow pages</u>: http://www.yell.com/ or http://www.yell.co.uk/

<u>Zineworld</u>: a directory for ezines and Webzines on the Net:
http://www.oblivion.net/zineworld/

Science, technology, engineering and space exploration

<u>Annals of Improbable Research</u>: covers often little-known yet compelling areas of scientific study: http://www.improb.com/

<u>Atomic Bomb making guide – in a nutshell</u>: for academic use only of course. Read at your own risk: I accept no responsibility for any medical conditions resulting from extreme boredom:
http://www.student.nada.kth.se/~nv91-asa/atomic.html

<u>Boeing</u>: about aeroplanes, modern weaponry and space vehicles: http://www.boeing.com/

<u>Moller Sky Car</u>: the world's first personal vertical takeoff and landing vehicle. Order yours today: http://www.moller.com/skycar/

<u>NASA</u>: the Office of Space Science: covers recent missions like the Mars Pathfinder and Hubble Space Telescope: http://spacescience.nasa.gov/

<u>National Geographic</u>: the online equivalent of the US-originated magazine: http://www.nationalgeographic.com/

<u>National Library of Medicine</u>: huge resource of medical and scientific information: http://www.nlm.nih.gov/

<u>National Space Science Data Center</u>: lots of information and pictures of space: http://nssdc.gsfc.nasa.gov/

<u>New Scientist</u>: the magazine on the Web: http://www.newscientist.co.uk/

<u>Popular Science</u>: online version of the magazine with the same name: http://www.popularscience.com/

<u>Science Daily</u>: up-to-the-minute research news from around the world: http://www.sciencedaily.com/

<u>Science Online</u>: information covering research projects, news, career guidelines and online discussions: http://www.sciencemag.org/

<u>SETI@home</u>: join in the search for extraterrestrial intelligence; you can download a free program and help find ET before the Borg arrive: http://setiathome.ssl.berkeley.edu/

<u>Spacelinks</u>: information on careers in the space business plus some slick Web design: http://www.spacelinks.com/

<u>The Planetary Society</u>: help search for alien life in the universe and learn all about things astronomical: http://www.planetary.org/

<u>The World's Smallest Web Server</u>: a Web computer the size of a matchbox: http://wearables.stanford.edu/

Shopping (general)

All Sports Retail: online version of the popular British sportswear retailer: http://www.allsportsretail.co.uk/

Amazon.com: for books, music, videos, articles, reviews: http://www.amazon.com/ or http://www.amazon.co.uk/

Asda: by the time this book is in print, maybe your local store has much to offer online: http://www.asda.co.uk/

Avon: wide range of skin care, make-up and fragrances plus many other products: http://www.uk.avon.com/

Barclaycard Online Store: Barclaycard's online Hi-Fi store: http://catalogue.barclaycard.co.uk./cgi-bin/audio.storefront

Black Star: an all-in-one UK video; covers a range of categories: http://www.blackstar.co.uk/

BT Internet: offers many links to brand name shopping sites: http://www.btinternet.com/

Dixons Online: electronic goods and accessories: http://www.dixons.co.uk/

eComet: popular British domestic electronic goods (mostly) retailer: http://www.comet.co.uk/

Elizabeth Botham: superb Yorkshire cakes and various delicious varieties available here: http://www.botham.co.uk/

Finding UK-specific shops on the Net: http://www.shopsonthenet.co.uk/ (see the facing page) and http://www.shopguide.co.uk/

Flowers Direct: possibly the UK's largest florist online: http://www.flowersdirect.co.uk/

Gap: http://www.gap.com/

Genie: a news, information and entertainment portal from BT Cellnet: http://www.genie.co.uk/

Giftstore UK: a wide range of gifts: http://www.giftstore.co.uk/

<u>Great Universal Stores (GUS)</u>: http://www.homeshopping.co.uk/

<u>Greetings Direct</u>: greeting cards online from the Cancer Research Campaign:
http://www.greetingsdirect.co.uk/

<u>Innovations</u>: an virtual shop containing the most popular gadgets:
http://www.innovations.co.uk/

<u>Interflora</u>: now there's no excuse for not getting that special gift of flowers:
http://www.interflora.co.uk/

<u>LastMinute.com</u>: for last minute travel, shows, and weekend breaks:
http://www.lastminute.com/

<u>LetsBuyIt.com</u>: discover all about co-buying: http://www.letsbuyit.com/

<u>Next</u>: http://www.next.com/

<u>Nike</u>: http://www.nikefootball.com/

<u>Safeway</u>: see what's new at your local supermarket online:
http://www.safeway.co.uk/

<u>Sainsburys</u>: http://www.sainsburys.co.uk/

<u>SayItNow.co.uk</u>: online shopping with a difference: dubbed as "Gifts and ideas for any occasion": http://www.sayitnow.co.uk/

<u>ShopGuide</u>: an online guide to great shops on the Net:
http://www.shopguide.co.uk/

<u>ShoppersUniverse</u>: http://www.shoppersuniverse.co.uk/

<u>ShopSmart.Com</u>: a wide range of shopping categories here including publications, clothes, gifts, health and fitness, tickets and events:
http://www.shopsmart.com/

<u>Somerfield</u>: at the time of going to print, only a limited range of shopping options at this supermarket were available: http://www.somerfield.co.uk/

<u>Tesco Online</u>: if you hate shopping or are too busy and you live in one of the UK areas supported by Tesco's online shopping service, you can shop for your weekly groceries here: http://www.tesco.co.uk/

<u>The Carphone Warehouse</u>: a superb resource to help you get the right mobile phone: http://www.carphonewarehouse.com/

<u>The Complete Outdoors</u>: outdoor gear and tackle here:
http://www.complete-outdoors.co.uk/

<u>The Co-op</u>: offers an impressive range of shopping options from this established high street chain: http://www.co-op.co.uk/

<u>The Highland Trail</u>: provides information about a range of unique and interesting products from Scotland: http://www.highlandtrail.co.uk/

<u>The Kite Shop</u>: relax and fly a kite: different kinds of kites available here:
http://www.kiteshop.co.uk/

<u>Ticketmaster UK</u>: here you can buy tickets for a wide range of events:
http://www.ticketmaster.co.uk/

<u>Toys R Us</u>: lots of toys available to buy for children of all ages:
http://www.toysrus.co.uk/ or http://www.toysrus.com/

UK Shops: shopping site: http://www.ukshops.co.uk/

UKShopSearch: the directory for UK-based online shops and UK-friendly global stores: http://www.ukshopsearch.com/

ValueDirect.com shopping network: http://www.valuedirect.com/

Wild Trak: lots of outdoor gear, climbing equipment and related stuff: http://www.wildtrak.com/

Xtra.co: popular New Zealand portal site: http://www.xtra.co.nz/

ZDNet: http://www.zdnet.co.uk/

Society and culture

alt.culture: Exploring the 1990s: http://www.altculture.com/

Amnesty International: helping people anywhere who can't ask for help: http://www.amnesty.org.uk/ or http://www.amnesty.org/

CanDo.com: a great Web community aimed at disabled people, their families, friends and carers: http://www.cando.com/

Car Free Cities: exploring methods to free our cities of car congestion: http://www.carfree.com/

House of Tartan: ideal for those who want to find out about and buy anything tartan: http://www.house-of-tartan.scotland.net/

RETRO: Covers popular themes from the last three quarters of the 20th Century: http://www.retroactive.com/

Shakespeare's Globe Theatre: http://www.reading.ac.uk/globe/

The British Library: browse a database of 20,000 artistic works from London's Guildhall Library and Art Gallery: http://collage.nhil.com/

The Cafe Society: a fascinating site mainly about photography and electronic imagery: http://www.cafesociety.org/cafe/

The Campaign Against Age Discrimination in Employment (CAADE): http://www.caade.net/

The History of the World: http://www.hyperhistory.com/

The Hunger Site: One mouse click is all it takes to feed someone with not enough to eat for free: http://www.thehungersite.com/

The Millennium Dome Experience: a superb Web presentation: http://www.dome2000.co.uk/

The National Society for Prevention of Cruelty to Children (NSPCC): http://www.nspcc.org.uk/

The RainForest Site: One mouse is all it takes to help protect more of the Rain Forest for free: http://www.therainforestsite.com/

ThirdAge: information and resources on third-age issues: http://www.thirdage.com/

UpMyStreet: discover key information and statistics about different areas of the UK: http://www.upmystreet.com/

Women.com: themes that are of particular interest to women everywhere: http://www.women.com/

Sport

All Sports Retail: get your kit on(line): http://www.allsportsretail.co.uk/

Arsenal Football Club: http://www.arsenal.co.uk/

Bluesquare: place your bets please; dubbed as a jargon-free bookmarker http://www.bluesq.com/

Boxing.com: if you're keen on boxing news, rules, facts and figures, you'll love this site: http://www.boxing.com/

British Athletics: an ideal resource if you want to see listings of British athletics clubs and links to other related sites: http://www.british-athletics.co.uk/

CarlingNet: the all-in-one football resource: http://www.carlingnet.com/

Chelsea Football Club: http://www.chelseafc.co.uk/

Cricket Unlimited: largely current cricket news:
http://www.cricketunlimited.co.uk/

Enterprise City: includes a useful list of soccer clubs online if you want to buy kit direct: http://www.enterprisecity.co.uk/

ESPN Network: covers popular sports in the USA: http://www.espn.com/

F1 Central: if speed racing and Formula 1 is for you, you'll love this site:
http://www.f1central.net/

Fastball: covers key topics, news and information on major league baseball
http://www.fastball.com/

Formula1.com: includes news, stories and features on Formula 1 racing:
http://www.formula1.com/

Golf.com: for golf news, background information and features:
http://www.golf.com/

Gorp: if you like participating in outdoor activities, the Great Outdoors Recreation Pages site is worth a look: http://www.gorp.com/

JD Sports: online version of this well-established high street retailer:
http://www.jdsports.co.uk/home.html

Leeds United Football Club: http://www.lufc.co.uk/

Lords Cricket Ground: to learn more about Lords Cricket ground and why not take a tour of the online shop while you're there: http://www.lords.org/

Manchester United Football Club: http://www.manutd.com/

Newcastle Football Club: http://www.nufc.co.uk/

Newitts: incredible range of sports items available:
http://www.newitts.com/online/

NFL.com: the (American) National Football League site. If you like American football, don't miss this one: http://www.nfl.com/

Rugby Football Union (RFU): lots of useful information about the game:
http://www.rfu.com/

<u>SkiNet</u>: a must-have resource if you're into skiing:
http://www.iski.com/

<u>Soccernet</u>: lots of up-to-date
information on soccer league
results, news, and events from
the UK and around the world:
http://www.soccernet.com/

<u>Sporting Life</u>: includes lots of
popular sports, news and
features: http://www.sporting-
life.com/

<u>Sports.com</u>: with a European
flavour and links to US-oriented
sports, includes the following
topics: soccer, cricket, golf, tennis, rugby, Formula 1, rally and
boxing: http://www.sports.com/

<u>TotalBet</u>: if you like to go
betting, this site in association
with Tote and Sporting Life offers lots of sporting topics to choose from:
https://www.totalbet.com/

<u>Wimbledon Tennis Tournament</u>: the All England Lawn Tennis and Croquet
Club site that is particularly popular during the Wimbledon tennis tournament:
http://www.wimbledon.com/

<u>Wrestling</u>: investigating ways to squeeze red juice out of oversized meat and
generally promote the virtues of pain – providing it's happening to someone
else of course: http://www.wrestling.com/

<u>XPC Extreme Sports</u>: if you like extreme sports, jump off onto this one:
http://www.extremesports.com/

Strange and bizarre (some adult themes)

<u>Area 51</u>: discover what's in those secret military bases in New Mexico
http://www.ufomind.com/area51/

<u>Church of the Subgenius</u>: covers extracts from The Book of the Subgenius by
J R "Bob" Dobbs, a strange pipe-puffing preacher with a lot to say (warning:
includes adult themes of dubious value): http://www.subgenius.com/

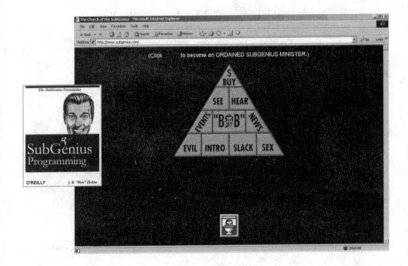

<u>Disobey</u>: a collection of dark and disobedient topics: http://www.disobey.com/

<u>Heaven's Gate</u>: discover how Heaven's Gate met the mothership hiding behind the Hale-Bopp comet: http://www.heavensgatetoo.com/

<u>Magic online</u>: behold, I am Simeon – proves I can read your mind; prepare to be amazed: http://www.caveofmagic.com/

<u>Morbid Fact Archive</u>: if you're broad-minded, prepare for some strange and bizarre reading; not for the fainthearted:
http://www.shocking.com/~despair/morb996.htm

<u>Phonebashing</u>: taking it out on innocent mobile phones:
http://www.phonebashing.com/

<u>Red Meat</u>: zany brainchild of cartoonist Max Cannon; for those who hold strong opinions about red meat: http://www.redmeat.com/

<u>The House of the Techno Discordians</u>: all about an "irreligious" cult who believe "God is a crazy woman" (their words, not mine – and my wife agrees): http://www.discordia.org/

<u>Universal Life Church – ordain yourself in seconds</u>: you've been telling them for years so why not become a legally ordained minister (USA) today: http://www.ulc.net/ or http://www.sotari.org/ordain.htm

<u>Waco Never Again</u>: information about David Koresh and the Branch Davidian cult and the notorious antics of the FBI: http://home.maine.rr.com/waco/

<u>YaHooka</u>: a site that suggests it is "The guide to marijuana on the Internet". If like me, you have no experience of marijuana, some surprises are guaranteed. Also includes a health and medical section: http://www.yahooka.com/

The Internet:
yesterday and tomorrow

Today, we're seeing the first tiny shoots of a communications network that is spanning the entire globe. So let's explore the rise of the Internet and make a guess at some of the Internet-related developments that might emerge to play an important role in our lives throughout the coming years.

How did the Internet come about?

The "cold war" era of the 20th Century was without doubt a tense time. Superpowers rivalled for domination and the entire show was fuelled by mankind's two basic emotions: greed and fear. In the 1960s, key people in the US military were charged with considering the unthinkable: the task of masterminding a communications network that could survive a global nuclear war. Originally, only military computers were linked to form a grid or an "inter-net" of various kinds of computers to form ARPAnet.

During the 1980s, universities and library computer networks were added to the military network to explore new possibilities and the term "Internet" was born. Gradually, others too realised the potential: business and commerce, schools and individuals during the following years "tried out" this new idea until hundreds, thousands, then millions of computers around the world were "connected" to the Internet. The 1990s saw the fastest growth ever of the Internet, arguably fuelled by governmental recognition when American Vice President Al Gore provided special funding to further develop and look more closely into what he referred to as "the Information Superhighway."

Also during the 1990s, the idea of a World Wide Web (WWW) emerged from the amazing and prophetic British researcher Tim Berners-Lee while working at the CERN Laboratory for Particle Physics in Switzerland. The WWW or "Web" as it is more popularly known, has developed into the most incredible, most visible and the fastest growing sector of the Internet!

Today, millions of computers have access to the Internet and commercial and individual interests have essentially "taken over" in a big way. This shows no sign of stopping; in fact, my guess is that our use of the Internet is only just beginning!

The Internet is set to become the dominant global communications channel of the 21st Century, providing a common "melting pot" for television, telecommunications and the sharing of knowledge in all its forms. This amazing growth rate has astounded many experts and continues to break records and smash limits while probably changing stock market patterns permanently. New ways of valuing businesses are emerging based on future growth potential rather than short-term profits. This growth is fuelled by ever-falling communications prices around the world – a trend set to continue. As the price of key technology and Internet access falls, more opportunities for millions of ordinary people in many countries around the world become available – and just like you, people are curious and keen to discover more.

However, as we have seen with recent computer virus scares, the great strength of the Internet is also its biggest weakness. The more people who use the Internet, the more we as a race come to rely on it, the more inter-connected our world becomes, the more precarious our situation. It only takes a single continually mutating computer virus to cause widespread chaos.

Perhaps the safest option is to somehow find a balance and understand that the Internet is just another tool for modern living, and not let the ever-increasing drive for self-interest and short-term gains blind us into thinking the Internet is the answer to every problem – it simply isn't!

The future of email

Currently most people send and receive email messages using plain text. However, voice – and video eventually – is set to replace text! Although clearly a better option for most people, don't pack away your keyboard just yet: practical video email is still some way off. However, when you "talk" your message, you don't need to use a keyboard or know how to type. In fact, voice recognition software – that really works – looks set to really take off.

So what does voice recognition technology really mean? How about "talking" your email message and letting your computer create the words and sentences, or simply "package" your message as a special file to be recovered at the receiver's end and simply played back? Sound good? Well even today, several companies already provide the software tools to do just that – maybe the end result is not yet ideal but at least it can work when set up correctly.

We can explore this idea more using pictures from a WebCam – a small video camera usually mounted somewhere near a computer monitor or television – and include a microphone, speaker and the right software to drive the WebCam. Then, you simply talk your message, click Send and the software does the rest. Your video mail moves at lightening speed across the Internet to your recipient. They play your message, perhaps a little envious at how good you look first thing in the morning. Or you can simply establish a video phone connection and both communicate using live pictures and sound.

If you're in business especially, maybe you'll still need to remember to dress in a way that your contact expects. The technology for all of this exists now, but a suitable take-up trigger needs a little more time to develop. Quite reasonably you may ask, why then bother with plain old email? Videophone technology already exists in early forms, so why not just talk in real time (live)? For one reason, your recipient may live in another time zone and probably might not appreciate a chat about the minutes of the last meeting at 3 o'clock in the morning in their time zone!

However, just like video recorders and DVDs, it's always possible to record a message and queue it for playback later. A video email-based system will probably develop as the amazing pace of technology development continues to put more stuff into smaller spaces while still increasing the rate of information transfer. Learning how to "do more with less" usually means saving money, so it is indeed becoming one of the leading mantras of the 21st Century.

Email, video and voice recognition technology will probably merge together to create a complete solution soon. The next generation of mobile phones are set to include a small screen on which you can see who you're calling as well as gain access to the Web – which is already becoming a standard feature in most new mobile phones today. Perhaps when finished with live calls, your mobile phone will be designed to automatically switch back to its default state: a kind of Internet stand-by mode. Whenever you want to go online, you'll probably have access to a miniature version of your favourite Web browser set up with all your favourite phone numbers, email addresses and Web pages stored.

Tomorrow: Internet2 and the Super-Internet

The desire to smash limits and see what lies beyond is part of who we are and what it is to be human. Likewise, the never-ending drive to invent ways to speed up the Internet continues. Right now, several organisations around the world are developing technologies that will form the next generation of the Net. Internet2 (I2), for example, is set to improve the flow of information between Universities and other research establishments in the USA – remember, that is how the Internet as we know it today first started to grow.

The coming merger between television and the Internet has created even greater urgency for devising a better way to move bucket loads of complex information like video around the Internet. Currently, Project Oxygen – the Super-Internet – is one scheme under development that seeks to provide the answers needed.

However, if completely free Internet access were to become widespread, those who provide the services would have to recoup their costs from somewhere. So advertising may provide part of the solution. Charging for access to Web sites may also result. And to follow the chaotic nature of the Internet, maybe we'll end up with a combination of several low-cost fund-raising solutions coupled with a mishmash of advertising that currently funds most television providers around the world.

So will we be switching on to "TeleNet" in a few years: a marriage of global television and the Internet? Only time will tell. If so, the current owners of that brand name may soon be glad of their excellent choice of words. Whatever develops will reflect the choices you, I, and billions of other Internet users make and the actions we take now and during the coming years. Thank you for using this book; I hope you have enjoyed it. Have fun and good luck with using *your* Internet (let's keep it that way). Please send your comments, feedback and suggestions to: publisher@ineasysteps.com

Jargon buster

<u>Access provider</u>: an organisation that provides individual access to the Internet. Also known as an Internet Access Provider (IAP), and Internet Service Provider (ISP).

<u>Acrobat</u>: software from Adobe used to create highly compressed publications in the Portable Document Format (PDF) to view on-screen or be printed.

<u>ActiveX</u>: self-running program components that can be downloaded and run in a Web page. Also known as ActiveX Controls.

<u>Active content</u>: often refers to a Web page containing components and self-running programs that can provide a variety of animated and interactive effects.

<u>Active Desktop</u>: a built in option within Microsoft Internet Explorer that enables a user to allow Internet Explorer and Web channels to manage the entire appearance of the Microsoft Windows desktop.

<u>ActiveMovie</u>: a Microsoft program often referred to as a Control that allows playback of various file formats for example: AVI, MPEG, QuickTime and Wav files..

<u>Address book</u>: a program used to store email addresses and key contact details.

<u>ADSL (Asymmetrical Digital Subscriber Line)</u>: a system that allows fast data communications over traditional telephone lines. The speed at which data is sent from an ISP to a user (downstream) is much greater than sending data from a computer to an ISP (upstream). Typically, data comes to your computer at about 8Mbps, while data goes away from your computer at 64Kbps.

<u>Analogue information</u>: computers, modems and the Internet help move information around. Computers understand information using only two levels: 1 and 0 (or high and low): this is called digital. The human voice is made up of various levels: this is called analogue. A modem converts information between analogue and digital formats.

<u>Anonymous FTP</u>: an FTP site that accepts the user log-in name: "anonymous" (without the quotes) and the user's email address as the access password. Many FTP sites that provide software and other files for download free of charge allow anonymous FTP.

<u>Applet</u>: a small computer program that connects or is designed to work with a larger "partner" program.

<u>ASCII (American Standard Code for Information Interchange)</u>: also known as "plain text", ASCII is a standard text format that all computers understand.

<u>Attachment</u>: a computer file that is included with an email message.

<u>Autoresponder</u>: an email message that is sent automatically in response to an email message sent to another specific email address. Also known as Autobot or infobot.

<u>AVI</u>: an audio-video file format developed by Microsoft.

<u>Backbone</u>: a main "highway" of the Internet that can carry a huge amount of Internet information or "traffic".

<u>Bandwidth</u>: essentially describes the amount and speed of an Internet connection and is measured in bits per second (bps). So when we talk about a high bandwidth connection to the Internet, we're saying that this connection can move more information each second compared to a low bandwidth connection. If more information is sent than can be processed, we experience delays and bottlenecks on the Internet. Internet Service Providers are always looking for

better ways to provide more bandwidth and therefore provide faster, more reliable connections to the Net.

<u>Banner advert</u>: a small advertisement often placed on the top or bottom of a Web page that when clicked links to the advertiser's Web site and which can provide income for the host Web site.

<u>Baud rate</u>: information transmitted from a modem continually changes between high and low levels. The baud rate is the number of these changes each second. Compare with bits per second (bps).

<u>Binary file</u>: computer files can usually be grouped together in two main formats: ASCII or binary. Essentially a non-ASCII file is a binary file. Typical examples include: programs (.exe files), images, word-processed documents, sound and video clips.

<u>BinHex:</u> a format often used in email programs to encode (convert/prepare) binary information to be sent on the Internet. Used mainly in Apple Mac computers.

<u>Bookmarks</u>: a bookmark is a stored Web address in Netscape Navigator so that you can return to a Web page later without having to enter the Web address you want. Microsoft Internet Explorer refers to bookmarks as Favorites.

<u>Bounced email</u>: an email message that is automatically returned to the sender – usually because the email address does not exist or is incorrect.

<u>Bps (bits per second)</u>: in order to measure data, we have to chop it up into pieces. A "bit" is one piece of data. Bps measures the speed at which two modems communicate. Compare with baud rate.

<u>Cache</u>: temporary amount of space used to store popular Web pages. Most Web browsers have a cache to help provide quicker access to Web pages that are visited regularly.

CGI (Common Gateway Interface): an interactive system installed on Web servers to automatically process information entered into Web page forms, guestbooks, and so on.

Channels: a method that can send a regularly updated stream of information from a Web site on a particular theme or topic to a "subscribed" browser. An interesting idea that to-date hasn't really taken off.

Client application: software that is designed to communicate with server software. For example, Outlook Express is an email client that 'talks' to a computer that handles email (mail server).

Cookie: a nice, tasty biscuit – no seriously, an Internet cookie is a small computer file that many Web sites send to your computer on your first visit to them, so that next time you visit, they can identify your Web browser (you) and say "Hi." Usually, you can turn off cookies in your Web browser, but then not all Web sites may work properly.

Deja News: a Web site with a regularly updated newsgroup archive and a search engine.

DHTML (Dynamic HyperText Markup Language): a language format based on HTML but which allows animated and interactive Web pages to be created.

Digital information: computers, modems and the Internet help move information around. Computers understand information using only two levels: 1 and 0 (or high and low): this is called digital. The human voice is made up of various levels: this is called analogue. A modem converts information between analogue and digital formats.

Domain name: identifies a Web site address. In "www.computerstep.com", for example, "computerstep.com" is the domain name.

E-commerce: performing business transactions on the Internet.

Email: electronic mail – messages sent on the Internet that may also include computer files as attachments.

Email address: a unique address to someone on the Internet. Typical example formats: "b.austin@mysite.com" and "info@mysite.com"

FAQ (Frequently Asked Questions): a Web or newsgroup document that includes a list of answers to frequently asked questions about a Web site, product or service.

Favorites: a Favorite is a stored Web address in Microsoft Internet Explorer, so that you can return to a Web page later without having to enter the Web address you want. Netscape Navigator refers to Favorites as bookmarks.

File Transfer Protocol (FTP): a standard way to send files around the Internet.

Firewall: security system for networked computers to control access into and out of the network.

Flame: an abusive email message or series of messages targeted at a single user.

Flash: a popular Web technology often used to create fancy Web presentations that can download to a Web browser quickly. A Web browser requires the Flash Player plug-in – now provided free with Windows 9x and Apple Mac operating systems.

Folder/directory: different names for the same thing – an area in your computer's memory to store a group of related files or documents.

GIF (Graphics Interchange Format): a popular Web image format created by CompuServe and designed for quickly displaying simple images made up of a few colours or shades like basic logos for example. Contrast with JPEG images.

Guestbook: A Web form in which visitors to a Web site can leave comments about their visit.

<u>Home page</u>: the main page from which you can navigate to all other pages in a Web site. Also known as Index page.

<u>Home Highway</u>: British Telecom's name for an ISDN-based Internet communications package. Becoming outdated with developments in ADSL.

<u>Host</u>: a computer that makes available specified services to other computers on a network.

<u>HTML (HyperText Markup Language)</u>: a language format used to create Web pages.

<u>HTTP (HyperText Transfer Protocol)</u>: a set of established rules for transmitting Web pages on the Internet.

<u>HTTPS (HyperText Transfer Protocol Secure)</u>: a more secure version of HTTP used for processing online credit card transaction or for handling sensitive information.

<u>Hyperlink</u>: an item on a Web page that when clicked allows you to move to another location on the same Web page or another location on the Internet.

<u>Imagemap</u>: a single Web graphic in which different parts of the image, when clicked, link to various other Web locations.

<u>IMAP (Internet Message Access Protocol)</u>: an advanced system designed to process and store incoming email on a mail server. May eventually replace the current dominant alternative: POP3.

<u>Internet Relay Chat (IRC)</u>: a system that allows Internet users to talk to each other live.

<u>Internet Service Provider (Internet Access Provider)</u>: see Access provider.

<u>Internet Telephony</u>: making telephone calls using the Internet.

IP (Internet Protocol): Every computer connected to the Internet has a unique number: an IP address. Typically, an IP address is made up of four sets of numbers separated by full stops, for example: 123.123.123.45. As words make more sense to us, we use Web addresses or URLs: "www.computerstep.com" is much easier to remember than 123.123.123.23.

IP address: a unique number given to every computer that accesses the Internet. *See also* IP.

ISDN (Integrated Services Digital Network): an agreed standard that allows information in digital format to be sent over the standard telephone lines. Typical connections speeds are 64Kbps and 138Kbps. See ADSL instead.

Java: a computer language that can run on any computer developed by Sun Microsystems.

JavaScript: a simplified version of the Java programming language that when used as part of HTML can provide a variety of special Web page effects.

JPEG (Joint Photographic Experts Group): a popular Web image format designed for quickly displaying complex images made up of many colours or shades, like photographs for example. Contrast with GIF images.

Junk email: messages that are received but not asked for or usually wanted. Often, junk emailers send get-rich-quick offers or highly suspect proposals. Beware: sometimes various scams may be disguised as junk email. My advice is to treat junk email as you would any other junk.

Kbps: Kilo or thousands of bits per second. Remember, a bit is a basic unit of computer data. Kbps measures how fast digital data is moved around.

Leased line: a fast connection to the Internet that remains 'switched on' permanently. Aimed at business users, Leased Lines are expensive.

Link: a shorthand name for a hyperlink.

Listserver: a server that provides and manages mailing lists.

Lurk: to read messages on newsgroups or mailing lists without taking part or sending your own messages or replies.

Mail server: a computer that provides email services to a variety of users.

Mbps: Mega or millions of bits per second. Remember, a bit is a basic unit of computer data. Mbps measures how fast digital data is moved around.

MIDI (Musical Instrument Digital Interface): a standard used for controlling sound cards, synthesizers etc. Rather than including the actual sound data, MIDI files contain key information on how to create the sounds required.

MIME (Multipurpose Internet Mail Extensions): the standard used to include binary attachments to email messages.

Mirroring and peering: a term often used by an ISP to indicate that additional Internet resources are used to ensure that the fastest connections possible to the Internet are always available.

Mirror site: a copy of a Web site. Mirror sites are often set up so that users have alternative ways to get the same information more quickly.

Moderated: a newsgroup, mailing list or conference that is supervised and monitored by a human. Moderators can remove irrelevant or abusive information to make the best use of available resources.

MP3: highly compressed file format for music.

MUD (Multi-User Dungeon): Internet-based multi-user game.

Netcaster: Netscape Web browser add-on program for managing subscriptions, channels and Active Desktop.

Netiquette: responsible Internet behaviour based on consideration for others. Created from network etiquette

<u>Net-speak</u>: a collection of jargon terms that often sounds like gobbledegook to someone unfamiliar with the Internet.

<u>Newsreader</u>: software that allows access to and use of newsgroups by providing a connection to a news server.

<u>News server</u>: a computer that makes newsgroup services available.

<u>Operating system</u>: the basic "housekeeping" software components that every computer needs to operate.

<u>Packet</u>: a chunk of Internet information. Information to be sent on the Internet is first chopped up into packets. The packets are then sent on to the Internet and different packets may travel different routes to arrive at the same destination. Each packet contains all the information it needs to reach its destination.

<u>PDF (Portable Document Format)</u>: a well known highly compressed standard used for displaying and printing formatted documents especially popular on the Internet. Probably set to become the world standard for electronic documents.

<u>Plug-ins</u>: add-on software components that are necessary to work with specific types of files.

<u>PNG (Portable Network Graphics)</u>: a highly compressed graphics format for use in Web pages.

<u>POP (Point of Presence)</u>: a local (call-rate) dial-in point to the Internet provided by an Internet Service Provider.

<u>POP3 (Post Office Protocol 3)</u>: an established set of rules that ensures you can send and receive email from anywhere on the Internet.

<u>PPP (Point-to-Point Protocol)</u>: an established set of rules that allows a computer to connect to the Internet using a modem. PPP ensures the connecting computer is given either a fixed or temporary IP address (see IP).

<u>Portal</u>: a Web site that acts as a doorway or introduction to many other Web sites that are sometimes grouped into categories.

<u>PSTN (Public Switched Telephone Network)</u>: the public telephone system.

<u>QuickTime</u>: popular video format from Apple.

<u>RealAudio</u>: file format from Real Networks that allows sound information to download quickly on the Web. Uses "streaming" technology – the RealAudio file can start playing while it is being downloaded to a visitor's browser.

<u>RealMedia</u>: a collective term to describe RealAudio and RealVideo files.

<u>RealVideo</u>: file format from Real Networks that allows video information to download quickly on the Web. Uses "streaming" technology – the RealVideo file can start playing while it is being downloaded to a visitor's browser.

<u>Search engine</u>: a collection of information about a variety of different Web pages including links to these pages.

<u>Server</u>: a computer that provides online access. Also sometimes called a host – example: Web host. Server software runs a server and communicates with users of the server who use client software.

<u>Shockwave</u>: a Web browser plug-in required to view files created with Macromedia Director – a popular Web design graphics and animation tool.

<u>SLIP (Serial Line Internet Protocol)</u>: an established set of rules that allows a computer to connect to the Internet using a modem and a fixed IP address. Compare with PPP – which has almost entirely replaced SLIP nowadays.

<u>SMTP (Simple Mail Transfer Protocol)</u>: currently the most popular standard for sending email and for transferring it between mail servers.

<u>Spam</u>: the practice of sending the same email message to many Internet users at the same time and who did not ask for the usually commercially-oriented

message, or of posting to multiple newsgroups in the same manner. Also known as Unsolicited Commercial Email (UCE)

Streaming: a fast Internet delivery technology that allows an audio and video file to be heard and viewed while it is downloading, rather than the user having to wait until the entire file has downloaded to their computer first.

TCP/IP (Transmission Control Protocol/Internet Protocol): the essential set of rules that govern how the Internet works.

The Net: the Internet.

Telnet: an agreed set of rules or protocol that allows you to connect to another computer anywhere in the world, in such a way that the remote computer thinks that you are using its own keyboard.

Unmoderated: a newsgroup, mailing list or conference that is not supervised or monitored on a day-to-day basis by a human.

URL (Uniform Resource Locator): the system used for finding a Web address on the Internet. A URL is also known as a Web address.

Usenet: the most popular face of Internet newsgroups for swapping messages, in which topics are arranged into specific groups (alt., biz., comp., etc.)

V34: agreed international standard for modems that operate at 28,800bps, 31,200bps and 33,600bps.

V42, V42bis: agreed international standard for error correction and data compression. Commonly used in modem specifications.

V.90: agreed international standard for 56Kbps modems that replaces the two previous standards: X2 and K56flex.

Video for Windows: standard Microsoft Windows format for playing video files. The Video for Windows Player comes as part of Windows.

<u>Web author</u>: anyone who designs, creates and publishes Web pages and Web sites.

<u>Web browser</u>: sometimes called a Web client, allows a user to work with and move around the Web and view Web pages. Currently the most popular Web browsers are Microsoft Internet Explorer and Netscape Navigator.

<u>Web host</u>: an organisation with a permanent live connection to the Internet and which makes Web space available for rent (usually).

<u>Web page</u>: a published document that is designed to be made available on the World Wide Web.

<u>Web server</u>: a computer that stores Web pages and makes these available to users outside of the organisation that owns the Web server.

<u>Web site</u>: a collection of related Web pages usually stored at the same location.

<u>Winzipped files</u>: computer files that have been compressed and converted into a single file using the popular file compression software WinZip.

<u>WWW (World Wide Web)</u>: the most popular and visible branch of the Internet now more commonly know simply as the "Web" and which contains millions of Web pages.

<u>WYSIWYG (What You See Is What You Get)</u>: describes modern computing methods like Microsoft Windows and Apple MacOS in which you see the effects of what you enter immediately.

Index

F

G

H

I

N

P

O

Z